The Maroon Within Us

The Maroon Within Us

Selected Essays on African American Community Socialization

Asa G. Hilliard, III

DuForcelf

Cover design by W. Paul Coates

Printed on acid free paper to assure long life

Founded in 1978, Black Classic Press specializes in bringing to light obscure and significant works by and about people of African descent. If our books are not available in your area, ask your local bookseller to order them. Our current list of titles can be obtained by writing:

Black Classic Press
c/o List
P.O. Box 13414
Baltimore, MD 21203–3414

Please include the title of this book and where it was purchased.

Contents

Introduction

You cannot continue to oppress a consciously historical people.

—John Henrik Clarke

Africa, the home of humanity, and the home of the world's first well-recorded high civilizations and cultures in Kush (Ethiopia and Sudan) and Kemet (Egypt), has seen millennia of development. Societies on the continent have had their successes, which is true of all human societies. Great nations have developed on the continent, some with highly influential cultures and others more localized. Africa received influences from others as well. However, that story is well known, while the story of Africa's influence on others is not well known today. Africa is still stereotyped as the "dark continent" implicitly, when not explicitly.[1]

African people have spread all over the world through early migrations of successive populations of homo sapiens and later by way of the slave trade. To a degree, some of the powerful cultural legacies of continental Africa remain in populations in the African diaspora, including the United States.[2]

People of African descent in the United States can only be understood when *both* the African cultural and Western hemispheric political realities are taken into account together. For example, for nearly four hundred years, the slave trade, colonization, segregation, and racism—highly sophisticated systematic strategies of oppression—have been the massive political and economic forces operating on African people. These forces have affected the culture, the socialization processes, and the very consciousness of African people.

In spite of all attempts to obliterate African culture, African Americans continue to exist as one of many ethnic groups in the United States. Many people—even many African Americans—are unaware of this fact, and have so little respect for African people that we are seen merely as a color group (Black), instead of both a color and an ethnic (African) group.

Like all other ethnic groups, we exist, and we have a right to exist. Contrary to the way that we have been presented in the mass media and in the schools, we have been a vital part of the human historical process over the ages everywhere. We have a past and a present that we have experienced together (culture), and we have a right and an obligation to know both. Like all other humans, we are shaped by past and present circumstances, by African and Western hemispheric experiences.

It is not merely socialization, but the nature of the socialization process for African American children, and for the whole African family, that is a topic of central importance at this time. Issues of ethnic identity, values, educational strategies, community responsibilities, and many more concern us. Issues emerging from our long and bitter struggle to achieve in the political environment that we occupy are also of concern. We cannot leave consideration of these things to chance. No one else cares.

Many of our people are unaware of the fact that the physical component of slavery, colonization, segregation, and racism ran parallel to an even more significant mental component. Physical confinement, exploitation, abuse, and murder were supported by systematic attempts at cultural genocide as well. Many students of our history believe that the subjugation of the African mind through cultural genocide *was the primary strategy* in the enslavement and domination process. The greatest fear of our oppressors is that we will become conscious, independent, and unified. When this happens, we will therefore be able to mount effective resistance, gain freedom, mobilize for development, and become serious competitors. This is why, although the African enslaved in the Western Hemisphere was fully clothed in a rich cultural heritage, the leaders of the slave society set about systematically to strip Africans of all the culture they retained.[3]

Those who enslaved us wanted us to be either culturally naked or dead. They wanted to take us out of the human historical and cultural process. They wanted to say that we had never done anything that mattered. They wanted us to think that we were wholly dependent on Europe for everything. They wanted us to view the European as the only creator of culture and the African only as spectator.

We can document this historical systematic assault on the African mind. This assault continues today and for the same reasons as before. In recent years, led by right wing ideologues, it has become even more intense and acute, as we have begun to rediscover the truth about our history and culture, and as we have become more conscious and independent. The negative response to African conscious-ness has been massive. It is reminiscent of South Africa's response to Steven Bantu Biko's Black Consciousness Movement and to the cultural force-feeding of the chil-dren of Soweto.[4]

To embrace one's culture is not to "go back to the 1500's." It is not to reject technology. It is not to reject appropriate social and cultural change. It is not to reject categorically "Western Civilization." It is not to disrespect the culture of anyone. To embrace one's culture is to do merely what any healthy group does.

Many of our people are actually unaware of the fact that the best minds of the African world have agreed on this very diagnosis of our problem over the centuries. Great thinkers such as ben-Jochannan, Du Bois, Chin-weizu, and Fanon have agreed that we have a conscious-ness problem because of the nature of our socialization. It is a surprise to many that we can be schooled through the graduate level and, no matter what the academic discipline, rarely, if ever, are the names and works of these great African thinkers presented to us. Who then, will tell African people about their ideas, warnings, and visions? Can we afford to forget our struggles, and can we function in ignorance of a comprehensive and critical view of our present status? Never again![5]

Many of our people are unaware that great minds in the African world have posed valid and comprehensive solutions to our problems. There is remarkable agreement even in the diversity among our great minds. We are not children who need to ponder over these things under the "guidance," supervision, and even leadership of sponsors from other groups. We must not take family matters to alien think tanks. Family planning must be done at home by the family.[6]

Many of our people are confused about the meaning of "race," "social class," and "culture." Those of us who place heavy emphasis on our color as the basic index of group identity, will begin to function with a severely limited reality. Although we share pigmentation from our African roots, and although our oppressors have used our color as a means to identify us for mistreatment, pigmentation tells us little about *who* we are. Social class tells us little more than pigmentation does, although some social scientists have spoken of the "culture of poverty," as if one's economic condition is the only meaningful experience. African people, like others, share also in ethnicity, which is cultural at its base.

It is a people's culture, their shared creativities and struggles as they have evolved over time and space, that defines their essence. Culture is the "tie that binds." If there is no shared culture, there is no group, no unity, no solidarity. This is why the engine of group oppression is always cultural genocide. As Ngubane has said, the primary goal of the colonizer in South Africa was not merely to take the land, but to change the Zulu (African) into a new person (European dependent). The Zulus, having no say whatsoever, were to become a European creation totally dependent on their creator. The real conflict was a "conflict of minds."[7]

Some people who are racially and culturally of African descent have been socialized in such a way that they do not have any strong sense of identity with African people. That is their option. However, this book is not addressed to them, until such time as their orientation may change. Some people of African origin will identifyracially with Black people but will not feel any cultural bond. That, too, is their option. This book is not addressed to them, until such time as their orientation may change. I do not mean this in any negative way. This is merely to recognize the reality that there is diversity in the African community, and to be clear about the audience that I do wish to address.

The primary audience for this book is the African family and community: those who identify with and acknowledge their cultural heritage, those who want to know more about it and who feel an obligation to pass on the cultural traditions of the family to posterity, those who are committed to a collective struggle to develop our communities, and those who are dedicated to an uncompromising resistance to oppression in all its overt and covert forms.

The idea here is that it is absolutely essential that the African community itself have an independent and well-developed idea about its priorities and strategies for socialization. Within broadly based social institutions, such as the public schools, some parts of our task can be addressed. But public schools, which are attended primarily by African American children, are charged with and are limited mainly to a common national curriculum. As citizens of this nation, we do have an obligation to master the common curriculum, but there are other parts of our task that can and will only be addressed by the African community itself.

Schooling refers to the common content, skills, attitudes and understanding required by the larger society. *Education* refers to a deeper level of understanding and enables learners to interpret the realities around them. *Socialization* refers to the process of assuming responsibilities for one's ethnic group based upon its teachings of its shared culture and destiny.

Community socialization is a prerequisite for unity and solidarity. It is essential, and will permit us to collectively improve the conditions of our people. We cannot, and we should not, expect anyone else to commit to our development as their priority. There is no evidence now, nor has there been any in the past, that the development of our communities is a priority for anyone outside of ourselves, nor should it be. We must do for ourselves, then we can help to enhance the quality of life for all humanity.

These essays, published and presented over the last 19 years, have been revised and updated where appropriate. They are offered as a contribution to the African American community in its struggle for self-determination, so that we may develop our communities economically, educationally, spiritually, and politically. Let us take a look at who we are, what has and is happening to us, and what we must do to take charge of our own lives.

Asa G. Hilliard, III
August 31, 1994

Anecdotal and Other Material to Illustrate the Expression of Behavioral Style

The report, "Alternatives to IQ Testing: An Approach to the Assessment of Gifted Children" included a great deal of material on the context within which questions about intellectual ability are raised. As a result, early in the report, a great deal of attention is given to the history of African and African American people, as well as to the history of mental measurement. The report dealt with the fact that any standardized mental measurement approach would be naturally biased. However, the bias was only one part of the problem. The matter of validity in the design of effective instruction was the other part of the problem. Nevertheless, the report to the California State Department of Education restricted itself to the matter of bias.

The report dealt with cognitive or behavioral style as one source of bias in standardized approaches to assessment. As a result, a good deal of the research was done to review the literature and to interview practitioners in a variety of human services situations in order to articulate the parameters of cognitive and behavioral style. This report compares European and African American cognitive and behavioral styles, using music, language, and religion as domains for consideration. The following chapter from the report is the primary treatment of that subject.

The Expression of Behavioral Style in Religion

By using African American religious practice and experience, and by contrasting that general experience with the general experience of European Americans, the utility of the construct of "style" as an analytical tool should become apparent. It should also be clear that each tradition springs from a unique historical development and can be understood only by reference to that history. E. Bolaji Idowu and John S. Mbiti represent the most recent serious study of African religion. Both have been trained in Western as well as in African theology and from that perspective offer very helpful information. Idowu makes an early observation of the cultural encapsulation of Western as well as African theology, and from that perspective offer very helpful information. He sees cultural encapsulation as a way of preventing Western theologians from understanding religion in any full sense.[1]

> Unfortunately, by and large, the theologian of today is a very handicapped person. To begin with, he still lives with the age-old erroneous notion that only one religion, namely Christianity, has theology, which makes nonsense of the linguistic, connotational significance of the word. Recently, the question of the degree of the Doctor of Divinity, one of the highest degrees to be awarded in the universities of Africa, arose and the demurrer was raised that the "D.D." had always been awarded in connection with Christian theology;"that, therefore, it might comprise a department whose avowed position was that of religion as a comprehensive discipline." The corollary to this is obvious: a Doctor of Divinity is incompatible with Islamic studies, and very much less so with a thing like African traditional religion.[2]

The opinions of external observers of African religious belief and practices not only reveal the misunderstanding and misjudgment of the African belief system, more importantly, these opinions are classical illustrations of observers establishing their own worldview as a "norm" and viewing other worldviews as "deviations" from that norm. Such an approach is similar to the approach in testing, which we have called "Type One Question." "Do you know what I know?" Idowu expounds on this misinterpretation of African religion in the following way:

> Other terms employed to describe African religion include: animism, totemism, fetishism, and naturism. We need not go into them here. These and the previous terms show clearly how little the outside world has understood African religion. Some of the terms are being abandoned as more knowledge comes to light. But the fact remains that African religions and philosophy have been subjected to a great deal of misinterpretation, misrepresentation, and misunderstanding. They have been despised, mocked, and dismissed as "primitive" and "underdeveloped." One needs only to look at the earlier titles and accounts to see derogatory language used, prejudiced descriptions given, and false judgment passed upon these religions. In missionary circles they have been condemned as superstition, satanic, devilish, and hellish. In spite of all these attacks, traditional religions have survived, and they dominate the background of African people and must be reckoned with even in the middle of modern change.[3]

Mbiti conducted an extensive study covering nearly three hundred people from all over Africa outside the traditionally Christian and Muslim communities. In all these societies, without a single exception, Mbiti found that the people have a notion of God as the supreme being, and that this was the most minimal and fundamental idea about God found in all African societies. Idowu found that in Africa as a whole, there are really five elements of African traditional religion:

1. Belief in God
2. Belief in the divinity
3. Belief in spirits
4. Belief in the ancestors
5. Belief in the practice of magic and medicine[4]

We have already indicated earlier that a complex and highly developed worldview and religious belief system was characteristic of the Dogon. The same can be said for other African tribes as well. Even a cursory review of the elements of an African belief system should show that these systems cannot be solely understood from the framework of a European belief system. This brings us to the fundamental principle of cross-cultural assessment. That is why the "Type Two Question," "What is it that you know" must always be asked if the truth about "intelligence" or "aptitude" is to be discovered.[5]

In describing African religion further, Mbiti makes the point that there is no line drawn between the spiritual and the physical. Mbiti goes on to say that life in the hereafter is conceived of in materialistic and physical terms, neither paradise to be hoped for, nor hell to be feared; thus a man's soul does not long for spiritual redemption or even for closer contact with God in the next world. This important aspect of traditional religion helps one understand why African religiosity concentrates on earthly matters, with man at its center. Mbiti also says that the African concept of time is extremely important, because traditional religion and philosophy are concerned with man in the past and present time, God occurring as an explanation of man's contact with time. Africans do not have a messianic or apocalyptic vision of God stepping in at some future point to bring about an upheaval of man's everyday existence. They do not picture God as having an ethical or spiritual relationship with man, instead, "man's acts of worship and turning to God are pragmatic and utilitarian rather than spiritual or metaphysical." In short, according to Mbiti, African traditional religion is not dualistic, and it permeates the totality of man's orientation to his environment.

Henry Mitchell has expressed a contrasting view that comes from Western thought. He sees the Western worldview as one where man, being the enemy of all things in the natural world, naturally strives to control and exploit both his environment and his fellow human beings. This is to be contrasted with the "sunny" African existence, for despite the hard work required of him, and despite such nuisances as tsetse flies, the African had external as well as internal reasons to be less hostile and more trustful of the universe and its Creator. Western religious belief can be described as one where the spiritual and the physical and even the life in the hereafter is conceived of in materialistic and physical terms.[6]

If Western religious belief can be described as one where the believer sees himself or herself as distinct from the parts of the environment, then we have one of the defining characteristics of the atomistic-objective style. The observer in this sense considers himself or herself to be less a part of the environment being observed. Mitchell points out that African religions have neither "founders" nor "reformers," and that they have neither "authorized versions" or "canonical scriptures." Their religions simply flow out of the life of the people.[7]

Clearly, this is a much more open-ended approach to belief, which would conform to many of the characteristics that we have listed as "synthetic-personal." Such an orientation contrasts quite clearly with religion that is expressed as "orthodox," "authorized," "disciplined," and "formally ritualized." Idowu agrees with Mbiti that the African situation is one in which life is not divided artificially into the sacred or the secular. Instead, the African tends to see reality as a whole, in which the things of the earth (material things and man's daily activities) have meaning only in heavenly (spiritual) terms.[8]

On the matter of formality, Idowu indicates that every cult has its set liturgy, and that the liturgy consists of the pattern as well as the subject matter of the worship service. These liturgies are, of course, unwritten. An interesting point for our consideration here is that if the participants in the liturgy are asked to recite outside the context of actual worship, Idowu found that very often they stumble or are inaccurate. The worldview perception and activity in this synthetic-personal style is such that things take on meaning and feel natural only *in a given context* and not abstracted from that context.

Idowu contrasts this attitude toward religious experience with contemporary atomistic-objective theological analysis.Worse still, according to Idowu, the theologian of today thinks of himself as modern if he adopts a laboratory method in the sense of researching and teaching without being personally and emotionally involved. Therefore he has become more and more theoretical and abstract to the detriment of the truth that he is expected to be speaking and imparting.

Mbiti says that Africans are notoriously religious, and each people has its own religious system as well as sets of beliefs and practices. According to Mbiti, religion permeates all the departments of life so fully that it is neither easy nor even possible to isolate it. Religions are not primarily for or about the individual, but have more to do with the community of which the individual is a part. Many beliefs and practices are to be found in African society, but they are not formulated into systematic sets of dogma that a person is expected to accept.

According to Mbiti, people simply assimilate whatever religious ideas and practices are held or observed by their families or communities. Where the individual is at any given moment, that is where his or her religion is, for the person is always a religious being, and it is this that makes Africa so religious. Religion is its whole system of being. Mbiti says further that one of the difficulties in studying African religion and philosophy is that there are no sacred scriptures. Religion in African society is not written on paper, but in peoples' hearts, minds, word-history, rituals, and religious leaders, like the priests, the rainmakers, the officiating elders, and even the king.

Therefore belief and action in African traditional society cannot be separated because they belong to a single whole. Traditional religions have not missionaries to propagate them, and one individual would not preach his or her religion to another. There is little if any concern with the distinctly spiritual welfare of man apart from the physical life, and no line is drawn between the spiritual and the physical. Even the life that is in the hereafter, is seen in materialistic and physical terms.

An approach or attitude such as that above is in clear contrast to a religion that requires *proselytizing, written scriptures, permanent dogma,* and *isolated religious practice.* Indeed, for people who experience religion only in such atomistic-objective fashion, it is virtually impossible to make sense of the African religious experience. As observers, they will find it hard to "see" an alternative approach, since they will be unprepared to accept it as valid.

The values of standardization, uniformity, precision, and codification of belief are clearly derivatives of a European tradition and worldview. In Africa, the expression of religious belief and practice was *approximate, thematic,* and *popular.*

With the oral literature of Africa, there is no "authorized" version of a tradition, any more than there is an official version of a Negro spiritual. Mitchell indicates that he had seen in his own sources as many as three versions of the same proverb in the original language. This means that a variety of versions produces a variety of interpretations in subtle ways serving to further complicate the already confused implication. Mitchell says that compounding this difficulty is a gap between English and the African language. Therefore it becomes understandable why the surveys of Black belief have not been attempted by more Black scholars in America. Mbiti is the only scholar to attempt a religious view of African folk belief.[9]

The experience of many African Americans in the United States cannot be understood except through recourse to a study of historical roots in Africa and a study of African retentions in the African Americans' experience in America. It is also recognized that in addition to African retentions, there is a new set of experiences that has been accommodated and integrated into the African American core experience. African Americans in the United States today differ in terms of the degree to which they participate in a "core" African American experience. This is due to the many different social environmental factors. However, by tracing the development of African American experiences and by comparing contemporary core African American experiences with worldviews and behaviors on the African continent, an understanding of contemporary African American behavior is possible. The same can be said of Chinese, Mexican, French, Native American, Irish, or any other cultural group.[10]

The early slaves in America did not, as some history has taught, come as empty vessels. The restricted experience of slavery, and later, segregation, far from eliminating all elements of an African belief system, actually acted to preserve many of those elements.

According to Mitchell, the early slave was not an eager animist who came without religious beliefs, instead, in many ways, the early slave was already a "Christian" believer and practitioner. His apparent openness to the Christian faith, actually came from his desire to follow his already strong religious bent in a manner that would be more consistent with his heritage. The slaves and not the masters took the initiative to translate there own African beliefs into English and into Christian terms. They were the ones who sorted through the Christian Bible and took the ideas that were useful to them in the new slavery experience. By the time the masters were finally willing to concede that slaves had souls, and satisfied that the Christian faith could be used to enforce obedience, and increase the slaves' market value, the slaves had long since established an underground version of the true faith anyway; they were well along on their own "invisible institution" or underground church.[11]

Mitchell says that this independence is evidenced by the frequent appearance in the recorded slave narratives of a strong preference for Black preachers rather than White preachers. The Whites who were able to preach with any success to the slaves at all, noted that the response that they got seemed to be to their tonality, gestures, emotions, as opposed to what they considered to be acceptable conduct. In their European American ignorance, they were unaware of the subtle cultural signals by which they had inadvertently affirmed African identity. Mitchell says that the sounds and signs that constituted the Black communication code were easily understood by the members of a largely independent slave culture, but were mistaken by Whites for gullibility and ignorance. In fact, the slaves were really culturally almost self- sufficient, and they were also very intelligent. They were perfectly capable of reading the White faces, and they knew how to sort out biblical ideas, as they proved more than one time when they responded with utter indifference, or even with foot-voting (walking out) after any particularly obnoxious proslavery sermon.[12]

Not only did a unique African American theology develop among many African Americans, it became the vehicle through which the distinctly African American behavioral styles were expressed. For example, it is quite clear that the predominant preaching style of early African American preachers and the preaching styles of European American preachers were quite different. If any investigator doubts this, it is very easy, even today, to demonstrate the difference simply by having European American and African American preachers representing the two traditions exchange pulpits.

Mitchell tells us that the Black preacher is more likely to think of the Bible as an inexhaustible source of good preaching material rather than as inert doctrinal and ethical material. The Black preacher sees the Bible as full of insights, as warm and wise, and as relevant to the everyday problems of a Black man. It gives a basis for unlimited creativity in telling of the rich and interesting stories, and these narrations always command rapt attention even as the eternal truth is being brought to bear on the specific Black experience with the struggle for liberation. In the Black community the Bible undergirds remembrance and gives permanent relevance to whatever illuminates discernment.

Mitchell says the Black preacher does not merely use the Bible, at best he lets the Bible use him. The preacher has an intuitive and flexible approach to the Bible and seems to be asking, "What is the Lord trying to tell me today in this passage of the scripture?" Or he may be asking, "What answer for today's need does the whole sweep of the New Testament give?" or "How may I see it and tell it in the language of my people?" Mitchell says that the Black preacher is not addicted to pat legalistic or literal answers; they simply do not work for him.

For Mitchell, the Black preacher avoids the dead and irrelevant formulations expressed in the language and in the visions of the past. If you ever catch a Black preacher using such a crutch, he is probably desperate for material and plagiarizing, or else he has lost some of his "Blackness" by studying in some White school of theology. Mitchell says that at his best, the Black preacher is not so concerned with historical "objective" truth as in what might be called religious truth. The Black preacher has no intention of making the Bible a textbook and science. According to Mitchell, he is probably not interested in science, rather he is interested in the Bible as a reliable index of God's will for man, and in this broad concern, science will find a proper place as merely one aspect of a large reality.

Mitchell says that perhaps the most significant single overt indication of African American culture or style as it pertains to religion is the *freedom of expression* observed in the pulpit and in the congregation of any given Black church. When an African American congregation resists White style and conformity and engages in free expression, it imports high importance to the *feelings* of the person. This valuing of *improvisation* and *feeling* and *resistance to conformity* are characteristics of the synthetic-personal style that permeates all aspects of the experience of the person who practices that style.

It is instructive to examine the freedom in the orientation of some African Americans toward religious scriptures and, by extrapolation, any written material. Once again, it becomes clear that *freedom, improvisation, creativity, expression* and *flexibility* are shown to be valued. Mitchell illustrates this even further by tape recording Black preachers who use manuscripts. He found that when they use manuscripts well, nearly all of them engage in interludes of completely *spontaneous elaborations* or illustrations, and that when this happens, the messages were plainly more effective than when the passages were simply read. It is important to note as we pay attention to Mitchell's analysis of "Black preaching" and "Black belief," that neither of these things is defined as an "incomplete European religious system." Rather the African American belief and practice grow out of a special tradition and has its own integrity. Another example from Mitchell will help to fill out the description of a dominant African American style.

Mitchell says that the most certain statement one can make about Black preaching style, is that nothing is certain or fixed. The first thing that must be said about usual mannerism, is that the Black congregation is indeed very permissive. The Black congregation will accept a wide variety of behaviors unrelated to the message even, in order—consciously or unconsciously—to give the preacher the freedom to be himself. One preacher whom Mitchell noted was in wide demand by Blacks and Whites, pops his suspenders when he is really caught up in his message; another unbuttons his collar and seems to dig his chin into his chest; another has proclaimed for years "bless my bones;" still another preacher starts his sermon only after a long and unbelievably intense, even stern, glare at the congregation. Where Black culture is concerned, Christians always enjoy mannerisms provided they are natural and that they add interest and signal freedom and authentic personhood in which the congregation can participate vicariously. Mitchell says that the Black preacher does not have to develop a striking mannerism as a trademark just to be counted valid, but on the other hand, he notes that it is not a handicap either if he just happens to engage in strange and colorful action that is peculiar to him alone. The Black preacher's individuality is celebrated and accepted and communicated by the congregation in a way that is enjoyed by everyone who has not "bowed to the ball of White conformity."

The descriptions that Mitchell has given can be observed in a great number of African American congregations. In the examples above, the following specific values or aspects of behavioral style (synthetic-personal) can be identified:

* Improvisation
* Expressiveness
* Emotion
* Flexibility
* Intuitiveness
* Imagination
* People focus
* "Individual" existing *in the group*
* Novelty
* Uniqueness
* Thematic

It is also important to note that many of these same characteristics would be strange, if not intolerable, to many worshipers in churches that follow European American religious traditions: Catholic, Lutheran, Episcopalian, Methodist Episcopal, and so forth.

Students of religion will note very quickly that some African Americans do not participate in religious traditions as described by Mitchell. They will also note that some European Americans appear to follow a tradition quite similar to that described by Mitchell. In truth, it must be said that while ethnic group membership is frequently associated with a given pattern, behavioral style, or religious belief, clearly there are overlapping exceptions to the rule.

African American Music as an Expression of the Synthetic-Personal Style

Perhaps no better documented area of the variety of human experiences in the United States exists than that of music. As a consequence, our examination of this area will be more detailed than the preceding area of religious belief and practice. As was the case with religious belief and practice, we can examine the area of musical expression and find, in at least three different ways, evidence for the contrasting style of atomistic-objective and synthetic-personal. At this point, the descriptions of the "obsessive-compulsive" style and the "hysterical" style by David Shapiro can be reviewed with much benefit. The following points are important to make:

1. The European American has tended to perceive the African American experience from the point of view of the "Type One Question." (Do you know what I know?)
2. The traditional concept of "norm" takes on fresh meaning when placed in a given cultural context, and has little or no meaning when interpreted from the "norm" of another culture tradition.
3. The values expressed in the African American musical tradition are almost totally congruent with the synthetic-personal style, Shapiro's hysterical style, Cohen's relational style, Hilliard's African American style, Weem's Black style, and several other expressions of style.[13]

Amiri Baraka, formerly known as LeRoi Jones, says that while the whole European tradition strives for regularity of pitch, time, timbre and vibrato, the African tradition on the other hand strives against such regularity. In the African language, circumlocution is preferred to mere statement, for a direct statement is considered crude and unimaginative. Ever-changing paraphrases, which veil the content of speech, are considered the mark of excellence in personality. Baraka says that in music, the same tendency towards obliquity and ellipsis is noticeable. No note is attacked straight on; the voice of the instrument always approaches it from above or below and plays around the implied pitch without every remaining on it any length of time— and then departs from it without ever having committed itself to a single meaning. Baraka says that this timbre is veiled and paraphrased by constantly changing vibrato, tremolo, and overtone effects, and the timing and accentuations "are not stated, but implied or suggested, denying or withholding all sign posts."[14]

Ben Sidran supports Baraka's description. He states that the White aesthetic was summed up by Benny Goodman who said, "I am such a bug on *accuracy* and *performance* about *playing in tune and want just the proper note values. . . in the written parts.* I wanted it to sound as *exactly* as the band could possibly make it." On the other hand, Ben Sidran notes that African American musicians even in the big band context develop idioms that relied on no written parts. *Count Basie's big band had up to 17 men playing harmonically and rhythmically advanced music without any written music!* It is noted that the Black player, even as he was becoming more involved with harmonic exploration, tended to use his "ear" rather than to read music. The African American musician played offbeat in order to avoid the stagnant feel of Goodman's on-the-beat. The Black musician chose to rely on increased vocalization or "tone impurity" to help to break through the passage detachment of big band work and to return to the emotional jazz idiom.[15]

White musicologists (analogous to cross-cultural assessment of intelligence) have always had great difficulty in understanding and explaining or interpreting African American music. For example, Baraka cites White musicologists of the eighteenth and nineteenth centuries, and even some in the twentieth century, who spoke of the "aberration" of the diatonic scale in African music. Apparently, the musicologists were unable to understand that Africans were not using a diatonic scale but an African scale, a scale that would seem ludicrous when analyzed by normal methods of Western musicology. Baraka shows that such misperceptions by cross-cultural assessors of African American musical tradition have continued to the present decade.[16]

Baraka criticizes the musicological analysis of jazz, which has come into favor, as having severe limitations. Baraka says that the notator of any jazz solo or of blues (or for that matter, the transcriber of blues' lyrics) has no chance of capturing what is in effect the most important elements of the music. For example, he says a printed musical rendition of a Louis Armstrong solo or of a Thelonious Monk solo will tell us almost nothing accept the futility of formal musicology when dealing with jazz. He says not only are the various jazz effects almost impossible to notate, but that each note means something quite different in relation to musical notation. The notes of a jazz solo exist in a notation strictly for musical reasons, but the notes of a jazz solo as they are coming into existence, exist as they do for reasons that are only incidentally musical.

Baraka says that Coleman's cries are not "musical," but they are music, and quite moving music too. He cites Ornette Coleman's screams and rants and says that they are only musical once a person understands the music his emotional attitude is trying to create, an attitude not only "real," but perhaps the most singularly important aspect of his music. Baraka points out that, "Mississippi Joe Williams, Snooks Engalian, Lightnin' Hopkins and others have different emotional attitudes than Ornett Coleman. But all of these attitudes are continuous parts of the historical and cultural biography of the Negro as existed and developed since there was a Negro in America." This was a music that did not exist anywhere else in the world.[17]

Once analyzed by Western standards, the Western critic or listener according to Baraka will then utilize his own Western standards as a "norm." For example, a Western listener will criticize *atonal* and *timbral* qualities of an African or an African American singer, whose singing has a completely alien end as a "standard of excellence."[18]

The African singer or African American blues singer may have a hoarse or shrill quality. Among some critics, this quality has been attributed to their, "lack of proper vocal training," disregarding or ignoring the fact that among Africans and African Americans, this quality comes as a consequence of a conscious desire that is dictated by the culture and that is designed to produce a calculated effect. Baraka points out that a traditional African American singer and a Wagnerian tenor cannot be compared to one another in any way: "They issue from cultures that almost have nothing in common, and the music they make is equally alien to each other." Baraka says, "For a Westerner to say that the Wagnerian tenor's voice is 'better' than the African singer's or the African American blues singer, is analogous to a non-Westerner disparaging Beethoven's *Ninth Symphony* because 'it wasn't improvised.'" The Western concept of the "cultivation" of the voice is foreign to African and to most African American music. In the West, "only the artifact can be beautiful. Mere expression cannot be thought to be."[19]

According to Baraka, purely functional music has songs that might, for instance, be used by young men to woo young women or by workers to lighten their labor, or by older men to prepare adolescent boys for manhood. On the other side of the coin, what some people call "serious Western music," with the exception of early religious music, has been strictly perceived as an "art." According to Baraka, one would not think of any particular use for a Haydn symphony, except for perhaps "the cultivation of the soul." "Serious music" (a term that could only have extra-religious meanings in the West), has never been an integral part of Western life, according to Baraka. In fact,

Baraka says, no art has been a part of Western life since the Renaissance, because of the triumph in the West of the economic mind over the imaginative mind.

It is particularly relevant to our consideration of behavioral style and its relationship to cross-cultural assessment that we note the "translation" phenomenon. This was discussed in previous essays when we described the person who uses the atomistic-objective style. As he or she encounters content or tasks from the synthetic-personal domain, we may expect an attempt to be made to "reconceive" and to "translate" the phenomenon or task into a more familiar framework and vice versa. For example, Amiri Baraka says that, "Although the White middle brow had known about Negro music only for about three decades, he was already trying to *formalize* and finally *institutionalize* it." For Baraka, it was a hideous idea. Ben Sidran spoke of the reaction of the White music critic (another example of "translation") when Blacks continued to follow developmental lines rather than the "rules."

For Ben Sidran, the Black musician, when he or she took the process of cultural definition into his own hands, infuriated a vast number of Whites. He cites two major trends that point to the growing hostility of Whites toward modern Black music. The first trend was the emergence of the New Orleans revivalist movement, which was spearheaded by White purists who tried to apply both aesthetic and economic pressure to hold back the growing wave of "modernism." Ben Sidran said the debate became so fanatic that the influential critic Hugues Panassie went so far as to refer to bop as "heresy." Yet this attitude, which Ben Sidran saw as not uncommon among White critics in the 1940's, also indicated the extent to which some Whites had become committed to Black music, because to refer to an idiom of Black expression as a "heresy" is to imply that alternative idioms of Black expression had been accepted as "gospel."[20]

The situation got so bad that musical criticism was only able to redeem itself many years later. Baraka points out that the characteristic criticism of "bebop" in jazz fan magazines like *Down Beat* was so bad that they only recently had to re-review the classical bebop records by such greats as Charlie Parker and Thelonious Monk. Then, at this late date, they have given them wild acclaim, because the first reviews seemed to be so wrongheaded.[21]

For jazz critic Rudy Blesh, the irrelevances of bebop are exactly what they seem; they add up to no unity, to capricious and neurotically rhapsodic sequences of effects for their own sake. Blesh says that bebop comes precariously close to complete nonsense as a musical expression, and instead of a culmination of jazz, bebop is not jazz at all, but ultimately a degenerated form of swing exploiting the most fantastic rhythms and unrelated harmony that it would seem possible to conceive.[22]

Quite clearly, this critic was not simply expressing criticism, but a whole value system that was totally antithetical to that which has been described here as synthetic-personal. This critic apparently sought "order," "permanence," "imitation," "conformity," "regularity," and so forth. It is also important to note not only that these were apparent values of the critic, but that this critic sought to impose those values on musicians whose expressions came from a totally different experiential frame of reference. They were unable to understand that there could be more than one "norm." Once again, this is analogous to the work of psychometric or other assessments that are made cross-culturally.

C. O. Simpkins, author of *Coltrane: A Biography*, criticized Nat Hentoff's statement as follows: "Hentoff's statement reveals at least three common failings of the critics of Black music, and possibly music of any culture. First, there is the arrogance which blinds him to the fact that he has not mastered the saxophone, and therefore is incompetent to make statements like 'Coltrane. . . continues to improve.' Secondly, he confuses inability with honest differences writing, 'Coltrane's tone is often strident at the edges and rarely appears *able* to sustain legato softness as Getz can.'" Simpkins says further that, "Hentoff seems not to have considered the possibility that each musician may have a particular sound because he likes it, not because he *can't* produce a particular sound." Finally, Simpkins says that "Hentoff would like to hear a certain type of 'softness,' in the record. This is a value judgment which indicates shallow thinking, not unique to Hentoff. He states that 'gentler' sounds are more complex and that 'power' in Coltrane's playing as 'spontaneous emotion' is less complex." Simpkins concludes that, "Hentoff seems to have one standard to which he would like every musician to adhere."[23]

What has been revealed in this examination of musical criticism is more the critic's personal preference or attitude toward what music is "supposed" to be than a description of what jazz is. The critic's criteria are applied not only to Black music, but to all American music as well. However, these criteria are simply one alternative among many for thinking about music. Clearly African Americans, in general, have come from a tradition quite different from that of Europeans. Ben Sidran has captured a part of the essence of the African American aesthetic. He shows that the ability to experience and to communicate "emotional" content on a broad level is a salient characteristic of the African American musical tradition. He points to "oral man's" failure to "detach intellectually" from experience. Ultimately, this has been a strong point in the survival of African American music in American culture. Note that this criticism is really a reflection of atomistic-objective values.

African American music can be described in its own right, without undue reference to the European American cultural stream. Baraka shows that melodic diversity in African music came not only from the actual arrangement of notes, but from the singer's unique vocal "interpretation." In the African tradition, the meaning of a word might be changed simply by altering the pitch of a word or changing its stress. This signal system carried over into musical expression. It has already been pointed out that African music is "functional." It is "improvised," "spontaneous," "social," "free," "emotional," "flexible," "expressive," and "intuitive." These characteristics are very close to the description that we have made of the synthetic-personal style.[24]

Taylor has summarized the contrast between Western and non-Western (African music) using Charles Keel's comparative chart. This contrast is also very close to our contrast of the atomistic-objective and synthetic-personal styles.[25]

Contrasts between Western and Non-Western Music
by Charles Keel

Characteristics	European/Western	African/Non-Western
Mode of construction	composed	improvised
Mode of presentation	repeated performance	single performance
Mode of understanding	syntactic	processual
Mode of response	mental	motor
Guiding principles	architectonic (retentive)	"visual drive" (cumulative)
Technical emphasis	harmony-melody-embellishment-vertical	pulse-meter-rhythm-horizontal
Basic units	"sound term" (phrase)	gesture (phrasing)
Communication	linguistic	paralinguistic analogues
Gratification	deferred	immediate
Relevant criteria	coherences	spontaneity

In the African American musical tradition, the "solo" is rare. As has been mentioned before, the "writing" or "phrasing" of much African American music transforms it into something else. For example, Janet Robinson-Murphy complained about how inadequate the song books were for the Jubilee Singers. Murphy indicated that there was nothing in the song books to show the singer that he must make his voice exceedingly nasal or undulating, and that around every prominent note he must "trill," and that he must sing notes that are not found on the scale; that he must on no account leave one note until he has the next one well under control. Oliver says he might be tempted to take breaths whenever he came to the end of the line or verse, but he should carry his breath from line to line and verse to verse, even though it might appear that he is about to burst a blood vessel. The rule is that he must drop from a high note to a very low note, and be very careful to divide many of the monosyllabic words into two syllables. He must intersperse his singing with peculiar humming sounds.

Another integral aspect of the traditional African American style in music is "playing by ear." Locke pointed out that the African American musician had a whole chain of musical expertise. He had to have a musical "ear" and an "instinctive" feeling for harmony as well as the "courage" and gift to "improvise" and "interpolate." Finally, he had to have an uncanny sense for "total effect."[26]

When musicians are required to read music in order to play, the dominant value that is expressed is "preconception"; whereas, when a musician masters the art of "playing by ear," the dominant value is "creative conception." At its best, as in the music of Ornette Coleman, or other improvising soloists such as Charlie Parker, their purely extemporaneous statements *cannot be reproduced by any notation.* Indeed, to do so would be a fundamental violation of the value system of their behavioral style.

Traditionally, the jazz musician's music has been created out of the interaction between the combo and the audience. Feedback from the audience has played a major role in that creativity. There simply is no way to notate feedback, to reproduce it, or to preconceive it. The values expressed in either style are appropriate to that style. To judge one by the standards of the other is pure insanity.[27]

Early African American music, like even earlier African music, was also primarily "communal." Primitive jazz was like most African American music that preceded it, since it was a communal, collective music. The famous primitive ensemble style in the days of early jazz, made room for "off-breaks" or small sololike statements by individual players, but the formal intent of these breaks was still dominated by the formal intent of the ensemble. They were simply quasi-melodic punctuations at the end ensemble chord. Baraka says that jazz, even at the time of Oliver's Creole band, was still a matter of collective improvisation, though the Creole band did bring a smoother and more polyphonic technique to the ensemble style.

Simpkins commented on Coltrane by saying he didn't wear socks and had not worn underwear since he was eighteen, because he disliked anything restrictive, be it music or clothing. When Coltrane was once asked about using Shoenberg's twelve-tone system in his improvisations, his answer was, "Damn the rules; it's the feelings that count. You play all twelve notes in your solo anyway." Coltrane would flop around his house in old soft shoes and with his shirt half un-tucked, in a comfortable and carefree manner. But once, in Philadelphia, he bought some stylish new shoes. They were so uncomfortable, however, that he wore them only long enough to show his mother.

One of the most time-honored aspects of African American music is "freedom" and "improvisation." Traditional African American musician detest cliches. They strongly resist confinement. Not only did Coltrane resist conformity in music, he refused to impose conformity on others. Simpkins said that Coltrane once commented, "Look man, I can't tell anybody how to play their instrument. I can just about play the saxophone; I'm busy working on that." Coltrane continued, "So don't ask me. Just music is the subject matter; this is what we're doing."

An interesting variation and approach to improvisation occurs often in many African American churches. Fauste has observed that often there is only a piano to accompany the singing in church, and that an interesting thing about the player of the piano is that he usually picks up the melody according to the key of the singer. This reverses the practice in orthodox churches where the instrumentalist first gives the key to the singer and the singer follows. It should be clear that the value of spontaneity is served to a greater degree for the singer if the singer has the "freedom" to initiate the desired key. In another musical tradition this might be intolerable. It's a matter of style!

Ben Sidran reports on an anecdote that is both comical and instructive about African American and European American musicians. King Oliver was the one who brought Armstrong up from the South, and with him Armstrong's first recording. They had an elaborate system of signals that they worked out to keep Louis Armstrong's improvisational techniques a secret from others. They would use these signals, for example, after playing when "alligators" would take out their pens and pencils and copy down Armstrong's music on their napkins, table cloths, and even shirt cuffs. Ben Sidran said that this professional jealousy had a very subtle effect on Black socialization. On the one hand, it seemed to stimulate and increase the importance of innovation, or at least of individualization within a normally group-oriented society, but on the other hand, the stress on the individual tended to alter the slightly warm and extended family pattern of socialization in the South, and to replace this group interrelation with smaller musical in-groups or clans. Ben Sidran says that this in-grouping may be the central cause of the exoticism of Black music in the urban ghetto, since each clan tried to outperform and suppress the rival groups with even bolder innovations. It can be seen through such examples that the African and early African American styles are evolutionary, are modified by, and modify any musical tradition that it touches.

It was mentioned earlier that "writing" traditional African American music operated as a constraint on the performers who came from an expressive tradition. It has been noted by some, that the advent of recordings produced the same restrictive effect. As Ben Sidran has indicated, not only did recordings "freeze" music and allow critical "distance" and "preconception" to develop, but because of the three-minute time limit of the early electronic recordings, the extended improvisations of the African American were curtailed. The musicians were forced to *encapsulate* their ideas, to prestructure their "improvisations" in order to fit the record. Moreover, they had to aim their music at a "technological" rather than a "human source" of *feedback*. This forced African American musicians to accommodate by developing a sense of *abstraction* and a new *professional distance* from their music.

A word should be said about improvisation. Occasionally, it seems to the Western observer that improvisations are totally free and that there are not "rules." In improvisations, however, the *theme structures the performance.* Oliver gives a vivid description of the drums. He says that the crossing of the drum beat must be established. After that is done, additional drums may be added, with the main beat of the bar coinciding with one of those already beating, but with a different rhythm, or in the case of the master drum, once the first two drums have established a cross-rhythm, he may do just what he likes. He usually creates a series of rhythm patterns whose main beat crosses at least one of the other drums. Oliver cites Professor Nketia, who says that the rhythms are conceived with patterns assigned to one drum or a pair of drums played by one man, or to many drums played by different men. In the latter case, a number of the same type of drum or different drum may be playing a particular set of rhythms together. They may also be played multilineally where a number of rhythm patterns are adopting different sequences of patterns in such a way as to set off some beats of their respective patterns. Then against these, patterns may be played hand-clapped often by two or three individuals or groups of people whose clap rhythms are also playing against each other while the "gong" or clapperless bells establish a metronomic time signature.

Oliver says that it is wrong to suggest that the master drummer can "do just what he likes," because the length and character of the rhythm phrases are determined by the function, the nature of the dance, and the "piece" that is being performed. Oliver astutely observes, "improvisation is, in fact, very strictly controlled." Then he quotes Nketia who said when describing the music of the Gah people, "the drummers of an ensemble cannot just drum what catches their fancy, they have to know what is required of them in respect to rhythm and tone, they have to know the basic parts assigned to each drum and how they are intended to be combined."[28]

A final word needs to be said regarding the matter of "emotionality" in African American music. The power and emotion of African American music is illustrated by Amiri Baraka by recourse to the imagination. Anyone who is familiar with the rhythm and blues orchestra leader and singer James Brown can try the following exercise. Imagine James Brown in the lobby of a huge bank singing his million-record seller, "Money Won't Change You, but Time Will Take You Out." As Baraka says, "If this is played in a bank, the total environment is changed. Not only the sardonic comment of the lyrics, but the total emotional placement of the rhythm, instrumentation, and sound releases an energy in the bank that summons images that take the bank and everybody in it on a trip; that is, they visit another place, a place where the African American lives."[29]

Once again, it can be seen through an additional dimension of human experience that the core behavioral style of a people causes experiences to be constructed around that specific group's cultural norm. It should also be seen that no real understanding of an "event or "behavior" is possible apart from a consideration of that event or behavior situated in its cultural context.

The Expression of Behavioral Style Through Language

Language is far from an incidental matter. No discussion of "intelligence," which is known almost totally through language, can be intelligible apart from a full appreciation of this culturally situated and embedded process. Shakespeare's Caliban and Prospero offers us an excellent model for consideration.

Janheinz Jahn uses Shakespeare's Caliban and Prospero as a metaphor for the colonial condition. He agrees with other authors that the two characters in *The Tempest* can be interpreted as similar to the relationship of two sides in a colonialist society. Even though Shakespeare would have had no knowledge of this, Jahn shows the parallels as very striking. For example, he saw that Prospero had actually given to Caliban a language, and with that language an unstated history of consequences, a history where Caliban had no knowledge of future intentions. The gift of language was not English, so much as it was speech and concept; it was a way and avenue towards other areas of the self that could not be reached by any other way. Therefore, the whole enterprise was Prospero's alone. He made Caliban aware of the possibilities, as a result. All of Caliban's future, since future is really the very name for possibilities, must derive from Prospero's exercise, which is also, according to Jahn, Prospero's risk.[30]

If there is no extraordinary departure that challenges all of Prospero's underlying assumptions, then Caliban and his future would belong to Prospero, and Prospero will live in the absolute certainty that language, which is his gift to Caliban, will become the very prison within which Caliban's achievements will be realized and restructured.

Jahn agrees with Lamming in thinking that if Caliban is really nothing more than a simple part of nature, then Caliban will never be able to break out of the prison of Prospero's language. All the culture that Caliban can obtain, as is Prospero's intention, must of necessity derive from Prospero's language and mentality, and everything that Caliban does thereafter must be derivative. But then, Jahn supposes, Caliban is also a part of culture, and a different one that is unfamiliar to Prospero. One can see Caliban attempting desperately to remember, but able only to grasp these fleeting memories in images rather than in words, for Caliban is deeply imprisoned in Prospero's language and in his own servile condition.

Jahn points out that once Caliban has recognized the limits and roots of Prospero's power, he might actually try some further unsuccessful revolts. However, if his urge for freedom remains unbroken, the idea is bound to occur to him in the end, helped even by the education that Prospero has given him, even though that may be defective. His mother's powers, the voices and the instruments and the riches that drop in dreams, all belong together; they form a culture, but one very different from the one in Prospero's book.

Caliban must wrench free from the dreams into reality, in other words, Caliban must consciously recognize things, and of course he must do this in language, alas Prospero's language, for he possesses no other. So Caliban captures in his own and Prospero's language, the culture that Prospero did not create and cannot control, and which Caliban has now seen to be his own. But, as Jahn says, in the process of change, the language itself is transformed, and begins to acquire different meanings, which Prospero had never predicted. Caliban becomes "bilingual." The language that he now shares with Prospero, and the language that he has coined out of it are no longer identical. Thus Caliban breaks out of the prison of Prospero's language, and arrives at a new point of departure.

Jahn points out that Prospero's lessons cannot be unlearned. As a result, Caliban will continue to understand Prospero's language; however, Prospero will only have a partial understanding of the language that Caliban now has created for himself. As long as Prospero keeps his old attitudes, he is bound to miss the essential parts, the little nuances and references, and everything that relates to Caliban's cultural background, and he will therefore misunderstand Caliban's new language.

Jahn seems to think that Prospero could have himself initiated into Caliban's new language, which has now been extended to take in new fields of experience. The primary condition for this initiation, is that *Prospero ask Caliban questions, and that he be willing to be instructed, and is in fact instructed. He must abandon his colonialist arrogance, and shed his claim to be the master race, and consort with Caliban at the same level.* As a result, Caliban's liberation will give Prospero an opportunity as well. That opportunity is the chance of turning from a tyrant into a human person, according to Jahn.

If it takes two points to make a line, a third point will help to verify the line. Having looked at religion and music, we will now turn to a third and final detailed example of how an understanding of behavioral style is required for any meaningful interpretation of human experience. Although there can be many other points along the line that we have been following, *language* is a particularly important point to consider, especially when it comes to the assessment of "aptitude." It is important because language is the primary tool through which we have attempted to obtain information about the "intelligence" or "aptitude" of other individuals. Any lack of sophistication in understanding how language works will preclude the possibility for rational analysis and assessment in cross-cultural settings.

Virtually all "IQ" tests depend upon language. Yet, there is no indication that any IQ test has been developed that takes into account the variations in vocabulary, syntax, paralanguage, or other aspects of language for which major cultural alternatives or styles exist. The psychometrist's insistence and dependence upon "standardization" seems to require an assumption of a *common vocabulary, a common syntax, common paralinguistic features,* and *a common cultural situation.* For it is only by making the erroneous assumptions that differences in performance can be compared in a "standard" way through "standardized tests." Yet, even a superficial examination, with a limited knowledge of linguistics, and sociolinguistics in particular, reveals that it is a *gross error* to proceed in that. We may not know all that is needed to remedy poor assessment. However, we can clearly see where major problems exist.

In education as with many other areas in the behavioral sciences, the primary tool for accomplishing professional tasks is the tool of language. It is remarkable indeed that so few educators or behavioral science helping professionals have studied this tool systematically. Fewer still have developed the expertise to apply it skillfully. Understanding language and how it works is not the same thing as being able to speak a language. The failure to understand this simple principle is at the root of much of the malpractice that occurs in the area of cross-cultural assessment. There have been sensitive and sophisticated observers of the dynamics of human *interaction.* Franz Fanon, a Martinican psychiatrist, was among the keen observers of human behavior who truly understood the dynamics of language and the effect that language had on communication and understanding.[31]

Franz Fanon has said that speaking means that a person is in a position to use a certain syntax, and to grasp a morphology of language. It means that the person is able to assume a culture and to support the weight of a civilization. For Fanon, any man who has a language will possess the world that is expressed and implied by that language. So mastery of language actually brings great power.

Some human service professional practitioners seem to have understood the problem somewhat. For example, attorneys at law have understood the critical need to master specific techniques of communication. For them, it is not simply a matter of speaking good English, although that is important. The successful practice of law actually depends upon the skillful *manipulation* of English, either written or oral, in order to create a mind-set, to structure relations, or to pinpoint meanings. More than that, as a part of the law curriculum itself, attorneys study the technique of asking questions in order to utilize courtroom or interview interactions, to maximum effect. Only recently have educators begun to pay systematic attention to their primary tool. Studies of questioning strategies are now quite common. However, there is a general ignorance in our field, of the knowledge and insights possessed by the sociolinguist. Those who function in the area of psychological testing, have paid a tremendous cost for this ignorance. However, the children who have been misassessed have paid a cost that is geometrically higher than that.

The understanding of sociolinguistic principles would have eliminated decades of misassessment of the intelligence of "primitive" peoples. It was Benjamin Lee Whorf in 1927, and for several years following, who understood the connection between language, culture, worldview and thinking. For example, Whorf indicated that Indo-European languages can be roughly calibrated English, French, German, Russian, Latin, Greek, and the rest, but when it comes to Chinese, Mathmia, and Hopi, calibration, says Whorf, is structurally difficult, if not impossible. Speakers of Chinese dissect nature and the universe differently from Western speakers. A still different dissection is made by various groups of American Indians, Africans and the speakers of other languages. Whorf and his analysis also put to rest the mythology about "superior" and "inferior" languages and thinking. For example, he noted that among the Hopi, events always include "space" and "time," since neither is found alone in the Hopi world-view. Therefore, his language gets along adequately without tenses for its verbs, and permits the Hopi to think habitually in terms of "space-time." Whorf goes on to indicate that to properly understand Einstein's relativity theory, a Westerner must abandon his spoken tongue and take to the language of calculus. However, a Hopi has a sort of calculus built into him. Whorf indicates that Hopi is a better language for scientific investigation than are the European languages.[32]

Relatively few languages of the cultures have attained to modern civilizations and promised to overspread the globe and cause the extinction of hundreds of diverse exotic linguistic species, but it is idle to pretend that they represent any superiority of type. On the contrary, it takes but little real scientific study of preliterature languages, especially those of America, to show how much more precise and finely elaborated the system of relationships in many such tongues, than is ours. By comparison with many American languages, the formal systematization of ideas in English, German, French or Italian seems poor and jejune. Why, for example, do we not, like the Hopi, use a different way of expressing the relation of channel of sensation (seeing) to result in consciousness, as between "I see that it is red," and "I see that it is new." We fuse the two quite different types of relationships into a vague sort of connection expressed by "that," whereas the Hopi indicates that the first case presents the sensation "red," and in the second, "seeing" presents unspecified evidence from which is drawn the inference of newness....

Does the Hopi language show here a higher plane of thinking, a more rational analysis of situations, than our English? Of course it does. In this field and in various others, English compared to Hopi is like a bludgeon compared to a rapier. We even have to think and boggle over the question for some time to have it explained to us before we can see the difference in the relationships expressed by "that" in the above examples; whereas the Hopi discriminates his relationships with effortless ease, for the forms of his speech have accustomed him to doing so.[33]

Whorf goes on to say that many American Indian and African languages abound in finely wrought, beautifully logical discriminations about causation, action, result, dynamic or energetic quality, directness of experience, etc., all matters of the functions of thinking, indeed the quintessence of the rational. According to Whorf, in this respect, Hopi far outdistances the European languages. Whorf takes issue with such words as "preliterature." He indicates that, far from being subrational, "preliterate" or "primitive" communities may show human minds functioning on a higher and more complex plane of rationality than among the so-called civilized man. Whorf indicates that we do not know that civilization is synonymous with rationality.

Steward Chase wrote the foreword to Whorf's book. In that foreword, he presented an excellent set of principles that have immediate practical relevance for assessments that depend upon the use of language:

1. There is no one metaphysical pool of universal human thought.
2. The speakers of different languages see the cosmos differently, evaluate it differently, sometimes not by much, sometimes widely.
3. Thinking is relative to the language learned. There are no primitive languages.
4. Research is needed to discover the worldview of many unexplored languages, some now in danger of extinction.
5. Somewhere along the line it may be possible to develop a real international language. Someday all peoples will use language at capacity, and think much straighter than we do now.[34]

Much more can be said regarding the principles of sociolinguistics, which have developed to a high degree since the time of Benjamin Whorf. Such writers as Roger Shuy, Rudy Troike, Orlando Taylor, Paul Harrison, Malachi Andrews, Ray Birdwhistell, Albert Scheflen, Irving Goffman, Seymour Fisner, Peter Farb, and Edward Hall, etc. have helped us to understand how language works. It is necessary to know this information. It is the height of professional folly to proceed in the development and use of tests of "intelligence," *which depend upon language,* without an appreciation of messages of linguists.[35]

Once we understand that cognitive and behavioral styles are reflected in the language that is spoken by the child, and by the professional as well, we can begin to use that information in order to structure assessment processes. One of the reasons that we have been so backward in the United States in understanding how language works, is that the traditional approaches to linguistic study have been largely from the perspective of the "atomistic-objective" style user. Vygotsky picked up this trend during the years 1924 to 1938.[36]

The atomistic and functional modes of analysis that were prevalent during the last decade tended to treat psychic processes as if they existed in isolation. Vygotsky says that methods of research were developed and perfected with a view to studying separate functions while ignoring their interdependence and organization in the structure of consciousness as a whole. This remained outside the field of investigation altogether.

Vygotsky felt that it was possible to trace the idea of identity of thought and speech from the speculations of the psychological linguists of his time, that "thought is speech minus the sound," to the theories of modern American psychologists and reflexologists who came to consider thought as a reflex inhibited in its motor part. Vygotsky saw that in all these theories, the question of the *relationship* between thought and speech lost its meaning. If they were one and the same thing, no relationship between them could arise. Vygotsky took a critical swipe at the method of analysis that was adopted by most linguistic investigators. The methods that Vygotsky criticized were congruent to the one that we have called atomistic-objective.

For Vygotsky, the first method analyzed complex psychological wholes into little elements. He compares this to the chemical analysis of water into hydrogen and oxygen, neither of which has the properties of the whole, and each of which has some properties not present in the whole. The student applying these methods to look for the explanation of some property of water, such as why it will extinguish fire, would find to his surprise that hydrogen burns and oxygen sustains fire. Discovering this will not help the student solve the problem. Psychology is in the same kind of dead end when it analyzes verbal thoughts into components of thought and word and then studies them in isolation from each other. By the very process of analysis, the original properties of verbal thoughts have been obscured. As a result, nothing is left for the investigator except to search out the mechanical interaction of the two elements that he is familiar with, in the hope of reconstructing, in some speculative way, "the vanished properties of the whole."

Vygotsky preferred an alternative to that approach. He thought that the right course to follow was to use a method of analysis that he called "analysis into units." By unit, he meant a product of analysis that, unlike elements, retain the basic properties of the whole and that cannot be further divided without losing them. Not the chemical composition of water, but its molecules and their behavior, are the key to the understanding of the properties of water. The true unit of biological analysis would be the living cell, since it possesses the basic properties of the living organism. When it comes to verbal thought, Vygotsky believes that the unit of analysis should be "word meaning." The importance of Vygotsky's approach is that, like Whorf, he recognized the complexities of the communications process, and that it could not yield to the kind of atomistic analysis that would permit the development of the kinds of assumptions that underlie contemporary standardized tests of intelligence. The implicit assumptions are that worldviews may be ignored, unique experiential pools may be ignored, and that meaning, in the abstract, may be unconnected to any cultural setting. It is hard to believe how anyone who understood the principles of linguistics, sociolinguistics in particular, could hold such a position.

This brings us to the use of language in contemporary assessment processes. A close examination of the intelligence testing process will reveal that virtually all the sociolinguistic insights have been overlooked. One of the consequences of such an unsophisticated look at the assessment process is that many children who actually have high ability are misassessed and are labelled as having low ability. But an even more startling consequence to many educators, is the fact seldom considered, that is, that children who are measured as having high "aptitude" or "intelligence" frequently have achieved that rating only because they resemble the culture of the person who asked the questions and they frequently have less ability than has been indicated. They are "false positives."

Children who come from educated families often will use words that actually conceal their ignorance, since they have learned that words please their parents, and the desire to please their parents comes to outweigh their desire to know. Sometimes these children will use words to hide their feelings, since sometimes parents make it clear that strong feelings are not appropriate in a household where adults are themselves controlled. Sometimes they will ask questions over and over, not as an honest search for information, but as a means to engage an adult whose generosity in responding to a child is most likely to occur in cognitive areas.[37]

One of the ways to keep from making errors in assessment is to apply the understanding of behavioral style to the area of language. Many investigators have noted such relationships. Without looking too hard, one can find the same values and elements reflected in language styles that have been described earlier in religion and music. These styles are reflections of basic polar personality styles, and the intermediate styles that were discussed earlier. For example, the dominant atomistic-objective style reflected in language in America calls for an approach to language that emphasizes the "permanent" meaning of words, "conformity" in vocabulary, "conformity" in linguistic structure, and a "narrow focus." This approach excludes "paralinguistic" features, "standardizes" the language, and views it as "abstract" and "disconnected" from a particular cultural context.

The evidence that these assumptions are working is found in the high and growing commitment among public schools and higher education for "literacy requirements." Discussions about the "literacy requirements" usually carry the assumption, not only that there is a standard language of convenience, but that there is a "standard" language, meaning a superior language, to which all citizens must conform. When a student does not demonstrate a familiarity with the "standard language," the prevailing assumption about the student is not that the student has "another language and experience," but that the student is "unintelligent." One is reminded here of the narrow perceptual range of the obsessive-compulsive and the obsessive-compulsive's inability to feel comfortable with novel experience. "Literacy tests" then are frequently used by assessors who express a particular behavioral style. It can be shown here through language, that *if the intent is to discover "intelligence" and not communicate conformity, the assessor will be compelled to expand the approach to include using any experience that any student has!*

For example, Williams has spoken of the discrepancy between evidence for intelligence in school and evidence for intelligence expressed through the child's normal experience. Black parents and teachers have noticed and expressed surprise and puzzlement over the striking differences in fluency between school and nonschool verbal behavior in their children. According to Williams, this difference can be accounted for by the students' free choice of language once they are removed from the rigidity of the classroom, and of course this freedom assumes the form of ethnotropisms widely used in the Black culture.[38]

For Williams, the metaphor is the most imaginative and creative device in the language. Metaphor is considered to be the supreme ethnotrope. It has the capacity for a developed sense of beauty and "ethnotropism" of language. Williams says that metaphor is a high level of abstraction and symbolism, a high level of logical analogy, and it describes whatever its meaning symbolizes. The metaphor is quite ambiguous and is usually resolved by contextual clues or convergent concepts and knowledge and expectation of the members of the culture. In the conventional standard usage of English one is taught to avoid unambiguous metaphors, because they obscure literal meaning.

The Black child who is accustomed to the metaphors described above, but who has no opportunity to use his or her understanding of those metaphors in order to express his "intelligence," is not "deprived" but is *being deprived by someone* of an opportunity to demonstrate intelligence that exists. Another example of a part of the rich experience of some African American youngsters follows. Dr. Ernie Smith gives a poignant, detailed description of his coming of age "in the streets."[39]

Ernie Smith describes a person whom he chooses to call Walter N. Walter was a top-notch player and a name, and he first taught Ernie how to be a pimp. "School Boy," which was Walter's moniker or nickname in the fast life, taught Ernie all of the psycholinguistics of survival within and outside the street culture. Ernie said that he especially emphasized the necessity of developing an ability to coach using linguistically "proper" English. This was not "stuff-playing" and "slum-hustling," which are hustles that require a proficient and very skillful use of paralinguistic, linguistic, and semantic clues that convey an ignorant personality, "sweet-mouthin'," "rappin'," and especially "mackin'." All of these require a complete reversal in roles. School Boy taught Ernie the nuances of the fast life, but he also persistently urged that he pursue and he strongly influenced Ernie's ultimate decision to complete a post-secondary education. This carried all the way through Ernie's earning of the Ph.D. in linguistics.

At one point in Dr. "Sweet-Ernie" Smith's life he was regarded by the school staff as "mentally retarded." He could only have been regarded so by a psychologist or other assessor who had a limited personal experiential pool and, therefore, failed to understand enough of Dr. Smith's experience as a real world experience. A skilled psychologist or other assessor would know how to let Ernie use *his own* experience as a vehicle to reveal his cognitive skills.

Sidran has said that one can easily understand why White or Western historians have tended to minimize or mit the study of "orality," since they are "writers" by cultural tradition, a tradition that places no value whatsoever on the absence of "literacy," and as such, they have little, if any experience of the orality. Also, Sidran clearly perceives, as did Benjamin Whorf many years ago, the fact that language and worldview are intimately tied together, and that worldview and language reflect the way individuals structure and participate in their world. For example, in the African American world view, Sidran indicates that the African American oral man stores information through physical assimilation.[40]

Sidran says that the African American oral man becomes the information, and that this process has similarities to physical intercourse on a very general level. Where Western communication theory is based on a notion that "speech contains much that is redundant to intelligence and therefore wasteful of intelligence," making it possible, for example, for cybernetics to reduce communication to digital yes/no systems, Black communication on the other hand maintains the integrity of the individual and his "personal" voice in the context of group activity. Therefore, the notion that voice tones are superfluous to communication is absolutely absurd within the framework of African American oral culture. The same principle can be applied to instrumental music where Western musicians were recognized for their ability to conform to and master traditional techniques. The African American musicians were highly regarded for their ability to invent personal techniques, and therefore to project their personal sounds. The personal techniques were a means whereby the personal sounds could be accomplished.

What we have here then is not only a different vocabulary and a different grammatical structure, when we look at two different cultures, but a different experience of reality itself. Frequently it is difficult, if not impossible, to translate the experience from one worldview or behavioral style to another. Experiences can easily be overlooked by an assessor who knows only one worldview while observing a person who participates in another worldview.

For example, Ken Johnson, a linguist at the University of California at Berkeley, pointed out in a private conversation that it is impossible to "signify" in standard English. Signifying is a part of the African American oral experience that takes on its meaning within a particular linguistic social context. Even if the African American speaker is bi-dialectal, signifying can only occur in the African American dialect. Further, no one who is not steeped in the African American tradition can signify! While it may be true that signifying is not valued in a school setting, and may not provide the student the opportunity to gain school credit, signifying has to be of interest to any honest psychologist or assessor, *if the objective is to determine the student's "ability" to function cognitively or at a high intellectual plane.*

There are many unique aspects to the African American linguistic experience. These distinct aspects must be utilized in any assessment of "intelligence." For example, in the African American linguistic experience, speaking is more "social" and less "individual." That is to say, "interaction" is expected in communication, even at the level of formal speech making. Mayers notes that, in Black orations, the closer the person is to the African American core experience the more likely there will be the expectation of the "call and response" sociolinguistic-linguistic inter-action.

The African American speaker expects to hear "back-talk," words of encouragement, or signals of agreement, such as "Amen." This is an elaborated linguistic code. Mayers says that the non-Black speaker would very likely feel interrupted by such a response, should that speaker be unlikely enough to receive it in the first place. The African American speaker, on the other hand, would be encouraged and rejuvenated by it. In addition to the expectation for greater audience participation, African American speakers place high value on the use of creativity in vocabulary and communication. Particular word meanings do not have to maintain themselves over time, in fact, to be "hip" is to be precisely the opposite, to be novel.[41]

Baraka points out that the adjective, "funky," once meant merely a stink to most African Americans (a stink usually associated with sex). Yet, this very word was used to certify African American music as meaningful until the word "funky" became fashionable, and as a result almost useless. The social implication then was that the old stereotype of a distinctive "Black smell," a stereotype to which White America had subscribed, could actually now be turned against White America. This smell, real or not, was made to be a valuable characteristic of being Black by the 1950s, and for many Blacks and Whites, it was the only strength left in American culture.

Some of this creativity was tied to a simple enjoyment of the use of language. In other ways, Black creativity in speech comes as a consequence of oppression. The use of indirection, obliquity, inference, and illusion is *related to the need to be calculating and conscious in social exposure.* According to Lorenzo Turner,

> When Blacks came into contact with Whites, they often found it useful to maintain a "low profile." Metaphor provides a convenient cover when they wished to do so—talking in riddles, as it were. For example, when metaphors are used by Whites to promote negative values about Blacks, Blacks turn the metaphors back on the users by assigning them the same negative values. At the same time, they assign to themselves the positive values in the metaphor; thus, metaphor serves well the function of deliberate ambiguity for Blacks. When Whites make mistakes in pronunciation,

> Blacks say *clumsy lips*, on the other hand, Blacks
> may say clumsy lips and mean by that a man who
> is "really rapping." Similarly, fuzzy mind or *child-
> like mind* may mean either a muddled thinker,
> or a "deep mind" thinker. The subtlety of this
> way of thinking typifies Black Talk.[42]

Taking into account the use of language as indicated in the discussion above, it becomes quite clear that two separate value systems are operating. It should also be apparent that it is useless, if the intent is to discover the ability of a person to function and to apply his or her intelligence to an environment, to insist that the basic language and information pool for that demonstration come from a totally alien environment. There is absolutely nothing in the current practice of standardized testing for intelligence that gives evidence that any of our information about style, especially as expressed through language, is either understood or applied. Quite naturally, a good business person who contemplates what is implied by an acceptance of the principle being discussed here, would recognize immediately the cost involved in taking such knowledge into account. Quite clearly, the *mass produced* standardized test is cheap. On the other hand, we have seen that the *mass produced* standardized test can function only by doing violence to the truth, when in fact, *the expression of intelligence in human beings takes place through their own learned language and culture.* This condition demands multiple bases for assessment.

Additional Areas for the Expression of Style

We have utilized only three examples of areas where information regarding the expression of behavioral style can be found: religion, music, and language. The number of areas that could be examined is unlimited. For example, there are clear distinctions in the approach to *humor* by the atomistic-objective style user when contrasted with the synthetic-personal style user. In the first case, frequently the humor in a joke is *in the play on words*. Stand-up comedians with "one-liners" are the best examples of atomistic-objective style humor. The anecdote is *abrupt*. It is *disconnected from any particular context*. The joke can be easily delivered in a variety of contexts, and, therefore, can be considered something of a "standardized" version.

On the other hand, among African American humor, the jokes frequently told would be considered funny even by many European Americans. For example, instead of the use of "puns" or "one-liners," very often the African American joke is delivered as an involved description of a social situation, and *frequently uses material in the context where the joke is told.* Usually, people who are listening will be the subject of attention. The person who is delivering the joke may simply spin a long and detailed description of some misfortune.

In the old barber shop routine, a joke may be told once, and then several more times within a few moments. Each time it is told, there may be a different emphasis, milking from the joke all possible nuances. *The participation of the audience is expected.* New endings to the joke may be provided. Someone, the initial joke teller or anyone, may actually build on the joke to the point where a new joke is created. *In such cases the humor is in the created situation rather than carried strictly in the meanings of words. The total situation is funny rather than the "logic" or the "illogic" of the connections among words.*

These differences are so real that it would almost take a blind and deaf person to be unable to recognize the distinction between European American and African American humor as is the case with any other area of human experience. Yet a "universal" question on the Stanford Binet has been a question about "absurdities." For example, "Bill Jones' feet are so big that he has to put his pants on over his head." The style user who likes to listen to word play has an advantage here. The real absurdity is that psychometricians or test makers cannot detect the culture-specific nature of this question.

It has been important to take this time to detail illustrations of expression of cognitive style in a variety of areas, primarily because of the implicit assumption among those who place high value on standardized test results and assume that there is no need to consider stylistic variations among users. Having developed these points in a general fashion, it is now possible to progress to the research on the development of an approach to an alternative to an IQ test for identifying gifted minority students.

The Maroon Within Us: The Lessons of Africa for the Parenting and Education of African American Children

Jordan K. Ngubane has commented on the role in southern Africa of missionaries, who sought, above all other things, to impose ideological destinies on the African. He stated that missionaries were interested mainly in forcing or persuading the African to define himself in terms that served their interests. Naturally, the missionaries were not interested in preserving harmony in the African's personality. They wanted to fill the African's head with ideas that would enable him or her to be exploited and humiliated by his or her own consent. Ngubane says that the African personality was locked in a "prison of the mind" in order to facilitate exploitation by White Europeans.

It is important to realize that the African had a comprehensive and coherent frame of reference. Ngubane shows that the ancestors of African people defined themselves, and had a tradition of self-definition that linked them to the person in the society. That person did not need to go outside his or her own society in order to define him or herself.

The topic of African parenting styles is both simple and profound. At one level it stimulates us to talk about techniques of parenting, such as discipline, conflict resolutions, etc. At a deeper level, it stimulates us to consider the historical and cultural milieu within which parenting takes place, and which gives parenting its definition and character.

While the label "minority" is popularly applied to certain cultural groups, "minority" in no way defines the people to whom it refers. History and culture do provide such a defining dimension. I must also note that while the particular "minority" cultural group I will discuss is African American, the principles of parenting that I draw upon can be considered as universal. They can be considered as applicable to all groups, including the "majority" European American group.

Please bear with me as I bring together the historical and cultural background, which can serve as a basis for interpreting the experience of African American children. The oldest records of human culture are found in Olduvai Gorge in Kenya, East Africa. All the physical and cultural evidence show that they were Black people, similar in virtually every way to the varieties of East Africans who still live in the area. Black Africans moved from the headwaters of the Nile near the great lake and the "mountain of the moon" (Kilimanjaro in Kiswahili) to the delta, building great architecture and developing religion, science, art, symbol, mathematics, medicine and a system of education. These cultural developments became the foundation of world culture, with the major impact falling on those areas nearest to the Nile Valley, such as Europe.[1]

From predynastic times, "Africans" dispersed in migratory waves all over the world. As early as 40,000 years before Christ, a continent that would later be named for an African princess, Europa (Europe), would yield the bones and carvings of the steatopygous "Grimaldi Man," providing the first evidence of mankind in Europe. The first kings and queens on record are in Nubia, south of Egypt. Of 30 dynasties or kingdoms in Egypt, it was the indigenous Black dynasties I through XII, XVIII, and XXV, during which the greatest creativity was evident. For example, all the great pyramids and the Sphinx were built before any major invasion of Africa from the outside. Worldwide explorations occurred during these times. Among the oldest skeletons found on the American continent are those that scientists classify as "Negroid." Long before Columbus and nearly one thousand years before Christ was born, Africans established contact with and influenced the cultures of the nation we now call Mexico through a people who are known as Olmecs. This was 145 generations ago. Later, West Africans also traveled to

America, North and South, four generations before the voyage of Columbus, who used a West African navigator to find his way. Columbus and other explorers, such as Balboa, would later record their firsthand observation of Africans who preceded them to the Americas.[2]

There was a brutal destruction of African civilizations, even in the name of Christ, and savage murder and enslavement of approximately 200 million people. This barbarism was unequaled in written world history. It brought millions more Africans to the Americas, North and South. During the long night of slavery, many thousands of slaves freed themselves and established Maroon camps, centers for independent living, the remnants of which still exist today.

Overt physical slavery for the remaining slaves was abolished in America only six generations ago. The legal sanction for segregation or apartheid in American public school education, a system that was created by African American exslaves, initiatives after slavery, was ended just a little more than one generation ago. Even during the worst of inhuman years of church sanctioned legally sanctioned, scientifically sanctioned, philosophically sanctioned American apartheid, many Americans of African descent took the initiative to resist, to do battle, to create, to lead.[3]

There have always been Africans or Black people in America who have been both physically and mentally free. We have also had far too many of those who have yielded their bodies—and worse, their souls— to people and systems whose purpose was to exploit, to take all and give nothing.[4]

During the period of the enslavement of African Americans (north and south), there were those who managed to escape and establish what would come to be called "maroon" villages and nations. "Maroon" comes from the Spanish word "cimarron," which referred to escaped cattle living in the wilds. The numerous maroon communities throughout the slave trading areas had a number of things in common. They were located in places that were virtually inaccessible to slavers. They used the harshness of the environment to their own advantage, leaving false paths and camouflages. They were self-sufficient. They were culturally distinct. They were most vulnerable to "rangers," "chasserus," or simply other Africans who had agreed to track and to betray them.[5]

Maroons were called by many names, including *palenques, quilimbos, macambas, cumbes, laderias,* and *mambises.* Some of the major leaders of the maroons were Bayano in Panama, Miguel in Venezuela, Domingo Bisko in Colombia, and Yanga in Mexico, leader of the province of San Lorenzo de los Negros, from 1609 to 1698. In Cuba, the maroon village was called "Poblado del Cobre" in Oriente Province. In Ecuador, Esmeraldas Province was dominated by the Zambas near the end of the sixteenth century for nearly 100 years. There were also maroon villages from 1672 to 1884 in the United States in South Carolina, North Carolina, Virginia, Louisiana, Florida, Georgia, Mississippi, and Alabama. In Brazil, there was a whole African state, called Palmares. Today, there remain a few of these communities and their remnants. Suriname, on the North coast of South America in the Caribbean, is an example. They remain unconquered, fiercely proud of their cultural heritage.

It was a maroon base from which sprang Toussaint L'Ouverture, the great liberator of Haiti and later a symbol for liberation in the world. L'Ouverture, a slave, raised an army of slaves that defeated about 50,000 troops from Europe's finest army, the army of Napoleon. It is said that the catalyst for the Haitian Revolution was a secret "voodoo" meeting in the Bois Caiman Forest led by Boukmans, calling on Damballa. Earlier, Macandal, a maroon chief, was accused of fomenting revolution. He was accused of planning to poison the French inhabitants of Le Cap in 1757 by distributing bags of poison among the Africans to be used at a certain time.

Pierre Baptiste Simon, a plantation freedman, well educated, had five boys and three girls. The oldest was Toussaint, born in 1744 on All Saints Day. Toussaint grew up reading his master's books, with his master's approval. On one occasion, a White man knocked his book from his hand and beat him bloody. He refused to let his blood-stained coat be cleaned and wore it until the beginning of the revolution, when he met the man again, and stabbed him to death.

Toussaint was 13 when Macandal was burned at the stake. By August 22, 1791, his organization initiated the first act of its freedom quest.

Nearly a hundred years later, Marcus Mosiah Garvey was born in Jamaica. Garvey was a descendant of the maroons, who became the leader of a cultural revolution among African Americans, and the prime stimulus for many African Americans, and African liberation movements in such faraway places as Kenya, Ghana, Zaire, and Zambia, as acknowledged by such African leaders as Kwame Nkrumah, Jomo Kenyatta, Joseph Mobutu, and Kenneth Kaunda. Information such as the above is a vital part of the history and culture of African American families. Most of it is unknown to all but a very few people. Therefore it cannot be presently used in the way that cultural groups normally use their history and culture. Yet, no other history or culture is true for African Americans.[6]

Escape vs. Maroonage

Let me pause to make a clear distinction between simple escape, or simple freedom and maroonage. Simple escape and simple freedom were liberty without an aim. Maroonage, on the other hand, was freedom for the purpose of survival and cultural continuity. We must also take note of the fact that not all slaves became maroons, or even aspired to do so. Some chose rather to make the best of the slave system. Between the poles of slavery and freedom, there are many modes of responding. Ralph Ellison has written about the person who is "invisible." Here, existence itself is primarily validated by the awareness of an oppressor. Price Cobb and Bill Grier wrote about "Black Rage," essentially unfocused individual reactions to oppression.[7]

In his novel, *Two Thousand Seasons*, Ayi Kwei Armah has painted a vivid picture of an even more dangerous reaction, the behavior of the Askari. Armah talks about the Askaris as killers who are willing to assault their women. He told the story of women running from their town as Askari hunters came from the grasslands with bows and arrows. He mentioned that the oldest women coming from the closest houses were the first to arrive at the sound of the noise, and that the very oldest woman, named "Nandi," threw herself into the path of the "slaughtering zombies." Ironically, she was the grandmother of the leader of the killing band. Because of her appearance in the midst of all the carnage, the Askaris came to a halt in their slaughter. Grandmother Nandi looked around and saw some women trying to defend themselves, and some already dead, with most of the Askaris ready to continue the carnage. The grandmother turned to the crowd and asked, "But for whom are you fighting still?" and then directly to her grandson, "Son of my daughter, whose work are you doing? Look, those who turned you killer, where are they? Look at them. That should have been your work, killing your people's killers, destroying your people's destroyers."

Then the grandmother assailed her grandson, telling him, "You did not do it, the work of your life. Instead you chose the work of walking corpses, killing your own people." And then the grandmother mused, telling her grandson how she could understand that when the masters were living, that they had power over the Askaris, but now that the women had killed the masters, she asked the powerful question, "For whom then are you still killing your people, Son of my daughter, for whom?" When asked this question by his grandmother, the Askari zombie leader could not answer. Armah said that his face contained a look of terror, hate, despair and loss. After which, with a shout, in the language of the predator, Arabic, the zombies rushed again. First the leader of the zombies killed his own grandmother, Nandi.

But perhaps it was W.E.B. Du Bois who has seen as clearly as anyone the central issue for the slave. In *The Souls of Black Folk*, W.E.B. Du Bois compares the "Negro" to the Egyptian, Indian, Greek and Roman, Teuton and Mongolian, and says that this Negro is a sort of seventh son who is born with a veil and gifted with a second sight in an American world that yields him no true *self-consciousness*. This world of oppression only permits the "Negro" to see himself through the revelation of the other world. This condition Du Bois refers to as "double-consciousness," in other words, always looking at oneself through the eyes of others and "measuring one's soul by the tape of a world that looks on in amused contempt and pity." Du Bois said that the "Negro" always feels his two-ness as an American and a Negro, with two souls, two thoughts and two unreconciled strivings; he has two warring ideals in one dark body. Du Bois says it is dogged strength alone that keeps that body from being torn apart. Then he makes the insightful statement that it is the whole history of the American Negro, this strife, this longing to "merge his double self into a better and more truer self."

The double consciousness problem is not the problem of a split personality in the Freudian sense, nor is it a Dr. Jekyll and Mr. Hyde transformation as popularized in the literature. It is an issue of the surrender of self-definition and responsibility. To be forced to wait until an image of one's self comes into focus in the eyes of someone else before there can be a "self-concept" is the final victory for an enemy over a slave. The mind is gone and a zombie remains.

Escape from Escape

There were the maroons who escaped. Then there were those who sought to escape from escape. They turned away from any quest for self. Excessive indulgence in entertainment, alcohol, and drugs were pathways. Many became a part of the academic and theatrical audience for degrading messages about African Americans, enjoying or attending if not accepting messages about Black IQ and Black comedians. Still others simply dropped out altogether into superficial mysticism or still more alien religion.

It is given that in our present state, self-knowledge is hard to develop. Further, one cannot know without bearing a responsibility for what is known. Escape from mental slavery has its costs. Accepting the unnatural as normal and without criticism is virtual insanity.

Gradually then, without the sustaining power of consciousness of a brilliant cultural tradition, goals become ecumenical (as in religion), Ivy League (as in education), the "standard speech sounds" (as in television newscasters' voices), and to be with "Dallas Cowboys" (not as in football, but as in hats, boots, and buckles).

When Daniel Patrick Moynihan said Black families were falling apart, he was talking less about African American families than about European American families, since African American families were extended at that time. When Kenneth Clark told us—twice now—that African American children selected White dolls over Black dolls, we were embarrassed and hurt, and we made excuses and rationalizations. While Moynihan and Clark were not right, they were not exactly wrong. Their main error was to look at the individual African American child, or the isolated African American family. If they had stepped back far enough, they would have been in a position to see something far more disabling. They would have been able to see remnants of our cultural substance being unraveled at an incredible rate. They would have seen that spirituals and gospel music are being discarded more and more in favor of anthems; that blues, soul, jazz, calypso, and reggae are primarily of interest to European critics and musicologists; that unaffected deep spirituality is rapidly being replaced by empty rituals. These things are merely the tip of the iceberg. African Americans remain one of the very few groups in the United States who do not honor their own cultural traditions, sometimes even when they are honored by others. If there is a major illness among African American people it is that we increasingly honor and utilize our culture less. All great nations and people do the opposite.

Amilcar Cabral in Guinea-Bissau was eloquent in his analysis by showing the role of culture in national liberation struggles. He argues that these struggles are always preceded by an increase in the overt expression of culture by the dominated population; it is a means of negating the oppressor culture. He says that whatever the conditions of a people's political and social factors under domination, "it is generally within the culture that we find the seed of opposition," which he said leads to the structuring and development of the liberation movement itself.

For Cabral, freedom from foreign domination means that the African could acknowledge the positive accretions even from the oppressor and other cultures; however, they would have to return to the upward path of their own culture, which would be nourished by the living environment and would negate the harmful influences that come from accepting subjugation to any alien culture. Therefore, if imperialist domination requires cultural oppression, then "national liberation is necessarily and act of culture."

Why have African Americans in general so willingly engaged in cultural surrender? I think that there are several reasons. We have tended to accept certain false dichotomies:

1. We have tended to equate sophisticated technology with culture, believing that such technology is exclu-

sively European and that to affirm African culture is to reject technology.

2. We have tended to equate modern with technology, and to value modern as if it were cultural "progress." At the same time, we have seen the affirmation of African/African American culture as a matter of retrogression. Further, we have seen African/African American culture as static rather than dynamic and adaptive.

3. We have tended to equate European culture with wealth and African/African American culture with poverty.

4. We have tended to associate education with the acquisition of all the cultural forms of Europeans, and find it hard to conceive of educated persons who *live* the African/African American culture.

5. We have tended to equate self-affirmation with the hatred of others.

6. We have tended to equate religion with particular forms of European interpretations of Christianity and have not seen our own people as religious.

7. Generally we have failed to study ourselves and to know our culture.

These are all errors. Because we have made these particular errors, we have been vulnerable to confused definitions of our problems in education. We have accepted a whole host of remedies for "problems" that we have seen as originating in individuals or in isolated families. We have accepted programs to improve the "self-concept" of "individuals," to diagnose an "individual's" learning disability, to put "individuals" into a mainstream, to work with "individual" adolescents about their pregnancies, to cure "individuals" from drug addiction, to respond to problems created for "individual" families that are "broken." At no point have we realized that a community or group may be culturally disabled because of the distortion or suppression of culture. And yet, any superficial study of strong nations and groups will reveal the degree of detailed attention and high level of resources that go into the study, articulation, dissemination, preservation, and institutionalization of cultural forms.

We on the contrary, have failed to understand the political function of culture. Franz Fanon showed us its meaning where language is concerned. He tells us that the very act of speaking a language means not only to grasp the rules of that language, but, in addition, to assume a culture, supporting the weight of the civilization itself. Therefore, a person who has a language has a world that is also expressed and implied by that language.[8]

Fanon says that every colonized people, in whose soul an inferiority complex has been deposited because of the death and burial of their local cultural originality, will find themselves face to face with the language of their oppressor. Therefore the colonized are said to be "elevated above their 'jungle status'" to the degree that they adopt the language of the colonizing country. As they become "Whiter," renouncing Blackness, renouncing their environment, they are frequently called upon to act as interpreters, as go-betweens brokering for Whites and their interests. They convey their masters' orders to their fellows, and as a result enjoy a certain position of honor.

The colonized experience what Fanon has called a "personality change, a new way of being." Every dialect is actually a way of thinking. Fanon even notes that Africans newly returned to the continent from France, have adopted a language quite different from that of the group into which they were born, and that this is evidence of a psychological dislocation and a separation. He quotes Professor D. Westermann who says that "Negroes' inferiority complex is particularly intensified among the most educated," and that these educated struggle with that complex unceasingly. The way that they do this is very often quite naive, such as "the wearing of European clothes, whether rags or the most up-to-date style, or using European furniture and European forms of social intercourse; or adorning the Native language with European expressions, or using particularly bombastic phrases in speaking or writing European languages." All of these, according to Professor Westermann, make the African feel equal to the European and help the African identify with European achievement.

But there are those among us who, because they have given no attention to the study of themselves, will, even while exhibiting African/African American culture, deny that such a thing exists. Wade Nobles, Na'im Akbar, Robert B. Hill, and Cheikh Anta Diop are but a few of those who have articulated the richness of traditional culture that still guides us. It must have been shocking to see Hill's figures comparing informal adoptions in European American families with those in African American families where children born out of formal wedlock were concerned. Although these figures would very likely be different today from 1968 to 1969, two-thirds of the White children born out of wedlock were placed in foster homes or given up for adoption. The figure was a mere 7 percent for African Americans. Time will not permit a detailed discussion of this matter. Suffice it to say that it is evident that diverse cultures still exists.[9]

In music and dance alone, Africans in both North and South have been the source of almost all the creativity during the last several decades. Samba, Conga, Rhumba, Pachanga, Cha-cha, Merengue, Pony, Twist, Jerk, Madison, Jitterbug, Scotch, Chicken, Popcorn, Body Language, Hucklebuck, Lindy Hop, Charleston, Tap, Slow Drag, Peck, Shimmy, and even rhythm for the Mechanical Man, are just a few of the dances that have been sources for social dancing around the world and the source of ideas for the finest Broadway choreographers. Calypso, reggae, high life, salsa, jazz, gospel, spirituals, and rhythm & blues, mean the same thing to the musical tradition. These are but the visible manifestations of a deep substratum of dynamic culture.

S.M.E. Bengu has described the plight as one of "Chasing Gods Not Our Own."[10] This was never more clear than in the case of Marva Collins and West Side Prep. After having lifted Ms. Collins to the national spotlight for teaching poor Black children in Chicago about Shakespeare, Dostoyevsky, and Dante, she was dismembered on the *Phil Donahue Show*. She was accused by innuendo of plagiarism, of lying about the use of federal funds, and even of failing to teach. I resent the treatment this teacher received. Her teaching skills speak for themselves. While I can see the value of teaching all children about the works that she selects, I would have preferred seeing some "Gods of our own." But that is not the main point. The main point is this: as that beautiful, dedicated teacher faced the mostly accusing throng, in her hour of siege, in the pain and anger, she called on Caesar, saying of the Black teacher who betrayed her, "Et tu Brutus," in Latin!! She called on Plato and Shakespeare! Only! I know that these are fine and great people. But in her deep hour of need, it was pitiful to me that she found no refuge in a single African or African American giant such as

* Ellison's *Invisible Man,*
* Du Bois' *Souls of Black Folk,*
* Fanon's *Black Skins, White Masks,*
* Morrison's *The Bluest Eye,*
* Frazier's *The Black Bourgeoisie,*
* Garvey's *Philosophy and Opinions,*
* Malcolm X's *Malcolm Speaks,*
* Robeson's *Here I Stand,*
* Cabral's *Return to the Source,*
* Nkrumah's *Consciencism,*
* ben-Jochannan's *Africa: Mother of Western Civilization* and especially,
* Woodson's *Miseducation of the Negro.*

Education of African American Children

At one time we knew how to educate our children. When I review some of those practices, I get a real sense of just how far we have drifted from liberated education, which was technically and culturally sound. My experiences in Africa and my memory of information educational practices in African American communities yielded much that we can use today.

African education proceeded from a fundamental respect for nature, and from a fundamental belief that humanity was clearly a part of nature. The whole educational experience emphasized meaning. Meanings were conveyed through symbols and rituals. The identity for the student was important. Names were virtually religious in their meaning. All students were expected not only to learn technical skills, but to deal with them in their social perspective. All students were constantly introduced to profound ideas through proverbs, analogies, parables, and stories with moral lessons. Students were given real responsibilities and were expected to be able to function on their own initiative at the same time. Students learned courtesy and respect for elders and others. Students were taught about their ultimate responsibilities. Students became a part of their age group as a social set. Their set is a fraternity that is meaningfully connected to an adult community. Memory was valued, but so was analysis and explanation, so was imitation, since they had great models.

I talked with my oldest son about his first six years of school in Liberia, Africa. He began to reflect and to recall experiences he had forgotten. I was pleased and proud when he told me, for the first time, some of the things he experienced in both formal and informal educational settings. He remembered hunting birds with a .22-caliber rifle in the mangrove swamp behind our house. His Liberian playmate asked him why he wanted to kill the birds. "Don't you know what rice birds do? They clean up. Frighten them away from the rice, but don't kill them." Asa vividly recalled his feeling of shame. He also recalled the frivolity of American students at the American School as contrasted with the serious hunger for meaningful education on the part of his Liberian playmates.

The vestiges of maroonage remain in the United States. Periodically they are revived in focused form: The Universal Negro Improvement Association of Garvey, the African Methodist Episcopal Church of Jones, Turner, and Allen, the Republic of New Africa, the Black Christian Nationalists, the Nation of Islam, the United States, the African Film Society, TransAfrica, the Pan African Congresses, African Liberation Days, the Harlem Renaissance, the West Coast, Detroit, Chicago, and Mississippi. These vestiges coexist with the cult of "gittin' ovah," "makin' it," and the cultural amnesiacs, so the African American community is not whole.

In many ways we are less whole today than were our grandparents. We did not move from something solid to something solid. We moved from a strong cultural identity to cultural confusion. In 1954, we were invited to disperse, to disorganize, to forsake cultural identity as the antidote to segregation. The original issue with the slaves was equity in resources and "cultural democracy," the right to be culturally distinct without abuse, or the right not to. The "integration" solution seemed so reasonable. We could get resources as long as we were taught in the same places where White students were taught, or so we thought. Yet since 1954 we have seen the invention of many new ways to deny resource equity, even while we sat in the same classrooms with White students. IQ testing, and now minimum competency testing, have been used in such a way that the results have been new forms of resegregation.

Through our attempts at achieving the goal of dispersion and disunity, we gradually began to lose the very thing that had sustained us before, a strong sense of history, culture, identity, and destiny. Our goals became simple access to whatever was offered to others. And so, whether it be religion, aesthetics, or education, we have "surrendered all rights and responsibility for creating definitions." In other words, we opted for the twoness, the double consciousness that Du Bois described so well. We chose, begged for, and got mental bondage, and most of us now live in voluntary servitude. Moreover, we raise our children and send them to school in the hopes that they will be like us.

Perhaps it would not be so bad if in our actions we had really chosen something, a particular alien culture. In reality we have chosen everything. We have chosen all religions except the "God of our fathers." We have rushed to embrace every novel value that emerges anywhere in the culture. We have no boundaries, not in the sense of protection from people feared or insulation from people who hate, but in the sense of self definition or identity. At the personal level we can conceive of "personality" without the individual automatically being seen as a threat to others. Culture is the personality of a group. Its existence should not in of itself threaten harmony of a collection of groups.

Historically, our people made choices. Some chose the plantation out of a fear that something was better than the unknown. Others chose maroonage. Those who did the latter saw the value of their own traditions and the direction of their current creativities. They sought no domination or degradation of others. Until this very day, the remnants of those groups enjoy a life of immersion in a way of life. We can't teach our children what our community does not know. We can't teach our children if we never call them together. We can't expect other people to care as much as we do to become prepared. We can't solve the problem without organization.

Parenting the African American Child

This brings me to the specific concern with parenting the African American child, and by extension, to the model of analysis, for the parenting of any child. From what has been said so far, it should be clear that I regard the matter of parenting to be situated in a much larger sociohistorical-cultural process. It is my belief we lose more ground each year in approaching the problems of parenting the African American child because of cultural surrender by African American people and the resulting loss in cultural definition. Our analytical models for all African American social problems are models that treat the problems as if the dynamics can be understood out of context.

The problem of an individual's experience of low self-esteem is not simply an individual's problem. The problem of disharmony between African American males and females is not simply a problem between two individuals or one that can be solved in any complete way by the two individuals. The problem of African American families, and especially parenting problems, are not problems that have their roots in individual families, nor can they be solved in any meaningful way by individual families. Temporary "make-do" adjustments to relieve stress and pain are possible. As individuals, couples, and families are experiencing more and more stress, and less and less unity, coherence, and meaning, our analytical processes, which are detached from cultural, social, and historical concerns, actually serve to push even more of us over the brink by emphasizing noncontextual problem solving.

For African Americans, all of our social problems, including parenting, include two major components:

1. A history of oppression
2. A cultural base

Therefore, we must understand how every social problem is related to these two things. When we perform our analysis with these things in mind, we will discover that the "oppression of African American people is not enough of a reason for setting a direction. We will also see that freedom from oppression is not good enough for African American people." Purpose and direction only come from immersion in a cultural base.

African Americans have been slow to realize that while America has done tolerably well in developing a national unity, it has never had a true cultural unity. There has never been complete melting in the melting pot. Most ethnic groups have known this as the ethnic politics of many large cities and even some states will reveal. Yet, while the cultural unity has not been achieved in the past, it appears to be evolving for the future. And yet, what a unity it will be!

Christopher Lasche has described the new mass culture that is emerging for the overwhelming majority of Americans of all ethnic and racial groups. He described Americans after the political turmoil of the 1960s as having retreated to the purely personal preoccupations. Since Americans had no hope, he said, of improving their lives in any way that matters, they began to convince themselves that what really mattered was psychic self-improvement. They began to get in touch with their feelings, to eat health food, to take lessons in ballet or belly-dancing, to immerse themselves in the wisdom of the East, to jog, to learn how to relate, to overcome the "fear of pleasure." Although Lasche saw these things as harmless, those pursuits elevated to a program and wrapped in the theoretic of authenticity and awareness, actually signaled a retreat from the politics and then became a refutation of the recent past.[11]

Indeed, Lasche says Americans wish to forget not only the 1960s, the riots, the disturbances from the new left, or the disruptions on the college campuses, to forget Vietnam and Watergate and the Nixon presidency, but they wanted to forget their entire collective past, even in the antiseptic form in which it is celebrated during the Bicentennial. He cites Woody Allen's movie *Sleeper* as typical of what was going on, and quotes Woody Allen as saying, "Political solutions don't work." And with resignation, Allen is quoted as saying, "I believe in sex and death— two experiences that come once in a lifetime." So Lasche saw living for the moment as the prevailing passion of those in the post 1960s era; he saw living for oneself rather than living for one's predecessors or for posterity, as central. He thought that Americans were fast losing a sense of historical continuity and a sense of belonging to a succession of generations that originated in the past and stretched into the future. As a consequence, society exhibits functional disorders, disorders that do not seem to suggest goals to which any of us would really aspire.[12]

Lasche said that today's Americans are not overcome by a sense of endless possibility, rather Americans seem to be overwhelmed by the banality of the social order that they have erected against possibility. Lasche saw Americans as internalizing social restraints that keep possibili-

ties within civilized limits. And as a result they feel themselves overwhelmed by an annihilating boredom, "like
animals whose instincts have withered in captivity." There
is no danger that they will revert to savagery. According to
Lasche, people today complain of an inability to feel. As a
result they try to cultivate more vivid experiences, they try
to "beat their sluggish flesh to life, they attempt to revive
their jaded appetites. They condemn the superego and
exalt the lost life of the senses.

He says that twentieth century peoples have erected so
many psychological barriers against strong emotion, and
have put so much energy into defending against emotion
as forbidden impulses, that they can no longer remember
what it even feels like to be inundated by desire. Instead,
they seem to be consumed more by rage that comes from
defenses against desire, and gives rise in turn to new
defenses against rage. Although Americans are outwardly
bland, submissive and sociable, Lasche believed that they
were seething with an inner anger for which a dense and
overpopulated bureaucratic society could devise very few
legitimate outlets.

African Americans continue to rush headlong toward
complete cultural surrender. Just a few examples will suffice. We have in the past and to a certain extent today,
believed that God could only be approached through the
Latin language (if we were Catholic), through old English
("thee" and "thy"), through English anthems, through
still bodies and quenched emotions, through music that
is read, through Hebrew history, through rational worship
(no real invocation in the invocation), and through receiv-
ing and not giving in our religious services. We are con-
verted culturally, if not spiritually, since there is little spirit
left. In the words of Bengu, we have been "chasing Gods
not our own." But where are these new Gods leading us?
Did we come through all of this just to be narcissist?[13]

The Bible scriptures and the African scriptures written
by Africa's holy men who lived in the heart of Africa before
there was an Egypt, tells us to honor "thy" father and "thy"
mother and "thy" days may be long upon the land that the
Lord "thy" God has given "thee."

From the attributes of God set forth in Egyptian texts
of all periods, Dr. Brugsch, de Rouge, and other eminent
Egyptologists have come to the opinion that the dwellers
in the Nile Valley, from the earliest times, knew and

worshipped one God, nameless, incomprehensible, and eternal.

When one reads the actual text from the *Book of the Coming Forth from Darkness into Light,* commonly known as the *Book of the Dead,* and other texts from the pyramids of ancient Egypt that come from the earliest kingdom, the Old Kingdom, the Pyramid Age, it is crystal clear that there was an uncompromising and abiding monotheism expressed in the words of the Egyptians themselves. When they talk about God being one and alone, and saying that no other existed with him, that God is the one who made everything, that God is a hidden spirit, that God is the spirit of spirits.

The ancient Kemetics, or Egyptians, spoke of God as the divine spirit, which had been from the beginning, and existed when nothing else had existed, and whatever existed was created after God had come into being. The Kemetics also believed that God was hidden, and that no person knew what the form of God was, that no person was able to seek out the likeness of God, that the very name of God remained hidden and was a mystery unto the children of God, although these names were innumerable, and no one even knew how many names the creator had.

God was referred to as the truth itself, living by truth and feeding on it. God is referred to in the text as the king of truth, which He had established on the earth. God is referred to as the giver of life, and as the one who breathed the breath of life into the nostrils of men and women. God is referred to as the father and the mother, and the father of fathers and the mother of mothers, who begeteth but was never begotten, and produced but was never produced, who begat himself but was never created. God is referred to as existence that endures without either increase or diminution. God is referred to as the creator of the earth and everything in it. God is referred to as the father of the gods, who fashioned men and formed gods, who was merciful unto all those who reverenced God, who heard all that called upon God, and God knew anyone who acknowledged him and rewarded anyone who served him, and protected all those who followed him.

Honor thy father and thy mother may be said another way, as ancient Africans also said, "Man know thyself." One must know parents and ancestors to honor, respect, and rely upon their models for guidance.

The African American parent like any other parent is a constant teacher, more by what they model than by what they say. To model cultural surrender, self-rejection, self-negation and shame, while exalting and honoring others is to teach children to be schizophrenic, or worse still, is to produce the double consciousness that Du Bois warned us about, seeing ourselves and measuring ourselves through the eyes of others. The real pity here is that it is so easy to do this. Both the child who fails, and worse, the child who succeeds become living examples of double consciousness.

A common goal of African American parents in the past has been to get their children to be just as good as them. Frequently, African American children were taught to be more European than the Europeans. There is something pitiful to me about any African American who can experience comfort in the state of cultural isolation that results, since cultural surrender does not, nor can it lead to authentic identity in a new culture, especially when the new culture may actually be composed of a multiple of European cultures.[14]

Cultural surrender or cultural destruction leads inevitably to the loss of any possibility for a group to mobilize on its own behalf. There can be no African American family in the absence of a cultural base. There is no culture of minority numbers, nor is there a culture of an oppressed group, or a culture of poverty. Those who accept the attributed identity of "minority," "poor" or "oppressed," have not only surrendered culture, they have surrendered history as well, leaving only the present political socioeconomic condition as the base for a deformed identity.

The short-term needs of many African American parents are simply to survive in an uncaring and sometimes hostile environment. The tendency to go it alone is great. Perhaps a few will "make it." Yet, the vast majority of us will be doomed to be perpetual members in the underclass since there is no master plan for rescuing the masses of us. It even becomes less and less clear that there is an "us."

To me, there is no mystery about what African American parents must do to create the environment within which African American children can grow and become competent.

1. Parents must study and know themselves (history and culture).
2. Parents must model the behavior that is expected of their children.
3. Parents must expose their children to the widest variety of experiences possible—systematically and critically.
4. Parenting is a large group process (among African Americans in the past) not a couples process. It has and should involve relatives and friends.
5. Parenting means involving children in the real world of work and play, joy and pain, and truth.
6. Parenting means participation by parents and children in organized groups that serve the interest of the larger group.
7. Parenting means giving children responsibilities and holding them responsible.
8. Parenting means listening well to what children think and feel.
9. Parenting means telling and retelling the story of one's people to the children so that they may experience continuity and know how to be.

None of the things above will happen unless parents are motivated to do so. This motivation comes from belonging to and committing to something larger than one's immediate nuclear family. Groups that have a cultural identity draw upon it and replenish themselves not only through study, but through appropriate rituals and symbols. Rituals and symbols such as naming, rites of passage, holidays, distinctive dress, etc., help to formulate and to crystallize ideals, values, rules, which give meaning to life itself. This is the basis for group cohesion and solidarity that is a prerequisite to group power.

Typical discussions about parenting have tended to emphasize such things as techniques for discipline, communication, behavior management and so forth, things that take place between the parent and the child. These are merely gimmicks that may not be rooted in anything basic. The important behavior is the cultural substance within which the parent and child are situated. Conscious orientation to that is a matter of survival and a matter of meaning.

Cultural surrender is more than a matter of rejecting one's father and mother culture. It means that one accepts a new definition as a person. The culturally grounded person is a creator. The culturally dependent person is a mere spectator, a receptacle for the creativities of others. To demand freedom from slavery only to use that freedom to commit one's self to a voluntary cultural servitude is to lose the chance to be human.

People who have no "parents" will never learn to parent. That is to say, people who have no awareness of a parent cultural identity have little meaning to offer to their children. Any group that participates in cultural surrender need not waste time with concerns about parenting. That is like rearranging the chairs on the Titanic.

Many African Americans will not feel the need to become aware of a cultural identity. They will be content to make up the rules as they go along, to beg others for their rules. I wish them well in their quest. Others will know immediately that it is just as important for African Americans to be culturally grounded as it is for others. It is also important that we be culturally grounded in an appropriate culture. The maroons among us symbolize the will to live and the faith in our own ability as creators.

If your God does not speak to you in your language, then that for you cannot be God. A good parent has a parent culture. The survival of a people is in their hands.[15]

Every person needs cultural definition. Every culture deserves to *be*. No one should be forced to be a part of any culture or even to pursue his or her own culture vigorously. Yet, the possibilities for good parenting are really tied to cultural and historical grounding.

In "Loco Parents"
or Retrieving Responsibility?

A people losing sight of origins are dead, a people deaf to purposes are lost. Under fertile rain, in scorching sunshine there is no difference: their bodies are mere corpses, awaiting final burial.

—Ayi Kwei Armah

Recently, I saw a television program on training sheepdogs. It made a great impression on me, so much so that I have used the story as an example in several speeches. It makes many points that are important for the education of our children.

In most places where people raise sheep, a special type of dog with a special type of training is used to watch a flock of sheep. If one of the sheep wanders, the sheepdog will bring it back. This dog will protect the sheep flock from all other animals, including other dogs. When the sheepdog is with its master, it is usually described as loyal, gentle, and intelligent. But the most striking part of the description to me is that the things that are said about the sheepdog's behavior are all from the point of view of the master and involve the master's needs. The dog's own needs are not really considered, other than to determine how those needs may be used by the master to make the dog do what the master's wishes.

How does this happen? How does a dog come to lose interest in its own independent direction or in the direction which, as a member of a "dog family," is expected to keep? The program on television showed how it is done. At birth, the puppy is separated almost at once from all the other dogs—from its brothers and sisters, from its family. It is then placed into a pen where there are nothing but sheep, including the young lambs who are nursing. In its normal drive to satisfy its hunger, it seeks out a ewe and tries to nurse from her, along with other lambs. When it is successful, it continues, and is then raised with sheep as a lamb until it is sufficiently developed to be trained. Notice here that it continues to look like a dog as well. It will leave the track of a dog and will have the speed and strength of a dog. Yet, while it has the intelligence of a dog, it will develop the mind of a sheep! Once that happens, it no longer acts like, or in the interest of itself as a dog, or in the interest of other dogs. Notice also that this dog has mastered the "basic skills," from its master's point of view. It would also have passed very high on the "D.A.T.," or "Dog Aptitude Test." Moreover, it will see its own brothers and sisters as "the enemy" since this dog does not know them as brothers or sisters.

Let's take a moment to review what this story teaches us. For the dog's master to work his will with the dog, he established a training, not an educational process that had certain key features in it:

1. The dog was separated from its family and group at an early age.
2. It was continually isolated from them during its learning years.
3. It was placed into a sheep's (alien) environment.
4. It was fed a sheep's (alien) diet.
5. It was given a "special education."
6. It was totally dependent upon the master and never allowed to hunt for itself.
7. All the decisions about its training were made outside of the family and without its consultation.

Now we can begin to see what must have happened to the dog so that it would dedicate its life to the service of others while seeing its own family as the enemy. Because of separation, it lost its people's collective memory or history. Without memory or history, neither the present nor the future can be interpreted. This is the first step toward developing dependency. The dog becomes totally dependent upon the knowledge and interpretations of others. Because of isolation from its "people," it can not learn the normal survival rules and agenda for dogs. It can not learn from the experiences of other dogs nor test its sense of reality with theirs. It even loses opportunity to learn dog "language" so that it can "ask questions" later on.

Because it grows up in a sheep's environment, it begins to live in a world of illusions, seeing itself as a sheep. Because it is nurtured on an alien diet, it comes to crave that diet and to depend upon those who could provide it, since it can not produce the diet for itself. Because of its "special education," it accepts training and confuses it with education (critical awareness). Because it is dependent, it can never challenge the master or "bite the hand that feeds it." Because none of the decisions about its training or education can be made by its parents, family, or community, and because it can only agree or disagree with what is provided, it becomes a living, breathing, highly skilled, and quite intelligent, robot. But to all outward appearances, few would ever know.

Dr. ET
as Africancentered Transformer

The creature stood in grass, his heart light flashing with fear. He was alone, three million light years from home.

—*Kotzwinkle*

Typically, the analysis of "mental health" problems is performed at the level of the individual only. There are a set of problems, however, that manifest at the level of the individual, but which are actually rooted in the group to which the individual belongs. I believe it can be demonstrated that a strong cultural identity is a prerequisite for the success of an ethnic group and the individuals within them. Groups that have a strong cultural identity also have structures and systems for communicating to their members an identity and purpose. The survival of a group's identity is directly proportional to the degree to which it can replenish its identity through education, ritual, and role taking. These dynamics operate even when only one cultural group is present. A strong cultural group identity is not a product of competition among groups; it is the product of the group's effort to interact with the world.

African Americans have suffered a loss of control over social institutions (e.g., educational, religious) that normally provide identity, definition, and replenishment. As a consequence, we now witness at the group level what has been described at the individual level as identity diffusion, or better, identity confusion. At the same time, many other groups have maintained and even enhanced their sense of group consciousness. It is the undifferentiated individual within the undifferentiated mass culture who is most vulnerable. Collective mobilization, even for group interest, is impossible in the absence of identity.[1]

Many African Americans today, like some other Americans, have lost their way "home" (a sense of peoplehood). They have joined in the emerging undifferentiated mass culture that Lasche has described as the "culture of narcissism." This culture of narcissism does not provide a model to which any intact cultural group can aspire, especially African Americans. Cultural surrender is too great a price to pay for approval in an oppressive society.

The mass media is only one of the social institutions that is available to create and replenish group identity. The control of images of Black people, generated by the mass media, remains firmly in the hands of non-Black people. One consequence of this is a grossly negative distortion of the true experiences of Black people, which deprives Blacks of the essential benefits of self-determined, guiding symbols. Television programs such as the *The Jeffersons, Sanford and Son, Good Times, Different Strokes, Martin*, and a host of other shows project clown images that form the bulk of the media representation of Black people.

A small group of dedicated and underfunded Black film makers continues the struggle to produce appropriate media images and symbols. Nevertheless, the masses of African Americans never see the results of these efforts and depend on distorted and fabricated media images. It is possible, however, to reinterpret the significance of such films from a Black perspective.

Alice in Wonderland, Gulliver's Travels, A Christmas Carol, and *Uncle Tom's Cabin* are but a few examples of movies that may be appreciated at a superficial or a more symbolic level. Other movies may be explored in the same way, even though the producers may not have intended this usage at all. *ET* is such a film. A unique examination of this film will unmask its relevance to Black culture.

Throughout, I will refer to ET as "Dr. ET," an idea that came from a colleague, Pamela Jones, in recognition of the fact that ET was a mature scientist. Although he was saved physically by children and was never respected, recognized, or accepted as a peer by other adults and scientists in the film, ET was more than just a lost space visitor.

In analyzing *ET*, I will examine the actions of Dr. ET, Elliot, and his people. This process will provide a method for interpreting the content of the film. I will also examine the film in a broader context, that is, the film's relationship to current movie trends and general media usage. The primary focus of this paper, however, is on the relationships between Dr. ET and the culture in which he finds himself—not as the author of the book and the director of the film may have intended, but as an exploration of its symbolic value for Black children and youths.

We must recognize at the outset that the mass media, in general, offers few positive experiences for Black children and adolescents. Yet, Black children and families continue to support the mass media as paying consumers. In fact, a disproportionate share of film and television viewing is done by African Americans. Still, the viewing selections for African Americans are almost all made from products that enhance the self-esteem and perpetuation of others.

The fact that Dr. ET will be presented as a positive symbol, and a more humane film than the usual Hollywood fare, should not be interpreted as an endorsement of *ET* as a positive film. African American children and families have and will spend millions of their scarce dollars to see this film in which only three or four African Americans appear. They will see a film that is mainly fantasy in a world where the crises for African people are such that full-time reality is demanded. They will remain customers, really prisoners of the whims or even the calculations of other people's definitions of both fantasy and reality. They will be influenced by a film with images and themes that will govern some of their thoughts and behavior in ways that we cannot even anticipate, and some that we can. Drawing from the images and themes of *Mother Goose, Alice in Wonderland,* Walt Disney, and all the typical cartoons that are available is certainly different from incorporating the messages of *Aesop's Fables, Anansi, Brer Rabbit,* and other traditional African stories that have moral, political, and social object lessons.

What is at stake? According to Paulo Freire, the primary defense of the mind is for it to struggle continuously for critical consciousness. No one should accept passively every concocted idea that is presented. If the content of a film cannot be changed, at least its use can be transformed. African American children and adolescents should never accept the role of mere spectator. Critical analysis—deconstruction, reconstruction, and transformation—of harmful messages must be a constant activity.[2]

The Cultural Significance of ET

ET can be seen as depicting the meeting of two cultures—the culture from outer space and the culture into which the spaceship lands. We may focus on the comparison of cultures and upon the interpersonal and sociopolitical relationships between the members of the two cultures. By focusing on these relationships, a direct analogy can be made between the focus of the film and the historical relationships between African people and their colonizers, both on the African continent and the African diaspora. These two themes, the meeting of cultures and the colonial relationship between them, can be analyzed and illuminated by reference to *ET*.

The distinctness of African culture in terms of world views (metaphysics), knowledge (epistemology), and values (axiology), has been well described. The dynamics of colonial relationships have also been well articulated and documented. Furthermore, the residuals of African culture in the African diaspora have been documented. Although not all African Americans either practice or retain the same degree of African culture, there is a core African culture that remains among many, even when unrecognized or unacknowledged.[3]

The United States is made up of many cultural groups and a growing common culture as well.[4] This common culture is ad hoc and without conscious direction, although it has an identifiable focus. Christopher Lasche has called it the culture of narcissism. As such, it represents a radical departure from African cultural traditions. We must be sensitive to the meeting of traditional cultures and the relationships among them and to the emergence of cultural amalgamation and our relationship to its antecedents.[5]

The new is not necessarily better, more developed, or more technologically advanced than the old. When choices are to be made, many choose "home," but with a sense of returning to the past rather than with a sense of creating a future from a solid cultural base. Joining a culture of narcissism simply because its progenitors are powerful is cultural surrender, which has dire consequences. For example, amplified explicit sex, slow-motion viewing of violence, violent sex, and human and environmental destruction are pervasive themes permeating mass media today, especially television and film intended primarily for children. The appeal of *ET* is due, in part, to the fact that it is a needed relief from the adaptation of pornographic brutality in films such as *A Clockwork Orange, Friday the 13th, Caligula,* and *The Blade Runner.* These themes are in stark contrast to the traditional mental diet of indigenous African people and to much of the remnants of African culture in the diaspora.

For example, we may begin with examining the old *Aesop's Fables* and continue to present-day, traditional African culture at home and abroad. Most of these stories are steeped in spiritual meaning, moral object lessons, and lessons for the development of mental skills.[6]

Systematic attempts to destroy African and African American history and culture have caused a break from "home." The study of Africa and African Americans, archaeologically, historically, linguistically, politically, and economically, has been uncompromisingly in the hands of colonizers. Yet, some of the resultant information can be used. Similarly, although the media images of African Americans are primarily created by and for others, these media creations can be reinterpreted, however, to serve beneficial purposes.[7]

The Symbolism in ET

The movie *ET* can be viewed and analyzed at a symbolic level. By accepting ET (the extraterrestrial being who was left behind) as a symbol of traditional African and African diaspora culture now situated in an alien environment, the film can be used to explore the historical and colonial relationships among African Americans in the United States. The film can also be used to examine issues of identity and cultural consciousness within the African American population. Thus, we can transform the film from simple entertainment to an important symbolic lesson.

At the beginning of the film, we are shown a score of space travelers (not invaders), who are interested in preserving botanical specimens from Earth (note, most space fiction movies are about "invaders.").

According to Kotzwinkle, the author of *ET the Extra-Terrestrial in His Adventure on Earth*, the travelers from outer space were not elves, instead they were creatures more scientifically minded, as evidenced by the fact that they were taking samples: a flower, moss, shrubs, saplings. Because of their "misshaped heads " and their "drooping arms and roly-poly sawed-off torsos" one might think of them as elves, but they were very tender in their approach to plants. They were "elfin botanists" from outer space, and they were free to work in peace. These space travelers are interrupted by an aggressive group of men in trucks. In the rush to flee the "invaders," Dr. ET is left behind as the spaceship escapes. It is Dr. ET's glowing red-heart response that tipped off the aggressive Earth men to his location (note the "Southern Cradle" [Egypt] emphasis on direct nonverbal communication through feeling as contrasted with words alone). Dr. ET, however, escapes capture. Elliot, a young boy, finds him by accident. The remainder of the film basically centers on the attempt by Elliot, and other children, to help the space visitor survive and return home.[8]

Elliot can be regarded as a symbol of openness, toleration, and acceptance within the West. He, a child, is able to gain the cooperation of his older brother, Michael, his younger sister, Gertie, and in the end, his mother, Mary, in accepting someone physically different from themselves. Luckily for Dr. ET, Elliot is a family member in a "broken home." Dad (a symbol for the adult male) was not in the house on the night that Dr. ET arrived, or it would have been a much shorter movie, as the behavior of all but one of the adult males was destructive.

Elliot makes initial contact with Dr. ET by providing candy as friendly reinforcement. In no time, Elliot is psychologically bonded to Dr. ET and can actually "feel his feelings." Moreover, Dr. ET's feelings tend to have great influence on Elliot's behavior, even when they are separated from one another. When Dr. ET gets ill, Elliot says, "He is sick, I think we are dying." Near the film's end, when Elliot thinks ET is dead, Elliot says, "He must be dead; I don't know how to feel, I can't feel anything anymore." We need not dwell at length here on the traditional role of African American culture as the soul of this nation. Think of the many musicians who have captured European American audiences by imitating the vocation of spirit by traditional African American musicians. By their own admissions, musicians such as Elvis Presley, the Beatles, Janis Joplin, and Tom Jones, modeled after African American musicians, most of whom never reaped the economic benefits of their creativity. Or think of the permanent fixture of "soulful" Aunt Jemima, or of the Black nursemaid who is ever so prevalent on television movies written by European Americans. These are typical images that are deeply embedded in the psyche of most European Americans, if we use television ratings as a measurement of American values.

Elliot instinctively knows about his own culture, and the likely fate of Dr. ET is discovered by adults. One character states, "If they catch him [ET] they will take him away." Significantly, Elliot responds, "They'll probably do a lobotomy on him or something." Recall the traditional attack on the mind of the African. Ngubane calls it a "conflict of minds"; Woodson calls it "miseducation"; Wright calls it "menticide." Each of these individuals viewed the "mind" rather than the body as the real target of those who enslave.[9]

When Dr. ET expresses his consistent desire "to go home," Elliot says at one point, "We could be happy here" (give up your people?), "I could take care of you" (be on public welfare?), "We could grow up together" (culturally assimilate?). Yet, with no disrespect to, or rejection of Elliot, his family, or even his culture, Dr. ET maintains his goal of returning home. The desire to return home symbolizes cultural identity and self-determination.

Dr. ET is definitely an analogue for the traditional core culture of African American people, even though many have departed from that culture. Dr. ET appears on the scene first as he carefully harvests living plant samples. Note ET's African traditional respect for, and identity with, nature: Dr. ET follows a trail of Reese's candies left by Elliot to attract him and returns some of the candy to Elliot. The latter behavior is a symbol of reciprocity that is typical of Africa and the Southern Cradle. Harmonizing with nature rather than destroying it, and avoiding needless consumption are also traditional African values and practices.[10]

Dr. ET has special powers, which are also typical of the Southern Cradle. He can make things live and grow. He has the power to heal by the gentle touch of the tip of his finger. He has powers to transcend apparent limits in order to escape restrictions, as when the boys' bicycles were made to fly at moments of danger. The flying reminds us of the transcending survival techniques of slaves such as the *Brer Rabbit* stories, which were really stories about turning weakness into strength, and the spirituals that were really coded without words. It is important to note that at no time were any of those special powers used wantonly, aggressively, or destructively.[11]

From the beginning, Dr. ET is a creative intellectual and an explorer of every environment, always going beyond the guidance of his teachers. Upon seeing a map of the United States, a globe of the world, and a picture of the solar systems, Dr. ET instantly points to his home. Moreover, he constructs an animated model of his place in the universe, a process that both awes and frightens his friend and protector, Elliot. As Dr. ET reads about a character in a comic book who cries for help, he feels his own need to be free. Simultaneously, Elliot, who is told by his teacher to place frogs in a "killing jar," senses ET's desire for freedom and initiates the release of all the frogs (freedom for one, freedom for all). Remember how many different groups gained because of the Black freedom struggle of the 1960s, such as the handicapped and the aged, women, and gays.[12]

Dr. ET learns what a phone is by watching television (an essentially nonreciprocal medium), and, in one of his finest moments, he transforms household items into tools for his own liberation. An automated toy spelling box, a television channel selector, an umbrella, a saw blade, an electric mixer, and some wire and string, are assembled as a receiver transmitter. This behavior symbolizes critical consciousness and reciprocity in communication.[13]

When the opportunity comes to test his communication system (he was helped to escape, costumed as, what else, a "spook"), Dr. ET's first self-generated sentence in English is "ET home phone" or "ET phone home." His whole orientation and all-consuming passion is to return home; he is never distracted from his goal. In the parting scene, standing before the spaceship from home, Dr. ET says to Elliot, "I'll be right there," pointing to a spot in the middle of Elliot's forehead—the mind, the "third eye," the pineal gland. In the book version, Dr. ET points to the heart.[14]

Nowhere in the film does the Northern (Europe) and Southern (Africa) Cradle contrast appear more vividly than in the scenes where Dr. ET appears to be dying. The intrusive brutality of detached, mechanical, Western medicine is dramatized by men in germfree spacesuits, the quarantine of Elliot's home and family, and the cold harsh instruments of modern medical practice. When an adult male tells Elliot, "I want him to live, too. What can we do that we are not doing?" Elliot responds, "He needs to go home." In other words, he needs his people. Elliot is able to say this without seeming to feel diminished by Dr. ET's self-affirmation, even though Elliot is obviously disconsolate.

Having said all of this we can conclude culture is the personality of a group. Without a cultural base, no group can really exist. The loss of desire for home by members of any group must be seen as pathological. The struggle to return home (i.e., the affirmation of cultural unity and identity) and the transformation of any environment to meet the objective must be seen as healthy.[15]

To promote one's self and group is not to be against others. Any system whose group identity and cultural unity is built on the basis of the degradation of others is limited; cultural diversity and democracy go hand in hand. Coercive cultural unity is undemocratic as well as unhealthy. Democracy is not merely freedom of movement but freedom to be a people.

ET is entertainment. *ET* can be symbolic as well. We may choose our meanings for the symbols. As long as major film productions remain beyond the influence of African Americans, existing media *must* be examined for the hidden truths that they may reflect unintentionally—home.

Pedagogy in Ancient Kemet

The surface has been hardly scratched in the study of history of Africa and its people. The rough outlines of that history are beginning to emerge as well-prepared African and African American historians have begun the painstakingly detailed work of documenting the African experience in antiquity. It is hard enough to trace the broad general outlines of the African experience, such as pedagogy, with any degree of clarity. And yet there is the need for us to do precisely that.

Our concern with the connection to our African past is really future oriented. It is not merely for sentimental or aesthetic reasons that we return. While it is true that no one can or should live in the past, it is equally true that all futures are created out of some past. Ancient Africans not only existed, they developed a way of life, the remnants of which continue to influence world development. As we view competing designs for human institutions and competing philosophies, it is incumbent upon us to come to that process as fully disciplined, and especially as creative participants. A review of our past will reveal that no people has a better place from which to start.

The intent of this essay is to draw the best possible picture of one small aspect of a total development process of ancient Africans in the Nile Valley region and in the Great Lakes region. Simply put, how did the ancient Africans design and carry out the educational process? What were the aims, the methods, and the contents of ancient African education? The best preserved records of cultural activity are to be found in Kemet (Ancient Egypt). As a result, a great deal of our attention must be focused on that point. However, it is always important to keep in mind the fact that ancient Egypt was, as Gerald Massey said, "merely the mouthpiece for a more deeply rooted African birthplace."

Anyone who is familiar with the material on ancient Egypt is well aware of the fact that there exist few if any books on the educational system of Egypt. Consequently, the reconstruction of what must have been a highly developed and vast system of education necessarily requires an approach that is highly inferential. Nonetheless, the inferences are not without empirical grounding. For example, the evidence that gives information about the educational system can be found in paintings, monuments, architecture, technology and, above all, in the hieroglyphic and demonic writings, which include stories, rituals, songs and so forth. In addition, the skilled eye can detect in the widespread African diaspora an extensive variety of cultural forms whose antecedents are clear matches to those of the Egyptian and earlier ancient cultural forms. And so we are not short of evidence for the fact that educational systems existed. Rather the task is to sift through a plethora of data in order to reconstruct a picture of the past.

It is important at this point that a few words be said about the general orientation that I consider to be essential to any understanding of the raw data or summarized interpretation of data about ancient Egyptian education. First, in doing our analysis we must always keep in mind the "antiquity" of African culture. Second, and just as important, we must always keep in mind what Cheikh Diop has referred to as the "unity" of African culture. In order to explain the culture, and particularly the educational system of Egypt, we must appeal not only to data in Egypt but to data about education from the cultural antecedents of Egypt. We must also appeal to manifestations of the core African culture, not only in the Egyptian part of the diaspora, but in the rest of the continental diaspora and later in the intercontinental diaspora as well.[1]

History

Briefly, let me summarize some of the main points of ancient African history with which most of us are now quite familiar. It is now clear from the archaeological record that the whole body of data supports an African origin for mankind. What is equally important is that the earliest record of what we call civilization developed first in the same areas where the earliest fossil remains of humans are found. That is to say, long before Egypt began, it was Black people in Africa along the southern Nile River valley, close to its source, who produced the first stirrings of "civilization," that can be documented.

Albert Churchward is merely echoed by Richard Leakey when he says that the first paleolithic man was a pigmy. This pigmy evolved in central Africa at the sources of the Nile River and valley. Churchward says that from there all others originated and migrated throughout the world. Churchward says that the sources of the Nile in the equatorial provinces, where the great lakes and the papyrus swamp were located, were regarded by the ancient Kemetic people as their "Ta-Nuter," in other words their holy land. It was called the land of the spirits of the gods.[2]

It was Henri Frankfort, among other students of Egyptian history and culture, who recognized from the evidence that Egypt's historical and cultural antecedents were to be found "south" of Egypt, deeper in the Nile Valley. Frankfort tells us that the roots of Egyptian unity go all the way back to the distant past. He says that the population of the Nile Valley was homogeneous physically and culturally, as much as any large group can ever be. He used the evidence from fauna and flint tools that suggest that the inhabitants descended in early neolithic times from surrounding desert plateaus, and argues that the physique of the inhabitants of the valley from the delta deep down into Nubia remains the same from predynastic to late historical time. These Africans shared a common material culture in predynastic times. There are indications that the material culture extended even into Libya and reached the Red Sea in the east. The features of their language and their ethnological resemblances connect the ancient Egyptians firmly with the Hamitic speaking peoples of east Africa, according to Frankfort. It seems that the Pharaonic civilizations arose on this northeast African Hamitic substratum. So for Frankfurt, the prehistorical inhabitants of the Nile Valley possessed a common spiritual culture as a correlate of the homogenous physical and archaeological remains.[3]

Of course, we are all familiar with the fact that the very first unification of the two lands was initiated from the south. John Jackson has said that Egypt's first golden age was actually started by an invasion from Ethiopia. He quotes Flinders Petrie as saying that a conqueror from Sudan founded the Third Dynasty, and many entirely new ideas entered Kemet (Egypt) at this time. This new movement culminated in the vast schemes of Khufu, who was a dominating personality and builder of the first true pyramid. According to Jackson, with Khufu the lines of Egyptian growth were established and the course of events became the subject of written records.[4]

And it is Yosef ben-Jochannan who often cites the records from the Papyrus of Hunefer where the Egyptians themselves announced that their home was to the south at the "source" of the Nile near the foothills of the "Mountains of the Moon" (or Mt. Kilimanjaro).[5]

Clearly what we are getting is the picture of highly developed civilized behavior long before Egypt began—to the south of Egypt. For example, hieroglyphic writing existed long before the First Dynasty in Egypt. Further, the hard evidence from such great monuments as the great "Sphinx" of Giza (or as Africans called it, Hor-Em-Aket), indicates that it was much older than the pyramids and probably much older than Egypt as a nation.

According to John Jackson, the Egyptians made their first appearance on the stage of history, somewhere between 8,000 and 10,000 years before Christ. He felt that this date should not be considered excessive, and cites as evidence the fact that the ancient statue now called the Great Sphinx was estimated by another French Egyptologist, Professor Pierre Hippolyte Boussac, to be at least 10,000 years old. Jackson cites the evidence from an inscription of the Pharaoh Khufu, who built the Great Pyramid, who tells how a temple adjoining the Sphinx, which had been buried under the sand for generations, was actually discovered by chance in his reign. The inscription that Jackson referred to was in the Boulak Museum in Cairo, and says that the Sphinx was much older than the Great Pyramid, and that the giant statue actually required repairs during the reign of Khufu.

John Jackson tells us that the Edfu texts is an important document on the early history of the Nile Valley. This text was found in the temple of Horus at Edfu and gives an account of the origins of the ancient Egyptian civilization. According to that account, civilization was brought to the north of Egypt from the south by a band of invaders under the leadership of a king names Horus, who was later deified and ultimately became the Egyptian Christ. The followers of this king Horus were called Blacksmiths because they had iron implements. According to Jackson, this early culture had been traced back to Somaliland, although it may have originated in the Great Lakes region of central Africa. In Somaliland, Jackson says, there are ruins of buildings constructed with dressed stones showing the close resemblance of the architecture of Somaliland to that of early Egypt. And then Jackson cites Professor Arthur G. Brodeur who speculated that the ancestors of the southern Egyptians came originally from that region, and that they entered the Nile Valley through Nubia and brought with them a well-developed civilization. That migration had occurred somewhere in the distant past before 5,000 BC.[6]

Looking again to evidence for a southern origin of Egyptian civilization, we must note the recent evaluation of material from archaeological digs taken just before the waters behind the Aswan Dam flooded Nubia. Margaret Drower points out that south of Abu-Simbel there were some conical mounds at Ballana, and on the opposite bank of Qostol. Excavations were made, and more mounds were examined, all with similar results. Eventually the actual graves of the kings were found, and they were described by Drower as "tall men, with Negroid features."[7]

And so it is very recently that establishment Egyptologists such as Bruce Williams at the University of Chicago, have begun to say that Egyptian civilization had a parent, perhaps more than one, and that the most likely candidate for direct parenthood is the Nubian civilization of Ta-Seti to the south of Egypt.[8]

Barbara Mertz has said that as far as she knew there was never a blond queen of Egypt. She mentions that one woman was believed to be blond or red-headed, but later evidence showed that she was actually wearing a yellow headcloth. There were never any other candidates for that description. What emerges clearly from the evidence is that "indigenous Black Africans" developed the whole Nile Valley, including Egyptian civilization.[9]

Culture

Cheikh Diop's concept of cultural unity is very important to us. It is a powerful explanatory construct, and it helps to guide empirical investigation. The concept of cultural unity helps us to link Egypt (East Africa) with the rest of Africa and the intercontinental diaspora. It cannot be emphasized too strongly that we are not limited to mere speculation on these points, as Diop's book on the cultural unity of Black Africa has demonstrated. There is abundant evidence for the cultural unity, both in antiquity and in the present.[10]

In West Africa, according to DeGramont, ethnologists who studied the Bozos say that the tiny island of fisherman actually came from Egypt 5,000 years ago and settled in the Niger bin. They have not moved or changed their ways since that time. These ways seem to be derived from the river people of the Nile, under the early dynasties, as is the language of the Bozos. The Bozos have maintained their spiritual independence from Islam and Christianity, and have kept alive traditions that originated before the fall of the city of Memphis in ancient Egypt. According to DeGramont, watching a Bozo ceremony with the dancers' heads covered with animal masks is like watching living hieroglyphics.[11]

I must emphasize that it was the "empirical" evidence that led DeGramont to such a conclusion. Similarly, the study of voodoo religion in West Africa reveals its similarity to ancient Egyptian religion, and to its offspring, European religion.

Maya Deren has said that the role of the mysteries named Legba correspond to those of the Egyptian Hermes, celebrated in Hellenistic culture. Since so many of their symbols are identical, the analogy can hardly be dismissed either as incidental or as a consequence of what anthropologists call "convergence." According to Deren, the similarities comprise a total image of the god and are furthermore symbolically consistent, even when rendered in the rites and myths, and as interpreted by "qualified Houngans." "In any case, no matter what the explanation may be, the parallel between the myth and cult in contemporary Haiti, and those not only of 17th century Africa but over antiquity are undeniable and abundant."[12]

We can look at another culture in West Africa. DeGramont in his book, *The Strong Brown God* ,was fascinated by the ancient West African city of Djenne, a companion city to Timbuktu in Mali, which he called an "African Venice."

He says that when the river was high, it could only be reached by boat, protected by water. Djenne was said to have resisted 99 sieges in the course of its history. According to DeGramont, if Pharaoh woke up in Djenne, he would think he was in ancient Egypt. They have clay houses and decorated facades with trapezoidal porticos and pointed glens and columns in low relief. The mosque that he saw was as large as a gothic cathedral, and was inspiring in its use of "primitive materials on a monumental scale." The people of Djenne are fishermen and traders, attached to their city and seldom leaving it, said DeGramont.[13]

It is amazing how often scholars who wish to understand ancient Egyptian culture, especially its religion, are driven to the study of other Black African populations who are descendants of ancient Egyptians or who descended from a common source as the ancient Egyptians. This was expressed explicitly by E. A. Wallace Budge and also by Henri Frankfort in his book, *Kingship and the Gods,* as he states that there are two ways to penetrate behind the words of the text. First there were alive at the time in Africa subgroups of people who, according to Frankfort, were the survivors of that great east African substratum out of which Egyptian culture arose. Among other things that Frankfort sought to study was how deeply the divine nature of kings affects both the ruler and his subjects. Once again, the essential point to be made here is there is an overwhelming abundance of "empirical" data to show both the historical and contemporary cultural connection between East Africa, including Egypt, and its continental and intercontinental diaspora.[14]

We need the linguistic terms from Noam Chomsky of "surface structure" and "deep structure" to explain the apparent diversity that exists throughout the African continent and, indeed, throughout the diaspora. Foreign explorers have been fascinated by what they considered to be significant differences among Africans, differences in the physiognomy of peoples, in ways of worship, etc. However, they have attracted to the surface structural manifestations. Clearly, an impartial investigation based upon empirical facts will demonstrate, as Cheikh Anta Diop and others such as Robert Thompson and Janheinz Jahn have done, that cultural unity is far more significant than is superficial diversity.[15]

If time permitted, it would be instructive to examine the records of African neighbors in what we now call the Middle East, in Asia, and in Europe. In doing this, we would see that during the early part of development of civilization the source of civil ideas was almost completely African. Three thousand years of unbroken development along the Nile Valley positioned Africans to have a major influence on the world, an influence that still continues.

Education

This brings me to my major task, which is to attempt to sharpen our picture of Egyptian education. We are hampered in our attempt to learn about ancient Egyptian education not only by the widespread loss of documentary materials, the destruction of social institutions and civilizations, including their library records, and years of prejudice and neglect; but also by the fact that some of the most important parts of the educational process were conducted in "secret." Much of the tradition was passed on orally to the prepared initiate.

We are indebted to such writers as George G.M. James, R.A. Schwaller DeLubicz, Robert Thompson, Albert Churchward, and others for helping to unveil some of this "secret" tradition. George James studied the reports of the establishment historians and collected fragments of accepted information, placing them in a new perspective. R. A. Schwaller DeLubicz studied the ruins of the Temple at Luxor and Egyptian symbolic writing and thought. Thompson studied cultural patterns of existing Bantu tribal groups, especially their religious practices. Churchward studied the evolution of the use of symbols from their source in the Great Lakes region and Nile Valley to the dispersion of the use of those symbols through the world. What I'm trying to show once again is that there is an empirical base for emerging descriptions of an ancient Egyptian educational system.[16]

As we look at the ancient Egyptian cultural patterns, we see that there was not only a cultural unity among apparently diverse groups of people. There was also an essential unity within the culture that was reflected in the intimate and harmonious ties between and among education, politics, economics, religion, and so forth. It would make no sense whatsoever to consider the educational process apart from a deep study of the worldview and religion of ancient Egypt. Ancient Egyptians lived close to nature, basically as a sedentary population under highly favorable environmental conditions. They were in a position to make repeated observations of natural processes over thousands of years. As clearly as anywhere else in the world, it can be seen in the Nile Valley that nature has regular processes of birth, growth, aging, death, decay, and rebirth. All nature seems to tell the same story. The behavior of the Mother Nile was cyclical. Within general limits, this behavior could be predicted. Indeed, the successful predictions of its rise and fall determined the degree to which its bountiful resources could be exploited.

The skies were almost always clear, providing an unparalleled opportunity for long-term systematic observation of the behavior of heavenly bodies. The enduring repetitive cycles obviously made a profound impression upon the ancient dwellers on the Nile. The Nile River in Egypt is but a thin ribbon in a vast land with a full population. From its beginning, Egypt was crowded and provided the basis for easy transportation up and down the smooth Nile River. Transportation on the Nile was assisted by the winds that blow from the north to the south, enabling travelers to take a current downstream to the north and to return to the south aided by the light breezes.

The ancient Egyptians observed movement, change, and life itself. What seems to have impressed them most was the degree to which a grand design appeared to be evident throughout the universe, enabling one who studied any part of the universe to understand the rest of it through the play of analogies. For example, the Nile was a river on the earth and the Milky Way was a "river in the sky." The observations of plant and animal life provided the opportunity to reflect on human life as well as with cycles of birth, growth, death, decay, and rebirth.

A major technology arose in the northern end of the Nile Valley. That technology is reflected in thousands of temples, tombs, pyramids and in writings and scientific developments and discoveries. The observational technology that produced the first zodiac such as that seen in the Temple of Dendera or in the Tomb of Seti I in the Valley of the Kings at Waset (Luxor to the Arabs and Thebes to the Greeks), gives evidence of a long line of development. The construction of the Great Pyramid at Giza, attributed to Pharaoh Khufu, with its 2.2 million limestone rocks averaging two tons each, some weighing as much as forty tons, giving ample evidence of a high level of technical development. This is especially true when we realize that until the present time, no one appears to have been able to repeat the feat.

But given these and many other examples of high level technical developments in Egypt, what is important is not so much the level of technical development as the "philosophical orientation of the users of the technology." The purpose of technology is to develop a greater understanding of man's relationship to nature and mankind's place in nature. This is in stark contrast to some contemporary expressions of technology. Today, we seem to seek technical developments for the sole purpose of "exploiting" the environment for personal gains in wealth and power. Sometimes the goal of technology is expressed merely as one of helping people or nations to know, but toward "what end?"

At this point we need to return to George G.M. James who has given an excellent summary description of the Egyptian Mystery System. The ultimate aim of education in Egypt was for a person to become "one with God" or to "become like God." The path to the development of godlike qualities was through the development of virtue. A person was seen as being essentially spiritual whose essence was housed in a finite body. It was the spirit that had an eternal existence. The capacity of a person to become godlike was determined by the degree to which the person was able to overcome certain natural impediments of the body. These were character flaws, and virtue was the antidote to character flaws. But virtue could be achieved only through special study and effort. According to James, the following 10 virtues were sought by students in the ancient Egyptian Mystery System:

1. Control of thought
2. Control of action
3. Steadfastness of purpose
4. Identity with the spiritual life

5. Evidence of having a mission in life
6. Evidence of a call to spiritual orders
7. Freedom from resentment under persecution and wrong
8. Confidence in the power of the master as teacher
9. Confidence in one's own ability to learn
10. Readiness or preparedness for initiation[17]

Even a brief study of this list of 10 virtues reveals just how different it is in character from typical educational objectives with which most of us are familiar. In *Stolen Legacy*, James goes into great detail to explain and to interpret the meaning of these 10 virtues.

George G. M. James also tells us that the center of the higher education system in ancient Egypt was located at the ancient Egyptian city of Waset, which means "the septer," after the town or name of province from which this small city developed. It was sometimes referred to as the city of Amun, which was the name of the great god. Apparently, Waset was so important that it was sometimes simply referred to as "The City." Waset was later given the name Thebes by European invaders, and after that, the name Luxor, by the Arab invaders. Various sections of the city of Waset had their own names. One section of the city was called Ipet Isut the translation, "most select of places." Later populations would refer to it as Karnak where a great temple now stands. Another part of Waset was called the Southern Ipet or sanctuary. Later, populations would refer to this section as Luxor, the name by which the whole city is now called.

It was at Waset (Thebes or Luxor) where the oldest records of a university headquarters existed. We may think of this as the main branch. Speculation places the age of this headquarters as far back as 3,000 B.C. There was another "grand lodge" in lower or northern Egypt dedicated to God in the name of Osiris. It was called the Osiriaca. This lodge had branches in other parts of the Egyptian sphere of influence. According to George James, several were located as follows: the Ionian Temple at Dydma, Euclid's Lodge at Megara, Pythagora's Lodge at Cortona, and the Orphic Temple at Delphi.

We begin to get some inkling of the high level of esteem for the Egyptian civilization and all that the Greeks and Romans felt for it by a review of the activities of the

Europeans when confronted with African civilization. It is hard to account for the behavior of European conquerors of Kemet except to note that they must have felt themselves to be in the presence of a superior civilization. They tried to imitate it.

Jill Kamil remarks that Ptolemaic rule was noted for its architectural activity, and that the Greeks tried in every way to add to the splendor of national buildings after one of the Egyptian priests had told Alexander that he was the son of the god Amon, and that he should revere him. The Romans also repaired ruins and built temples in the traditional style, but it was a losing battle, since the past could not be recaptured. Thebes, according to Kamil, could hardly hide its well-worn wrinkles; a time-weathered quality lay over the metropolis.

Not only were buildings copied, European kings and people joined the African religions in Africa and in Europe. It was this "African religion" of Isis, Osiris, Horus, and Amen (Amon or Amun) that remained one of the major religions of Europe until the national government of Rome installed Christianity as the state religion, after the Council of Nicea, nearly three hundred years after the death of Christ.

Parenthetically, we can illustrate at this point the close connection between education and religion. We can also show some antecedents of western religion. In doing this, we take our material directly from the remains of the monuments themselves, in this case, the Temple of Luxor.

As Kamil states, the temple contains a birth room, and in that birth room on the left-hand wall in three rows is the story of the conception and birth of Amenhotep. In one row, the god Khnum, is making the baby Amenhotep and his guardian spirit on a potter's wheel while the goddess Isis sits in the presence of Amon. In the middle row, the ibis-headed god, Jehuti, God of Wisdom, leads Amon to the queen's bed chamber. Here, Amon approaches her in order to beget the child whom Khnum has already molded. After the delivery, Amon will stand with the child in his arms in the presence of the goddesses Hathor and Mut. Shown in the top row are the infant king being suckled, the infant king's guardian spirits, and his presentation to the god Amon by Horus. Horus promises him "millions of years like Ra."[18]

Here we have then—in the Eighteenth Dynasty—a visual record of the virgin birth of Amen-Hotep. We find the same scene portrayed in the mortuary temple of Hatshepsut. Once again, it is in the birth colonnade of that temple.

The birth colonnade corresponds to the Punt Colonnade. It was constructed to allay concern about the legitimacy of Queen Hatshepsut's claim to the throne. Here we see the theory of her divine origin: the ram-headed Khnum is shaping Hatshepsut and her Ka on the potter's wheel, while being instructed by Amon; it is Amon who has impregnated the queen's mother, Ahmose, with Hatshepsut.

The careful listener may wonder why we skipped a period in the Twelfth Dynasty over as far as the Eighteenth Dynasty. It must be noted there that during this period of time, the government of Egypt was in the hands of invading kings, the Hyksos from Asia. However, their reign is less important than it might be for a very simple reason. They seem to have had little to offer to Kemet.

As Elizabeth Riefstahl has observed, the Hyksos had very little culture of their own, and as a result they readily adopted the Egyptian arts and customs and to some extent even the religion of the Egyptians. The new Hyksos rulers took over the titles of the Egyptian kings, and like those kings referred to themselves as "sons of Re," the ancient Egyptian solar god from whom all pharaohs claimed descent. Riefstahl also mentions that some scant remains show that the Hyksos added to and embellished some Egyptian temples, while they destroyed others. Through what little survives from the Hyksos period in the way of art and architecture, we see a decline in skill. What papyri from that period remain, however, show that learning in the temples continued undiminished.[19]

Certain authors have looked at the initiation system that still exists in West Africa. It is good to do this because that system is a direct outgrowth of the more ancient initiation system that was utilized in the Nile Valley. Contemporary information and historical study of the initiation in West Africa reveals that the process operated in the following way. According to Pierre Erny in his book, *Childhood and Cosmos*, the following things were included in the initiation process:

1. The initiates were physically segregated from the regular activity of daily life.

2. They retreated from their familiar environment to an environment that enabled them to get more directly in touch with nature. This symbolized a move from the infantile situation into a situation that would allow for more maturity.

3. The initiates joined with other initiates of the same age and shared their lives in common, since the common living experience was also a common learning experience.

4. The initiates were separated from their parents in addition to being separated from the large community.

5. The initiates had to renounce all that recalls the past existence.

6. The initiates were then taught by the old men and old women of the village or town.

7. The initiates frequently went nude or wore clothes made of grass to symbolize the clothes of the first men or women.

8. The initiates underwent purification baths.

9. During the course of initiation, a number of tests of audacity, courage, fasting, flogging, hazing, mutations, scarifications were conducted. (The purpose of the test was to give the opportunity for the initiates to demonstrate a refusal to take life as it is given as a way of opening the mind to beauty, joy and ecstasy.)

10. Initiates learned a new and secret language.

11. Initiates were given new names.

12. The initiation processes symbolizes a rebirth.

13. The initiation process included a number of exercises and things to be learned such as physical and military training, songs, dances, how to handle sacred things such as math and tools.[20]

Dadisi Sonyika summarizes the initiation process into seven steps.[21]

1. Separation
2. Location in a sacred place
3. Symbolic death and burial
4. Testing or revelation
5. Testing
6. Resurrection (symbolic)
7. Reintroduction or reincorporation of the initiate into the larger community

It can be seen from the study of Isha DeLubicz's work, *Her-Bak*, that the West African initiation process, as described by Sonyika and Erny, is quite congruent with the initiations that are described by DeLubicz, based upon the study of documents, carvings, and paintings from ancient Egypt. At its base, initiation is a comprehensive education system. In addition to the narrowly vocational aims one can discern in the ancient Egyptian and ancient African educational system, the goals were the following:

* Unity of the person, unity of the tribe, and unity with nature
* The development of social responsibility
* The development of character
* The development of spiritual power[22]

It was these higher aims that drove the educational process. Vocational skill training was merely a small part of the whole process.

In the ancient Egyptian educational system, little thought seems to have been given to the question of the "inept intellectual capacity" of a person. Much more attention was given to the character as an impediment or as a facilitator of educational development. While learning was obviously done by individuals, the picture that we get of the method used is that it was a collective rather than an individual effort. The educational process was designed in such a way that it seemed to be a true rebirth that occurs through successive series of personal and social transformations.

Initiates were deeply immersed in a comprehensive process. It was an interactive process. There were interactions among students and interactions between student and teacher. The process was full including much time for stories, examination of signs, symbols, the use of proverbs, the use of songs, dances, and so forth—all combined to convey values and to convey a special view of the world. Teachers or "masters" modeled the behavior that they expected the initiates to learn. The masters were alert and in a position to react to and to nurture the direct experience of students in order that they could learn higher level lessons.

At its base the educational process was a religious process in the broadest sense of that word. The entire living environment was organized and constructed to the smallest detail as a teaching environment. The architecture was symbolic to the smallest detail. Even the layout of buildings within a city carried symbolic meaning. Clothing that was worn, names that were given, everything had multilevels of meaning. This indicated a full-time commitment to the goal of personal transformation through education.

The best single description of education in ancient Egypt is given by Isha Schwaller DeLubicz. In two books, she presents her findings through the use of an initiate, Her-Bak. DeLubicz and her husband, R. A. Schwaller DeLubicz, spent nearly 15 years on a detailed study of the Temple of Luxor and its environs. R. A. Schwaller DeLubicz has written numbers of important books on that work. In the *The Temple in Man* and, *Symbol and the Symbolic,* the DeLubiczs tried to "enter into the mentality of the Egyptians" by an in-depth study of their records, both written and archaeological. In Isha Schwaller DeLubicz's books, almost all narrative is supported by illustrations of temple carvings, drawings, relief carvings, and building configurations, primarily at Luxor and Karnak Temples in Waset.

It must be kept in mind that both Luxor Temple and Karnak Temple are built on the site of older temples! For example, the "White Chapel," the oldest part of the Eighteenth Dynasty temple at Karnak, is a reconstruction from fragments that were made by crushing the old chapel. The small places were then used as "seeds" from which the new Temple of Amon would grow. The fragments were found in the third Pylon of the Temple of Amon. The older temple, the White Chapel, was built by Sesostris during the Twelfth Dynasty (1950 B.C.) as an offering to the great Black God Min. Both represent extensions of religious and educational practices that were known from the beginnings of Egyptian civilization.[23]

While no one can be certain of all the details of ancient Egyptian culture, one must respect writers such as the DeLubiczs who do not stray far from primary sources, as best they can be understood.

The Aims of Egyptian Education

We must keep in mind that the Egyptians made no separation between "church and state," or for that matter, between religion and life. They lived a totally religious life, just as is the case with traditional African religions today. Therefore, education was religious at its base.

The lower education system, no matter how unstructured, allowed for a natural progress along a path that reached certain choice points. Having started along a path of advanced education, a student could reach the major choice of his or her life, according to Isha Schwaller DeLubicz, the "choice between leadership and high positions or knowledge and wisdom." The student who chose ambition also chose limits. It was said that "ambition does to intuition what weevils do to wheat." On the other hand, for one who was able to sacrifice personal ambition, the act of sacrifice was said to "defend consciousness against the deadly effect of the search for satisfaction." For that person, the path leading to wisdom was open. The initiate could reach the outer Temple or "Peristyle" where "utilitarian" knowledge was mastered. However, once admitted to the Inner Temple, the initiate learned about symbols and came to know him or herself. Undoubtedly, as George G.M. James, has so clearly shown, Greek students of the African "mysteries" came to respect this goal, "man know thyself," which has been falsely attributed to Socrates, the Greek latecomer of dynastic times. The highest aim of Egyptian education was for one to become godlike through the revision of one's own "Neter," of how God is revealed in the person.[24]

Methodology in Egyptian Pedagogy

Serious education began by putting the initiate on the path of observation of nature. Usually the initiate would be assigned to a master as an apprentice. But the purpose of the apprenticeship was for the student to learn the laws of matter (materials). It was the knowledge of these laws that separated the master craftsman from a mere worker. So the "observation" of nature was really a participatory observation. Revealed in any craft were nature's laws. During the apprenticeship, the initiate was confronted with problems of conscience. This would allow for the development of a sense of responsibility and judgment. At the end of a successful apprenticeship, the initiate was offered the chance to choose between the two paths, "political power" and "wisdom."

Heavy use was made of proverbs, songs, and stories. Direct or symbolic lessons were taught through these. It was the fundamental belief in the unity or interconnectedness of all things that made the use of analogies such a powerful pedagogical tool "for above is exalted by below." The use of proverbs and analogies permeates African and African diasporan culture today.[25]

Parenthetically, it is interesting that racist psychologists claim that Black people are not capable of "Level II thinking," the kind of abstract thinking that is reflected in proverbs and analogies. To the contrary, this is our strong suit. It is the mismatch in experiential content between such psychologists and African Americans that causes them to miss the extensive use of proverbs and analogies among us.

The African reader of ancient Egyptian writings will find familiar methodology in the use of such things as the sayings of Ptahotep, Fifth Dynasty, (circa 2350 B.C.)

> Do not be arrogant because of your knowledge, but confer with the ignorant man as with the learned, for the limit of skill has not been attained, and there is no craftsman who has [fully] acquired his mastery. Good speech is more hidden than malachite, yet is found in the possession of women slaves at the milestones.[26]

Then there are the teachings of Kagemni that are contained along with the teachings of Ptahotep in the "Prisse Papyrus." The teachings of Ptahotep say such things as the following:

> ...The submissive man prospers, the moderate man is praised, the tent is open for the silent man, and the place of the contented man is wide. Do not talk [freely], for the flint knives are sharpened against the one who strays from the road; there is no hastening, except indeed against his misdeed.[27]

The instructions of Amenomope are estimated to have been written during the Eighteenth Dynasty just before the Amarna period, possibly during the reign of Amen-Hotep III. These sayings have close parallels to later Hebrew scriptures in the book of Proverbs.

> The hot-headed man in the temple is like a tree grown indoors; only for a moment does it put forth roots. It reaches its end in the carpentry shop, it is floated away from its place, or fire is its funeral pyre. The truly temperate man sets himself apart. He is like a tree grown in a sunlit field. But it flourishes, it doubles its yield, it stands before its owner; its fruit is something

> sweet, its shade is pleasant; and it reaches its end
> as a statute.[28]

When we look at the "Memphite Theology," writings that are estimated to have been composed at the beginning of the pyramid age, we see something remarkably similar to the method of Karl Marx, the dialectic, complete with the use of contradictions. In the Memphite Theology, writings on stone at Memphis in Egypt, we find the doctrine of the four elements and the four qualities. This "law of opposites" (the relationship between pairs of elements) sets up the conditions under which creativity occurs. The Pyramid texts also use the principle of opposites in the description of the African "pantheon," or place of "the Gods." Like the later Greek and Roman copies, there was an Ennead—a pantheon of nine Gods, or more correctly, a diagram of nine aspects of the one Great Neter (God).[29]

Egyptian Aspects of God

Atum

Shu (Air)   Tefnut (Moisture)

Geb (Earth)   Nut (Sky)

Osirus   Isis   Seth   Nephthys

In early times the Sun-God had his own family of gods that was also the supreme council of the gods. This group, which had its chief center at the Temple of the Sun at Heliopolis, was the Ennead, "the Nine," consisting of four interrelated couples surmounted by one common ancestor. This Ennead or "Nine" may be placed in contrast to the "Eight," for "Eight" comprised elements of cosmic disorder, whereas the "Nine" contained only progressive steps of cosmic order: air and moisture, earth and sky, the beginnings on earth.

The Content of Egyptian Pedagogy

I have already referred to George G. M. James' list of curriculum content. Those courses—grammar, rhetoric, logic, arithmetic, astronomy, geometry and music—were the liberating or liberal arts. They supported the quest of the initiate for the highest form of self-knowledge. The initiate would study for "form," "name," "place," and "symbol" of things. Having done that, it was believed that the "function" of things would be revealed.

The important thing to remember is that "nature it-self," the environment or the person, was the basic content for study. In addition, the study of nature was facilitated by the study of symbols, stories, proverbs, songs, puzzles, rhythm, and the sacred writings of the Mdw Ntr (hieroglyphics). These studies also gave insight into human nature, which was as shown before, merely the study of one aspect of nature.

In the final analysis, the ancient Egyptian sought MAAT (truth, justice, and order). To be more correct, I should say that they sought to become one with MAAT, the cosmic order.

The window to what was a well-developed education system is through ancient Kemet. Even though the best records in antiquity are found in Kemet, the picture is not yet complete. Suffice it to say that ancient Kemet was an African culture and it shared then, and shares now, in the greater cultural unity of the African continent and in the diaspora of ancient African people.

A careful study and reconstruction of this aspect of our African past can guide the reconstruction and development of educational aims, methods, and content appropriate to the children of the sun. As Gerald Massey has said, "Truth is all powerful with its silent power/if only whispered and never heard aloud/But working secretly almost unseen, except in some excommunicated book/Truth is like lightning with its errand done before you hear the thunder."[30]

Saving Our Children

Several years ago in Bay City, Texas, a memorial monument was unveiled and dedicated to my father who died a short time earlier. He had been a high school principal, as had his father before him.

On the site of my father's first principalship—at a school named for his father—graduates, former faculty, and friends gathered for the unveiling of the monument. After the official program was over, an old gentleman who had been a member of my father's first PTA interrupted the closing remarks and asked to speak. He appeared to be in his 80s and frail, though mentally very alert. The crowd became silent as Mr. Robert Hart began his brief remarks.

> Now some a y'all might not know this, but the ground you're standin' on used to be very wet. Children used to be playin' out here with mud and water comin' up over they shoe tops. Me and my brother, Prince, and Mr. Green Farris had some good mules. So we got our mules and scraped up some sand, and we put those children *On Dry Ground*!! That's all I got to say.

My ears jumped into my throat as his words reminded me of all the African American men and women that I have seen who saw what had to be done, who have taken the initiative, and without hesitation or a backwards glance have done what had to be done, against all the odds. Like them, Mr. Hart knew what he had to do. He *had* to make *dry ground* for the children.

That was back in the 1930s. Needless to say, the school that I referred to was a segregated school for African Americans. Jim Crow laws were explicit. It would be nearly

25 years before the 1954 Supreme Court decision, *Brown vs. Board of Education,* would outlaw official school segregation, 35 years before the upheavals of the 1960s, and nearly 60 before today.

One would think and hope that with time and with national enlightenment that we would have completely escaped from the ravages of slavery, segregation, racism, and poverty. Yet, as we shall see, heaven has not yet come upon this earth for African Americans, nearly 130 years after the signing of the Emancipation Proclamation, a period in which the greatest number of European immigrants have gone through their torture to full socioeconomic status.

More than a year ago, Dr. Barbara Sizemore and I were asked to chair the National Association of Black School Educators (NABSE) Task Force on Black Academic and Cultural Excellence. The task force's research led us to conclude that there is cause for alarm when our children and their education are concerned. Indeed, there is cause for alarm when our people as a whole are concerned. The picture is not bright, whether you are looking at achievement test scores, dropout rates, suspensions, expulsions, the decline in the numbers of African American principals and teachers, or other school-related problems. The picture is equally bleak when we look at our children's support system in general, whether we review the statistics on African American male employment, child abuse, adolescent pregnancies, adolescent and young suicide, or troubles with African American families.

How long it will take us to realize that all of our children are in deep trouble, not just the ones who are out of work, on drugs, or in trouble with the law? Perhaps even more serious, our children lack a clear and meaningful identity, purpose, and direction. Ask those who are deeply involved with adolescents on a regular basis what they see. The most sensitive observers that I know do not bear good news. For example, a mother in New York, who is deeply involved in sponsoring youth activities and who is tuned in to the informed dialogue of average youths says this:

> I see too many youngsters who are angry, confused, and depressed, especially the young men. They are ready to "throw down." They ain't taking no shit. The teenagers focus on trying to be a man, but they don't know how. They're just

going on guts. Many of the young sisters are taking all kinds of abuse from the young brothers.

It's a shame. Children got so much to say and ain't nobody listening.

Another observer is a psychologist in California who used to counsel presuicidal adolescents. She says that they, and to a lesser extent, most African American children, had important things in common. She said, "Asa, they are just out there. They are just floating. They have no boundaries. They don't know where they begin and end." Many of those who are most in trouble are those that are "making it" by popular standards such as work or school grades. Yet our children are not on *dry ground.*

These and other symptoms of difficulty are tied to the external stresses of poverty that continue unabated (nearly one million African American families have fallen into poverty since 1980) and the stresses of racism, which have taken on new forms.

W. E. B. Du Bois said at the beginning of this century that, "The problem of the twentieth century is the problem of the color line." The main difference between then and now is that in recent times the line has been drawn in "invisible ink." To come to conclusions that result in the failure to employ and, in the decision, to dismiss thousands of qualified African American teachers mainly on the basis of biased standardized, multiple choice, paper-and-pencil test scores, is to draw the invisible color line. To fail to find a solution to the employment problem for nearly one-half of the African American male population, and to fail to see these appalling numbers as a crisis demanding immediate attention, is to draw the invisible color line. To fail to deal with television programs and films that continue to defame, insult, and distort the images of African Americans on a daily basis, all in the name of the one great media god "the ratings," is to draw the color line in invisible ink. To fail to overhaul the whole school curriculum so that it fairly reflects upon the African American in more than cosmetic ways, is to draw the color line in invisible ink. To continue to question the intellect of African American children who have been deprived of opportunity, is to draw the color line in invisible ink. To have your nation invade Grenada to "restore democracy," go to war against Nicaragua, both openly and clandestinely, to "restore democracy," and yet sit in the United

Nations Security Council, unwilling or unable even to verbally condemn the apartheid policies of the tyrannical, racist, slave state of South Africa, is to draw the color line in invisible ink. To say that apartheid is "repugnant," but to abstain from voting in the UN to oppose it, or take other actions that count, is to smile while allowing the color line to be drawn.

As painful as the color line may be, visible or invisible, our real problem as leaders in education has to do with whether or not we know that it is there or not. We must never forget that all change is not progress. There are those among our people who say that we have left them, as we have walked the pathway of individual success. They say that we hear the siren sounds of Babylon. They say that the chump change that we naively call "wealth" has plugged our ears and blindfolded our eyes to the plight of the masses of our people.

They say that we believe, like George Jefferson, that we will have actually "moved on up to the top," when we finally get a "deluxe apartment in the sky." Many of our people have begun to wonder if we recall the sacrifices in blood, sweat, and tears that they made as

> Stony the road we trod
> Bitter the chastening rod
> Felt in the days when hope unborn had died
> Yet with a steady beat
> Have not our weary feet
> Come to the place for which our fathers sighed.
> We have come over a way that with tears has been watered
> We have come, treading a path through the blood
> of the slaughtered,
> Out from the gloomy past
> Till now we stand at last
> Where the white gleam of our bright star is cast.
> —James Weldon Johnson

It should be clear to anyone who looks closely that the years of poverty, slavery, segregation, racism, and the invisible color line have begun to take their toll. Like Muhummad Ali, the years of heavyweight blows to the body and to the head make it hard for kidneys to do what the kidneys are supposed to do and for the head to do what the head (mission control) is supposed to do. Extraordinary stresses can make you lose your memory, your sense of direction, but most important of all, you may lose your sense of direction, but most important of all, you may lose your sense of identity. In short, you will lose your *dry ground.*

In the *Souls of Black Folk,* Du Bois warned us about the sickness of "double consciousness," of having no true self-consciousness, of having to see ourselves through the eyes of others. Like Du Bois, Woodson saw the consequences of miseducation that produced this dependent consciousness. It leaves a people ripe for manipulation and exploitation. It makes us turn to and try to impress the wrong audience. It causes us to seek rewards from strangers. It prevents us from mobilizing our resources together.

We do not control the institutions that educate and socialize our children: the schools, the mass media, the law, etc. A possible exception can be made for some of our churches and a few other organizations. Yet our children *are* being schooled and socialized, but not by us. Moreover, we adults are also being schooled and socialized, by someone other than us. For example, I know that you have heard the statistics that children watch more than 22,000 hours of television, on the average, during grades 1 through 12, while they attend school for 12,000 hours. But the gross shame and pity is that we adults watch more television than do our children! We are truly their models. What models!

Previous reports about "excellence," with rare exceptions, were reports about *efficiency* in meeting certain "standards." Yet no serious look was taken at the "standards." They are the same "standards" that have been around for years. When we see things as standards at all, we should see them as minimal. They do not begin to address the needs of African Americans.

The NABSE task force report was explicit and uncompromising about academic "standards." We spell out in criterion terms, not in floating normative terms, what we expect from the schools *for the masses* of African American children in mathematics, language arts, and foreign language. We do this because it is right, even though we know that the pious platitudes about excellence spoken nationally are not followed by the real dollars that are necessary to produce excellence. For example, no state and no one in the national government have announced any plan to pay to produce the teachers and the conditions for adequate instruction of American children in foreign languages or in writing skills.

Our task force's report is unique. It is a message about academic quality at the *maximum competency* level. It points out that such excellence is already being achieved by a handful of African American educators. In other words, we call for the most rigorous standards of academic quality. Only the *Paidea Proposal* and the College Board report, *What High School Students Need To Know*, come close to our vision here. But we go much further!! We speak to the unique needs and conditions of African Americans. No report, other than two by the NAACP, has begun to address our special needs systematically.

When we looked closely at the condition of our people and our children, we saw that we would be boarding a "ship of fools" if we scrambled wildly to join the crowd on many of the "excellence" ocean liners. But we remembered that "all that glitters is not gold," and that "everybody talking 'bout heaven ain't goin' there." We remember that some ships are not what they are said to be, are not headed for our port of call, and may have no round trip passages available. We remember this from our first experience with foreign ships.

Interestingly, the first American slave ship was called "The Rainbow." But there was no "pot of gold" at the end of it for us. We did not see "birds flying high" over it either. Vincent Harding in his book, *There Is A River*, reminds us that other ships that delivered us here into slavery included those with the following names: "Brotherhood," "John the Baptist," "Justice," "Integrity," "Gift of God," "Liberty," and last, but not least, "Jesus." Just sailing on any ship may result in a trick rather than a treat, and not just on Halloween.

It is to the everlasting credit of our NABSE president, that brilliant educator and leader, Don Smith, and the NABSE Board of Directors that this task force was established and charged with looking at *Black, academic,* and *cultural excellence.* So we have spoken out of concern for African Americans. We have spoken about traditional general *academic* concerns, and for excellence there. Now we wish to speak to the matter of *cultural excellence* for African Americans.

Years ago, Franz Fanon, that great African Martinican psychiatrist, showed us clearly one of the functions of group culture. He showed in his book, *A Dying Colonialism*, that when the French government was at war to colonize Algeria, they used the services of scholars such as anthropologists to find a way to weaken the capacity of Algerian people to resist. The scholars recommended a frontal assault on male-female relationships and on Algerian religion, as well as on other cultural practices. They directed some of their attention to the veil worn by Algerian women. They couched their language in words about women's liberation that no right-acting person could oppose (remember the deceptive names on the slave ships). Yet France was not interested in the liberation of Algerian women. They wanted to create disunity among Algerians in order to enslave *both* the Algerian male and female.

Chinua Achebe, in his novels *Things Fall Apart, No Longer At Ease, Man of the People*, and *Arrow of God*, has shown how the destruction of the cultural fabric of a people is tantamount to the destruction of the people themselves.

Amilcar Cabral, fighting for independence in Guinea-Bissau, saw that there was a powerful relationship between the ability of his people to resist colonial domination and the maintenance of their unique cultural forms. These were not static cultural forms. They were forms that, while based on their past, grew out of a group's present struggles to advance as a group.

T. A. Lambo, a West African psychiatrist, has shown that those Africans who maintained their cultural traditions were more healthy psychologically than those who did not.

Jordan K. Ngubane of South Africa has shown that a distorted and alien religion was used to pry the Zulus away from their ancient religious forms, not to save Zulu souls. It was used to soften the Zulu for the military conquest and slavery that followed and continues till this very day.

Price Cobb, African American psychiatrist and coauthor with William Grier of *Black Rage*, is the founder of a new American movement in psychiatry, ethnotherapy. It is based on the proven idea that a person's cultural makeup is a primary resource in moving from mental sickness to mental health.

Why should we make such an issue over the matter of African American culture? To put it simply, we see an accelerating erosion of our culture and with it, of our capacity to use our own cultural traditions for our political, social, economic, and spiritual benefit. We are not, in general, passing on to our children those things that will give them a clear sense of identity, purpose, and direction. These things cannot be taught to them by strangers. To the extent that this is attempted, our children will suffer. Moreover, we see the flood and mud of value-poor, popular, mass culture covering over our creativities once more, as they have done in parts of our ancestral home, especially our ancient African Nile Valley cultures such as the remnants that lie under Lake Nasser in Nubia. *We need dry ground.*

The symptoms are clear. To see you in your green on St. Patrick's Day, saying your prayers with the sad belief that God speaks only in Old English (thee, thy, thou); singing or chanting your Mass in the Latin language; joining others in calling your own sacred ancestors "pagan" and "heathen"; struggling hard to master English literature; speaking the French language with pride; abandoning gospel music, body movement, call and response, and other traditional ways of communicating those things most deeply felt in our churches; shedding tears over European symphonies; straining your toes in ballet, and even doing a little hee haw; in this, I wish you well and take no issue. But is this all that you are? Is that "excellence" to you?

To me, there is something peculiar and pathetic about an African American psychiatrist who is an expert on Sigmund Freud and who is ignorant of Franz Fanon. It is peculiar and pathetic when an African American educator has read and remembered much of John Dewey and none of W. E. B. Du Bois. It is peculiar and pathetic when the African American teacher of literature is comfortable with Chaucer and has to ask who is Chinweizu and how to pronounce his name. It is peculiar and pathetic when the African American bibliophile loves the novels of Ernest Hemingway and has never heard the name Zora Neale Hurston. It is peculiar and pathetic to see an African American physician raise his or her hand and take the "Oath of Hippocrates" and grow misty-eyed and inspired over the glory that was Greece, not knowing that the Greek "Father of Medicine" is but a poor copy of the ancient

African God of Medicine, Imhotep, the world's first mul-tigenius. Where is our *dry ground?*

Given the current definition of "excellence," so popu-lar in our nation, you can have 1200 on the SAT and 18 on the ACT and not know there exists a body of excellent African and African American literature. You can score in the ninetieth percentile on the Graduate Record Exami-nation and know nothing of the unparalleled creative tradition of African Americans in music and dance. You can earn a Ph.D. from an Ivy League university and be ignorant of the fact that Africans and African Americans have asked and provided answers to profound questions about nature, man, and culture. Most national merit schol-ars are ignorant of the path- breaking developments by African American mathematicians, engineers, chemists, physicists, and biologists from the research on the atomic bomb to that of the space program.

What I am saying is that most of the definitions of excellence are not excellent, they are deficient. They are largely devoid of sensitivity to African Americans' special problems and to African American content. Under these popular definitions, an African American student could be "excellent" and not know where Africa is, what nations are there, who the leaders are, what the problems are, and how the problems relate to him or her.

It is this cultural retardation in African American his-tory and culture that leaves our children unable to tell the difference between *excellent technical talent* and *excellent role models.* It is the same retardation that leads some of our most brilliant and talented children to become pied pipers of cultural and spiritual death.

Are you surprised when your children are raised by television, movies, advertisements, insensitive schools, and no "ole-time" churches, that what you get back is truly pitiful? You gave a bright, beautiful, talented child to the world. Yet when he came home to you, he gave no sign of recognition. While he was away, he made some changes in the way that he looked. He found a way to fix his hair texture, from rough to Jheri-curled ringlets. He asked the doctors to put the knife to his nose. He also asked the surgeon to cut his eyes while he was at it. His steady date was a new girl, I think her name was Brooke Shields. He also picked up some new parents along the way. It is reported that he said that Henry Fonda was his ideal father image, and that he wants Jackie Kennedy Onassis to do his memoirs. His role model (given all the problems that our people have to face) is Peter Pan! I guess he lived in Hollywood too long, so it is not surprising that he took some of his hard-earned riches to reproduce the Disneyland fantasy in his backyard at home. Really now, Donald Duck? Goofy? Mickey Mouse?

Then one day he got a chance to make the video disk *of his own choosing*, since it cost him $25 million of his own money. His choice was a killer, it was called "Thriller"— just what our people needed. People whose daily lives are filled with violence and horror. His next release was called "Torture." It is a free country. What are our children to do when our children's major role models with rare opportunities choose options that fail to affirm African Americans, who are degraded on a daily basis. The role models are still bright, talented, and beautiful *individuals* who feel no obligation and have no direction to lead or serve the masses of us whose conditions change very little, if at all, over time. Where is our *dry ground?*

Maybe it's too much to hope that we can grow young kings and queens who will know enough and care enough to understand the difference between a Michael Jackson and a Stevie Wonder, between a Gil Scott Heron and a Prince. Our situation as a people is too critical and precarious to afford us the luxury of members who have the opportunity to serve, but feel no need to do so. It is the artist, the poet, the musician, the dancer, the actor, and the novelist that sends messages to our people. The question is, what messages do they send? They cannot send what they do not know. They will not know that which we do not live and teach.

In my opinion, the gifted or excellent African American child is one who

1. can speak an African language.
2. knows "our story" from the beginning to the present.
3. has the ability to understand, to explain, and to enjoy our artistic creativities.
4. has the ability to identify independent African American leadership.
5. has the ability to communicate with his or her own people as well as with others.
6. can locate our primary written records in libraries, bookstores, and research centers.

7. has a sense of identity as an African American.
8. has a sense of obligation to one's people.
9. has a sense of commitment to one's God.
10. has done his or her academic and cultural homework.

Unlike so many educators, we do not believe that African Americans have more "learning problems" than anyone else. We do not believe this because we know of too many cases where the effects of slavery, poverty, segregation, and racism have been reversed almost overnight. We also know of too many places where the brutal attempt at brainwashing treatment never took. We have watched as "qualified" behavioral scientists with "excellent" credentials, time and time again, have failed to see what we are about and have misrepresented our reality. It has taken well-prepared scholars to wade through the distortions. For example, Dr. J. Herman Blake has a fascinating chapter "Doctor Can't Do Me No Good" in Wilbur Watson's book, *Black Folk Medicine: The Therapeutic Significance of Faith and Trust.* He described the work of a brilliant fisherman among the Gullah Sea Islanders.

The Sea Islanders off the coast of Georgia and South Carolina live in a place where they obtain much of their food from the waters. As a result, people have become sensitive to weather and tides in ways that many of us would take for granted, and their sensitivities even seem incredible to the outsiders. Many of the Sea Islanders have the ability to predict weather for 24 to 36 hours before the weather comes, and they will be correct most of the time. They are able to tell if it will rain, when it will rain, and during the rainstorm they can tell how long and how severe the storm will be. Much of their ability is based on a combination of long years of experience and an understanding of wind and cloud formation.

One resident gave Herman Blake a detailed description of how he learned the skills from his mother, who kept stressing the importance of understanding winds and their direction and force. This knowledge of weather was combined with the understanding of tidal flows. The people knew when the tides would be high and low, and whether the tides would be strong, and combined with wind knowledge, they then knew when to expect rough waters. They were intimately acquainted with the processes of nature, and they actually participated in those processes. They used the knowledge that they had developed for fishing and determining when to venture out on the waters in their small vulnerable boats.

Blake found that many elderly people reported that they could use wild porpoises to herd fish. They did this by having two men go into the water in a boat, one took a net and the other would row. Then they would beat on the boat with a certain rhythm, and if there were porpoises in the area, they would swim toward this beat. The rower controlled the boat, and the other man threw his net into the school of fish that were running from the porpoises. By throwing some of the fish that were caught back to the porpoises, the men were able to keep the porpoises circling and thereby keep the fish bunched tightly for the net that they were casting. Blake said that even today some men use a modified version of the practice while they stand on the docks.

Our people did not come here devoid of intelligence, history, or culture. Rather, we had already built the foundations of world civilization. To look at the remnants of African culture after two thousand seasons of invasion and colonization and to judge a people from that is either ignorant or malicious, sometimes both. But it is dysfunctional for our people to feel shame over our cultural heritage, when we should feel immense pride.

Where do we begin to right the wrongs and to repair the situation? Once again, our answer should be quite different than what has been presented in the popular reports on "excellence." Our children will never be academically and culturally excellent until our adults are. African Americans have a special need. We need a massive mobilization of all of our resources toward the reeducation of ourselves and those who would lead the children. Our own memories must be restored. Our own sensitivities to our present cultural greatness must be revived. Our own hunger for self-determination as a people must be resurrected. As educators, we must stand on *dry ground*.

We can and must expect that our regular schools in this nation carry the burden of general skills education. We must expect that they do so with appropriate respect for us as a people and for our traditions. At the same time, cultural excellence will come only as a result of our own efforts. Much of this work must be done after school. We must drastically expand our efforts at systematic ongoing reeducation among our people. We must engage our children in formal after-school academic and cultural education. We must reintroduce celebrations, symbols, and rituals that carry our cultural messages and fix them in consciousness. We must also give close attention to the academic and cultural schooling that our children receive during the regular day. No one will do the important cultural things for us. We must do them for ourselves.

Let me reiterate in the strongest possible terms: neither my comments here, nor the report of the task force, should be construed in the slightest to downplay the important role that the regular schools must play, or our demands for equity in those schools. We are owed full support for a high-quality academic education. We can never be repaid for the lives, blood, and labor of our ancestors. I spent less time on the obvious need for academic quality of regular schools in the report only because I take it for granted that this is an overdue bill.

I must also reiterate the fact that African American children are fully capable of mastering our rigorous criterion levels of performance for high school in 12 years. If *some* of our teachers and principals can push our children to excellence, then we expect the same of schools everywhere. We will not accept the excuses that the children and their families are the problem.

I am not calling for the impossible. I am calling for an expansion of what has already been carried out. Surely, we can support, expand the work of, and listen to the leadership of Hannibal Afrik and the Council for Independent Black Institutions, of Evelyn Moore and the National Black Child Development Institute, of Haki Madhubuti and the Institute for Positive Education in Chicago, of The Institute of the Black World in Atlanta, of Ayin Agiougy and The Marcus Garvey School in Los Angeles. With existing resources, we can form small study groups at will, such as Amenta in Los Angeles, First World Alliance in New York, Kemetic Institute in Chicago, and the Bennu Study Group in Atlanta. I suggest the following educational and cultural projects.

* You can change the curriculum of whole school *systems* to reflect more accurately the experience of your people, as was done in the public schools in Portland, Oregon.

* You can start and build a museum of African American history as is being done in Atlanta, and as has been done in Chicago (The DuSable Museum).
* You can make movies like the one made by Delta Sigma Theta Sorority, Inc.
* You can start education and development efforts in your churches as did the Allen A.M.E. Church in Jamaica, New York; the Wose' Community Church in Oakland, California; and the Shrines of the Black Madonna in Detroit, Atlanta, and other cities.
* You can reintroduce the well-developed, culturally appropriate, and spiritually correct rites of passage through your church, as Ebenezer Baptist Church in Atlanta is doing.
* You can convene national conferences to share knowledge, as did the Institute of Pan-African Studies in Los Angeles and the Kemetic Institute in Chicago.
* You could host a Nile Valley Conference to restore our memory of ancient Africa, as did the Bennu Study Group and the Morehouse College Chapel and School of Medicine's Program for Human Values.
* You could just as easily make your pilgrimage to your ancient Holy Land, as you travel to Europe to enrich its coffers.
* You can sing your own songs a little more in your churches and get out of your autistic catatonic posture when your folk speak and sing to you in your own language.

I am struck by the fact that so many African Americans nationwide are seeing the same things that the task force saw. For example, Fred Hord and Pansey Atkinson at Frostburg State College in Maryland have developed a written document that is remarkably similar to parts of the NABSE report on Black Academic and Cultural Excellence. Even the title, *Save the Children*, is close to ours. There was also a plan developed recently by Ms. Anna Walker of Oakland, California, called B. A. T. A. (Black Americans in Training for Adulthood). It is an attempt to develop a national effort to implement many of the very ideas that we have identified. These and other efforts were developed independent of the Task Force.

In conclusion, as Mr. Robert Hart and his friends did for the children of Bay City, Texas, nearly 50 years ago, we, all of us *together*, must take action on many fronts simultaneously to put our own children on *dry ground*!!!

Kemetic Concepts in Education

Long before the colonization of the African continent by European nations, and long before the first-recorded invasions of the African continent by any nation outside the continent, Africans had developed the most sophisticated system of education to be found in early records. Those records show that the African system of education, especially its classical expression in ancient KMT (later called Egypt by the Greeks), was the parent of other systems of education, especially early European education in Greece and Rome.[1]

According to Plutarch, the wisest of the Greeks, Solon, Thales, Plato, Eudoxus, Pythagoras, actually came to Egypt and "consorted with the Priests." Plutarch also included Lycurgus. He goes on to say that Eudoxus received his instruction from Chonuphis of Memphis. In other words, Plutarch not only tells us where Eudoxus went to school, but specifies his major professor while there, as he did with Solon, who received his instruction from Sonchis of Sais, and Pythagoras from Oenuphis of Heliophis. Then Plutarch says that Pythagoras both greatly admired and was greatly admired by the priests; he copied their symbolism and occult teachings, and incorporated his doctrines in enigmas. "As a matter of fact, most of the Pythagorean precepts do not at all fall short of the writings that are called Hieroglyphics."

Long after invasions of and colonization in ancient Africa by outside nations, Africans maintained sophisticated systems of education. They maintained sophisticated systems appropriate to their environment even under harsh rural conditions. We can still see some of those systems today in traditional communities. It was these systems that were the priority targets of colonizers. Only when they were destroyed would Africans be weakened and confused to the point of serious vulnerability.[2]

Much of the present indigenous African education system is a part of a "secret" oral tradition, as was the case in ancient KMT. Knowledge was "secret" only in the sense that advanced technical ideas and skills would be taught only after a rigorous program of study had been mastered. This was nothing more than a recognition of something important about the learning process. It would mean little to give "secret" knowledge to an unprepared learner. He or she would not understand it.[3]

Over the full course of African history, a number of African civilizations and nations were destroyed by external conquests. This has led such writers as Ayi Kwei Armah to describe in *Two Thousand Seasons* the nearly two thousand years of destruction and decline of African nations, mainly by outside invaders.[4]

Any examination of education in ancient KMT must take into account this relationship of Africa to the rest of the world, especially to its conquerors. Yet because of the traditional ignorance, neglect, defamation, and destruction of African history and culture by outsiders over centuries, the reclamation and restitution of African history today is a very difficult task.

Education Under Black African Rule

My main purpose is to present a brief description of parts of the education system of ancient KMT when it was under native African leadership. While the population of KMT was somewhat ethnically and racially mixed, even in the early kingdoms, it was southern Black African leadership that founded KMT and governed it during its golden ages. For example, out of thirty dynasties or kingdoms, it was during the first seven dynasties that most of the pyramids were built. It was during the Eighteenth Dynasty that the most magnificent temples and tombs were built. It was during the Twenty-fifth Dynasty that there was a restoration of ancient ways. These were native African dynasties. Generally we may say that the native dynasties were Dynasties One through Twelve, Dynasty Eighteen, and Dynasty Twenty-Five. The Nineteenth and Thirtieth Dynasties did have large-scale building programs that imitated earlier native Africa culture. They added nothing new. Rameses II of the Nineteenth Dynasty did increase the scale of some architecture during his rule, but it was in essence the same type of architecture that his predecessors had created.

Operating Framework

The following statements will set forth the operating framework for this article. A more detailed treatment of evidence for these assertions has been presented elsewhere.

1. According to archaeological finds, the oldest hominoids in the world lived in Africa several million years before they appeared anywhere else in the world. Most of the bones of ancient man were found in sites that cluster around that great central eastern African lake Nyanzaa (named Lake Victoria by Europeans) on the equator. Only the last one million years do we find that hominoids were on other continents.

2. The oldest recorded civilizations to date is Nile Valley civilization.

3. The oldest nation on record to date was the Nubian nation Ta Seti, located to the south of KMT. Remember also, it was a king of the south or Upper KMT who united KMT and founded its First Dynasty.

4. KMT was Africa's greatest recorded classical civilization.

5. KMT was the natural extension of inner African culture.

6. There was in ancient times and there remains today a cultural unity between KMT and the rest of the African continent.

7. The native African populations were a Negroid people.

8. Ancient African nations influenced other civilizations worldwide.

9. KMT was a Black African nation during its most important development periods.

10. Africans in the African diaspora, including the Americas and the Caribbean, retained and still retain varying degrees of African culture. That culture is reflected in family patterns, language, religious belief systems, artistic creativities, etc.

Sources of Evidence

While few historians have specifically written about Kemetic education, there is a good deal of direct and indirect evidence that helps us to bring a good picture of it into focus. The sources of evidence include the following:

* Sacred texts written in Mdw Ntr (renamed hieroglyphics by the Greeks): pyramid texts, papyri, coffin texts, etc.
* Monuments: pyramids, tekenu (renamed obelisks by the Greeks), and stellae
* Carvings
* Paintings
* Pottery
* European "classical" writers, some of whom were eye-witnesses (Greek and Roman)
* Similarities between the ancient and contemporary cultural practices of inner Africa (religion, family practices, symbolic structures, education, etc.) and ancient KMT

Foreign (Asian) Invasions as the Destruction of High Culture

Considering the brevity of this essay, I have decided to begin my description of Kemetic education at one of the peak periods of its development, the New Kingdom, the Eighteenth Dynasty. This was the kingdom that included Thutmoses III, the great conqueror; Akhenaton, the world's first apostle of nonviolence and who is falsely regarded as the originator of the idea of monotheism; Hatshepsut, the most famous woman to rule KMT or any other ancient nation as a "King"; and the popular but inconsequential young pharaoh, "King Tutankhamen." These were native Africans who, led by Sequenenre the Southerner of the late Seventeenth Dynasty, had expelled the Asian Hyksos invaders from KMT and reestablished African rule.

It is very important to note that these Asian Hyksos invaders, also called shepherd kings, represented a dramatic interruption in the creative Kemetic cultural traditions. They were alien and made no recognizable lasting contribution to the culture of KMT, even though they ruled for five dynasties.

According to Breasted, the invaders, who were called "Hyksos," left so few monuments that even their nationality was the subject of much debate. Breasted says that the documentary materials bearing upon the Hyksos are so meager and limited in extent, that anyone can easily survey and judge the question for themselves. Steindorff said that the Hyksos left no literary evidence of their occupation of Egypt, practically no large monuments at all. The little that we know about them has been gleaned painfully from a group of scarabs (beetle-shaped amulets), cylinder seals, and a few other isolated objects: there was a tiny sphinx with a royal head and a Semitic face in the act of clawing to death an Egyptian; there was a dagger with a remarkable representation of animals on the handle; there was a fragmentary writing palate. And according to Steindorff again, the only truly monumental relics of the invaders are several blocks from a stone building found at Gebelein a few miles south of Thebes, which contain the names of the Kings, Khyan and Apophis Owoserre.

After this long cultural lull, the native Eighteenth Dynasty came as a revival of the African culture of the first twelve dynasties, and indeed the culture of the predynastic period.[5]

Kemetic Education

The center of the Eighteenth Dynasty government was at Wa-Set, or Wo-Se', meaning in Kemetic, "The Septer." Wa-Set was renamed "Thebes" by later Greek invaders. It was renamed "Luxor" by still later Arab invaders. In Wa-Set were two gigantic temples that contained the most highly developed education systems on record from ancient times.

One temple, the Southern Ipet (place), now called by the Arabic name the "Temple of Luxor," was located in the south of the city of Wa-Set. It was connected to the largest temple of ancient times, the Ipet Isut, called Karnak by the Arabs. These magnificent buildings existed long before there was a Greece, and even longer before Greeks would conquer KMT under Alexander the Great. Nearly a thousand years after the Greek invasion, the essentially Asiatic-Arabic population under Islam would take over KMT.

Ipet Isut meant "the most select of places," or "the holiest of places." It was both a center of religion and education, since the two could not be separated in the minds of the Kamites. It housed an elite faculty of priest-professors. It has been estimated that at one time there were more than 80,000 students at all grade levels studying at Ipet Isut University. Temples were at the center of religion, politics, and education.[6]

Ipet Isut was like all other lesser temples in KMT's Nile Valley. Every temple had a faculty and a library. This was true, not only in the Eighteenth Dynasty or New Kingdom, it was also true in the oldest kingdoms as well, kingdoms that flourished before the invasions. For example, libraries were an important part of Old Kingdom culture.[7]

Myer says that in one of the tombs at Gizeh, a great functionary of the Sixth Dynasty actually has the title "Governor of the House of Books." Myer says that this simple mention, thrown incidentally between two or more elevated titles, would be sufficient to show the extraordinary development at that time of civilization, since it would mean that they not only had a literature, but that it was large enough to fill whole libraries, and that the libraries would be so important, that a functionary of the court would be required to preserve a royal library. Maspero, according to Myer, said that the library officials can be found as far back as the Fourth Dynasty, approximately 2,500 years before the birth of Christ.[8]

The faculty was called Hersetha or "teachers of mysteries," and were divided into departments, as follows: (1) Mystery Teachers of Heaven (astronomy and astrology), (2) Mystery Teachers of All Lands (geography), (3) Mystery Teachers of the Depths (geology), (4) Mystery Teachers of the Secret Word (philosophy and theology), and (5) Mystery Teachers of Pharaoh and those who examined words (law and communication).[9]

Ancient KMT was a high-tech society. It required armies of educated people. The first step in the formal process of general education was training as a scribe, which was a highly honored profession. The route to sacred or secular office was through the scribal schools.

Scribes began their work by copying existing great works. The Mdw Ntr (hieroglyphics) expressed the great ideas of the age. There was no Dick, Jane, and Spot there— no Mickey Mouse and Donald Duck, no Cinderella, and Jack and the Beanstalk, no Goldilocks and the Three Bears. Scribes were introduced to serious matters from the outset. Though they may not, and probably did not, fully understand what they were copying initially, they gradually came to know the greatest historical and spiritual tradition in the history of mankind.

The process of education was not seen primarily as a process of acquiring knowledge. It was seen as a process of the transformation of the letter that progressed through successive stages of rebirth to become more god-like. Disciplined study under the guidance of a master teacher was the single path to becoming a new person.

The education system was an open admission system that was not tied to heredity. There is not a son for the Chief of the Double White House; there is not an heir for the Chief of the Seal.[10]

The "Double-White House" was the Pharaoh's capital. In other words, in order to be educated, the Pharaoh's children, like all others, had to follow the difficult path of hard study on their own. For example, Amenhotep, son of Hapu, was of lowly birth. However, he is identified as the architect-priest who designed the basic plan of the great temple of Ipet Isut.[11]

Kemetic educators were first and foremost serious students of natural phenomena, especially in the native African dynasties. It was the long, painstaking study of everything in nature that led Kamites and other Africans to the belief in the essential unity of all things in the universe, and to a belief in one supreme God. This belief was held in KMT from earliest times. According to the great Egyptologist, E. A. Wallis Budge, who studied all the ancient Kemetic literature, the study of that literature reveals that there was never a time when Kamites did not believe in one Great God (monotheism). This God was nameless, incomprehensible, and self-created. Kamites believed that any facet of nature could be studied to cover principles of nature's operations, or put another way, aspects of God. This allowed for the use of many natural objects as "symbols" of divine principles. It was the ancient Kamites' attempt to live in harmony with nature's principles, or God's manifestations (not many gods or polytheism) that led them to develop the earliest moral teachings and forms of worship to institutionalize those teachings.[12]

Anyone who reads the ancient texts will detect the universal preoccupation of native Africans with the sacred. The overall aim of education is exemplified by the NTRU (driving principles) Tehuti and Maat. Tehuti (renamed Thoth by the Greeks) was the masculine wisdom principle of God. Tehuti also represented writing and learning. Maat was a feminine principle of God and represented truth, justice, and righteousness. By following such pathways as these and others, Kamites hoped to become more like the Supreme Creator, who was hidden.

Some students of ancient KMT have described the education system as "practical," as lacking in a desire to pursue "knowledge for its own sake," as if the "pursuit of knowledge for its own sake" represented a higher and more advanced concept than "practical" education. Kemetic education can be described as "functional," a blend of "theory and practice, a holistic" education. I remain unconvinced that "education for its own sake" or "learning for the love of learning" is a more loftier goal than education to become more like the Supreme Creator. Put another way, should education be for its own sake or for God's sake?

The European Response to Kemetic Education

Ancient KMT was conquered first by Asians, later by Europeans, and finally by an Arabic-Asian population. However, under Greek rule, beginning with Alexander the Great in 323 B.C. and lasting through the Roman Caesars to the time of Roman Emperor Justinian, circa sixth century A.D., a strange thing happened. Before the Greek invasion, Greek students and settlers had been going to KMT for years to learn religion, architecture, and the arts and sciences. For example, the Parthenon on the Acropolis is merely a late copy of African architecture like the Southern Ipet and Ipet Isut Temples, which had been developed in KMT at such places as Wa-Set. Yet even after winning their wars with KMT, Greece and Rome became and remained captives of Kemetic culture, especially its religion and education, for nearly 650 years!

It took years of calculated struggle for the Romans to destroy Kemetic education. These struggles were initiated by rulers with such edicts as those issued by Theodosius, 380 A.D., and Justinian, 527 A.D. They had to burn down African temples or universities, and destroy or tame the priest-professors to annihilate the leadership of KMT. Kemetic religion and education were led by a priesthood that was not Roman. Emperors from Constantine onward did not want foreign leaders as competition, especially for the minds of the people. Christianity became a state religion with a native Roman leadership.

All over KMT today, one can see the results of Greek and Roman conquerors' efforts to copy the culture that they conquered. They rebuilt African temples (church/schools) and joined the African religion. They carved their own images on the African temples. They showed themselves being blessed by African Gods, wearing African clothes and performing African ceremonies. A visitor to KMT today must wonder as he or she gazes at the many massive African temples that were rebuilt by the Europeans, why did they go to such trouble? Noble Europeans even had their bodies mummified in the African way! They took home the African religion of Isis, Osirus, and Horus. African religion remained very popular and prominent until suppressed by the royal edicts. Even then, the influence of Africa remained. For example, the city of Paris, France is named for Isis (*par Isidos* or Place of Isis). Notre Dame Cathedral is actually built on the site of the older Temple of Isis!

The last Kemetic college, Philae at the First Cataract, was closed under orders from Justinian in 527 A.D. After this, the classical education of KMT died out or went underground. Many of the Kemetic educational concepts did not die. They remained in more or less disguised form in the education systems of European conquerors. George G.M. James, in *Stolen Legacy*, has examined traditional histories of philosophy and has shown as did Plutarch, that many of these authors acknowledge that the wisest of the Greeks were students of African teachers in Kemetic universities. They were given a "liberal arts" education, which became the prototype for later Greek and Roman education systems. In Greece, "the Trivium" of grammar, rhetoric and logic were practiced. In Rome, "the Quadrivium" of arithmetic, astronomy, geometry, and music were added. Taken together, these were the "seven liberal arts," the foundation of western higher education. They also remain in the traditional education system of Nile Valley migrants to all other parts of the African continent.[13]

Our reasons for looking at the ancient Kemetic system of education are many. The following reasons are but a few of them:

1. Kemetic education is our best window to ancient African education continentwide.
2. Kemetic education is the parent of "western" education, and therefore it must be understood if ancient and modern western education is to be understood.
3. Kemetic education is a system that can and, in my opinion, should provide guidance for the organization of the education of our people today.

African Americans have been asked over the years to sit as spectators in silence, in awe, in wonder, and in admiration of the ancient and modern cultures of other peoples. We have not been asked to follow that ancient African dictum, "Man, know yourself!" Were we truly to know ourselves, we would be able to use our own traditions and experiences as the basis for creative problem solving in today's world. To do otherwise is to become cultural schizophrenics, split personalities, trying vainly as Du Bois has said, to view the world through the eyes of others, who look on us with amused pity and contempt, "while we chase gods not our own."[14]

Many of those who view us thus have been partners in the design of an educational process that has withheld from us our birthright, a knowledge of ourselves. It has been said, "He who steals my purse steals trash. But he who steals my good name, steals that which does not make him rich but make me poor indeed." But "truth crushed to the ground" will rise again. In the words of Gerald Massey:

> Truth is all potent with its silent power
> If only whispered, never heard aloud
> But working secretly, almost unseen.
> Save in some excommunicated book;
> 'Tis as the lightning with its errand done
> Before you hear the thunder.

We have a special opportunity and a special responsibility—an obligation. It is not enough for us to be bright and competent. We must also have purpose and direction.

It is not enough for us to "make it" on our own—to save ourselves. As Abena says in Armah's novel, *Two Thousand Seasons,* "There is no self to save without the rest of us."

Socializing Our Children
for the Resurrection of African People

milcar Cabral has pointed out in *Return to the Source* that foreigners can easily dominate a people by material means; real domination, however, can occur only by the "permanent organized repression of the cultural life of the people concerned." In other words, a foreign idea or domination in the real sense can only be guaranteed if there is a "physical liquidation of a significant part of the dominated population." Cabral goes on to say that when a dominator takes up arms to destroy a people, it must also destroy, neutralize, paralyze its cultural life. "For with a strong indigenous cultural life, foreign domination cannot be sure of its perpetuation."

There is a hole in the ozone, which is that thin layer of gas that surrounds the earth and protects us from the most harmful ultraviolet rays of the sun. This is the first time in human history that we have had this happen. Some authorities say that many low-pigmented children will not be able to play outside in the sun in a few years. Already, skin cancer among Whites is at epidemic levels. This happened before any expert realized that it would. It cannot be cured. Moreover, we do not seem to be able to stop doing what we are doing to create the problem. We release fluorocarbons into the atmosphere along with other pollutants. This is done as a part of the process of manufacturing and consumption of such things as refrigerators and aerosol sprays. No one seems to know how to stop this harmful practice. This is something that the experts did not foresee.

In October 1987, the stock market crashed. The drop in stock prices was larger than any before. Experts did not foresee the crash and even now cannot explain it. Some say that among many factors, there is the matter of computer trading. Computers were supposed to be making decisions without the benefit of nonprogrammed human judgment. Just think: experts say that the burden of decision making for the national response to the threat of a possible nuclear attack is also on the computers. At least one computer expert who was involved in the development of the defense technology said that he believed that we will eventually blow ourselves up.

Quite simply, the experts do not always know. Many of us trust them to know. We are not likely to find the answers to the problems of African people by asking the same people who put the hole in the ozone, who let atomic energy get out of control (Three Mile Island and Chernobyl), who can't control the stock market, who can't stop polluting the earth, and who don't seem to be able to teach our children even the basic things like reading and counting. We must learn to trust our own wisdom again.

Our attention is drawn to our children when it should be drawn to our people as a whole. We must understand the real meaning of self-destructive behavior. Real "self-destructive behavior" occurs when we identify so strongly with our oppressors that we do to ourselves the worst that they could do to us. That is, rather than wait for our culture to be destroyed, we commit cultural suicide and enter voluntary cultural servitude, uncritically embracing alien cultural forms, even destructive and incoherent ones. In the process we lose the "glue" or the "tie that binds" us together as a people. At worst, group solidarity crumbles in the face of a love affair with individualism, an individualism that loses its cultural moorings.

We had a glorious beginning. Africa is the mother of the whole human family. Africa is also the mother of civilization. For thousands of years, African people were the premier teachers on the earth. A single nation in Africa, KMT (Egypt), demonstrated more than three thousand years of unbroken civilization. Native Africans were responsible for this—a feat unmatched in human history.

For thousands of years, Africans were the envy of the world, attracting the curious traveler, the serious student, the religious and political exile in search of sanctuary, the homeless in search of nurturance, and even the prodigal son or daughter, who had left in search of greener pastures.

Unfortunately, Africa also attracted the greedy. The Assyrians, the Persians in the sixth century B.C., the Greeks in the fourth century B.C., the Romans in the first century, B.C., the Arabs in the seventh century, A.D., and more recently, numerous European nations, have hungered for African wealth, human as well as material and cultural. Africa, home of the arts, the sciences, religion, and spirituality, nurtured human wonders of the world, only to fall prey to an endless succession of greedy invaders. Even now, the great powers of the world are poised and are active in their quest to own Africa and Africans.

The European colonization of Africa and enslavement of African people are but the most recent in a long line of body blows to the continent and to African people in the African diaspora. No matter where African people are today, their potential is unfulfilled. Look at the 60 million Africans in Brazil, millions more in the Caribbean, Fiji, Papua New Guinea, Dravidian India, and millions more in the United States of America. Look at the African continent itself. Africans have been under siege or in a deep sleep.

When we look at the remnants of nations, at our disorganized and disoriented people in disarray, we must wonder if it is possible for an African people to take their place once more on the world stage as peers. Can that enormous creative potential be released once more? Is the sleeping giant doomed to dream of bondage?

I am concerned because we seem to be riding in the caboose of a train that is not headed for our destination. I am concerned when I find that African Americans seem to be trapped in the rhetoric: logic, models, and problem definitions of mainstream America. We are neck deep in paper reports that seek to present problem definitions and propose solutions for the social problems that face the nation. The parade of "problems" is endless as they flow from the fickle minds of public policy analysts. On a given day, the major problems for African Americans may be child abuse, substance abuse, teen pregnancy, Black-on-Black crime, school dropouts, school suspensions, basic skills deficiencies, the Black family crisis, and a host of others. All anyone in the general society has to do is to announce a new problem and we move like clockwork to demand that we get a piece of the pie in order to be able to present the Black version of it. I am concerned because the problem with these "problems" is that they are not problems at all, but symptoms of problems. When we confuse symptoms with problems, we will not be able to find a remedy, and will squander scarce resources on meaningless activities.

I call the list of "problems" symptoms, because they are the predictable consequences of sustained, systematic, formal and informal, direct and indirect, overt and covert oppression and its legacy. This is not to deny the seriousness of the symptoms and the debilitating effect they have had upon the African American community. However, these symptoms have been with us for hundreds of years now. Psychologists, social workers, anthropologists, and educators have made professional reputations for themselves and have grown wealthy "serving our needs" by addressing these symptoms. Yet the symptoms persist! In fact, they must persist as long as we fail to come to terms with the true nature of the problem.

Our problem is the disintegration of a sense of peoplehood. Pure and simple, we have reached a point in our history where we have been socialized to see ourselves as individuals and cultural neuters. We socialize our children to be the same way. As we become more and more isolated, alone, and culturally undefined, we lose the capacity to see group problems. Gradually the sense of belonging diminishes for so many of us, so there is hardly an "us" at all.

Without a sense of "we," collective action is nearly impossible. Without a sense of we, collective action that may be possible will be limited and superficial. *We* can fight oppression together if *we* exist. But beyond fighting oppression, *we* can draw upon a common culture to fashion a new world, if *we* do indeed belong to that common culture. There really is no escape. Either we belong to a people or we belong to no one. Many of us try to belong to new groups or to the mythical "mainstream." Such attempts are accompanied by a profound sacrifice—the sacrifice of thousands of years of cultural heritage. The aesthetic loss is bad enough. Yet there is also a painful psychological, political, and economic cost as well. The lack of group unity is a guarantee of group vulnerability.

It seems to be very difficult for us to apply this reasoning to ourselves. We readily admire the solidarity of the Asians, the Mormons, the Jews, and other groups that have accumulated wealth and power and that provide certain types of leadership in the United States and in the world. Yet we do not seem to appreciate the meaning of their group solidarity, even when it is a loose solidarity.

It is because we are so misled about the nature of our problem that we miss the opportunity to pose the paramount issues that we need to address. Let me take just a few moments to suggest some priorities that we should be mobilized to address. I think that you will see immediately that these priorities are significantly different from the list of symptoms that I presented earlier. I think that you will see that it is highly unlikely that we will ever see these priorities on a national agenda for us, as long as we wait for others to set the agenda.

1. *Reality*

I believe that we and our children need to be informed about the world as it really is, and not as the various propagandists would have us believe it is. We need to be able to distinguish friends from foes. We need to be able to distinguish facts from falsehoods. We need to be able to distinguish what gives life from what causes death. For example, many of our children are unable to decode the negative messages about them in the mass media. Many are unable to distinguish between and among the famous African American role models. Treating fame as if it were our highest value, many of our children indiscriminately revere Michael Jackson, Jesse Jackson, and Reggie Jackson. They see the fame but not the game.

The siren sounds of cultural death are cloaked in the garments of life and presented to willing, nay eager and hungry audiences. The life of struggle, courage, sacrifice, commitment, and principle is submerged by an avalanche of images of role models that provide cheap thrills. "Profiling" and "chilling out" is the frequent response that our projected role models give to the multiple crises facing our people. Yet the real world will not go away.

2. *Identity*

More and more African Americans seem more and more confused about who they are. There is less of a deep sense of belonging to one's people. This is not surprising. There is precious little in the society to teach African American children about themselves. Where can our children go to discover or to be taught about these things? What models can they find to imitate? African American children cannot be expected to know more about these things than their parents and significant others. And the masses of African Americans suffer from amnesia in greater or lesser degrees with respect to our history and cultural forms. We do not do what all successful groups do—make systematic provisions for instructing all of the young in the things that they must know about their own people. A strong and clear group identity is not possible without the systematic study and practice of one's history and culture.

3. *Purpose*

The public schools today merely promise to provide training so that students can master the basic skills. For some of our children, help is given to master the advanced skills and information. Yet, nowhere in any of the reform literature on the schools have I seen any reference to helping young people develop a purpose in life. Under optimum community socialization, many community members interact in various ways with each child to help the child reflect upon the highest meaning of schooling and socialization. Going to school to get a job is not enough. Getting a job so that the nation can regain its competitive edge is not enough. I would like for many of our children to come to feel that our welfare as a group and our traditional values should figure into their formulation of a purpose. I would like to think that our children would not be mere prisoners of mass common ideas. I want them to hear and to heed the call of destiny.

4. *Information*

I want our children to be exposed to special information and to have special enriching experiences—information and experiences that expose them to the wider society. I want them to go places and see things—things pertaining to African Americans and to others as well. I want them to see the stock market in operation. I want them to see a genetic engineering plant in operation. I want them to see how Hollywood makes movies. I want them to see the vast numbers of Americans—few African

Americans among them—who go out into the woods on the weekend and take their "survivalist" training seriously. I want them to hear excerpts of *all* of the speeches that are made in the United Nations. I want them to talk to someone from the African National Congress. I want them to talk to African American actors and actresses about their struggle to get dignified roles. I want them to talk for a long time with lots of retired African Americans about their struggles for dignity in real life. I want them to get to know well at least one true African American and one true African hero. You see, they don't learn that in school.

5. *Responsibility*

Learning is making decisions and acting upon them. The decisions must be about real things, things that have consequences. Too many of our children never have to be responsible for things that matter, with the possible exception of their own personal survival on the streets. Children who balk at responsibility are of little value to themselves or to others. They can never learn to trust their own powers and abilities if they are never called upon to try. We do not conduct the education of our children in structures that require that they meet real responsibilities. They learn to follow orders, but they miss the experience of having someone really depend on them.

It is clear that a growing number of us agree with this problem definition and have made serious moves to do something about it. Witness the rapid proliferation of study groups. Many are modeled after some of the most successful ones in the nation: Amenta and The Institute for Pan African Studies in Los Angeles, The Kemetic Institute in Chicago, The Bennu Study Group in Atlanta, and The First World Alliance in New York. Witness the growing number of new African and African American museums and the expansion of old ones in such cities as Detroit, Houston, Atlanta, and Washington, D.C. Witness the widespread use of African names in our communities. Witness the growing number of churches and other organizations that have initiated rites of passage study programs and naming and graduation ceremonies. While such activities are far from universal, their magnitude is significant.

If our children are to get the education and socialization they need, it will take much more than these scattered efforts. We need to have a systematic, structured, sustained program. Such a program must be under the *independent* control of communities in which they are located. Realistically, this means that we must rely heavily upon volunteer work. There should be activities for our children that are over and beyond their public school programs. Practically, we need a streamlined program that develops the essential skills and provides a carefully designed cultural education.

It may come as a surprise to some of us that African people have thought about the great questions in life for thousands of years, including questions about the design of the educational process. Indeed, we have superior models to consider. The oldest human records are found in Africa. They include descriptions of a deeply spiritual, aesthetic, intellectual, and technical educational process. Its greatest manifestation was at the ancient University of Ipet Isut (the most select of places), in the city of Waset (known today as Luxor), in the nation of ancient Kemet (Egypt). The gigantic stone pillars of the magnificent and gigantic structure that housed the ancient educational system still stand today. No evidence of a comparable institution of comparable age (as early as 2000 B.C.) exists anywhere else in the world.

Ipet Isut University was the parent unit of the world's first recorded national system of higher education. It also served as the model for later systems of higher education throughout the ancient world, including the educational system in Greece. For example, George G. M. James in his book, *Stolen Legacy*, has defined the essential curriculum of the ancient African education system. The content included the foundation subjects of grammar, rhetoric, logic, arithmetic, astronomy, geometry, and music. Grammar, rhetoric, and logic were copied by Greek students. They took these subjects home to Greece. These subjects were called The Trivium in Greece and became the foundation for their higher education system. The Roman students in Africa copied the remaining four: arithmetic, astronomy, geometry, and music. The Romans called these four subjects The Quadrivium and added them to The Trivium to make up The Seven Liberal Arts.

The ultimate aim of Kemetic education was for the student to become godlike by acquiring ten virtues through the study of the seven liberating disciplines. The Ten Virtues were as follows:

1. Control of thought
2. Control of action
3. Steadfastness of purpose
4. Identity with the spiritual life
5. Evidence of having a mission in life
6. Evidence of a call to spiritual orders
7. Freedom from resentment under persecution and wrong
8. Confidence in the power of the master as teacher
9. Confidence in one's own ability to learn
10. Readiness or preparedness for initiation

It is well known to historians of philosophy that Plato was said to have spent 12 years as a student under African teachers in the Kemetic Mystery System. Plato took some of the virtues and left others. He took numbers one and two and called them *justice.* He took the number three and called it *fortitude.* He took the number four and called it *temperance.* He took numbers five and six and called them *prudence.* These are Plato's four Cardinal Virtues. What he left behind is as significant as what he decided to keep.

The design of African education was not confined to the northeast corner of the African continent. Before and after the decline of Kemetic civilization, in the face of many invasions and migrations, Africans elsewhere on the continent preserved the forms of ancient classical Africa, adding their own unique creativities as they built new classical civilizations in other places. For this reason, we do have available to us today the real essence of ancient African systems of education reflected in the traditional cultures of Africa. It is not because they are African, or even because they are ancient that we have reason to give serious consideration to these systems. It is because they were and are good and useful. Even a brief look at what our ancestors have said will show the wisdom of what these systems were about and their meaning for us at this very moment, in this very place.

Today, we can tap this ancient tradition by closely examining living Africans. Piere Erny in *Childhood and Cosmos,* Jordon K. Ngubane in *Conflict of Minds,* Marcel Griaule and Germaine Dieterlin in *Conversations with Ogotemnli,* and in their second book, *The Pale Fox,* have given in-depth views of the remarkable ways that Africans organized education and socialization in diverse parts of

Africa. African people in the Caribbean and in the United States still, in our most traditional institutions, retain some of the approaches to socialization that we see today in traditional African society. This retention of culture can be seen in the aims, methods, and contents of independently designed education and socialization. Particular forms and contents that we see in Africa do not matter as much as the principles that they reflect.

It is possible to identify the common principles of African systems of education and socialization that can serve as a guide for the design of our own modern system. These basic principles may be listed as follows:

> *Separation* - The beginning stages of education and socialization are marked by a clear separation of the child from the routine of daily life. It is understood that the separation has a deep meaning.
>
> *Observing nature* - The child is placed in an environment designed for a maximum exposure to nature. Nature itself is regarded as a teacher.
>
> *Peership* - Age mates are the important peers. The education and socialization process is above all a social process. Children are expected to master all requirements together. They begin and end the process together.
>
> *Rejection of the childhood* - Children are required to show that they have put away immature things and are ready for the lessons and responsibilities of more mature people.
>
> *Listening to the elders* - The elders play a major role in education and socialization in traditional African societies.
>
> *Purification rituals* - Baptism for symbolic purification is practiced.
>
> *Tests of character*
>
> *Use of special language*
>
> *Use of special names*
>
> *Symbolic resurrection* - Graduation or the completion of rites of passage represents transformation and the reincorporation of the child into the full community.

There would be nothing in the use of these principles that would keep our children from mastering modern technology. Nor is there anything here that would keep our children from learning about other groups in the world. However, the use of these principles would cast the education of our children in a more humane light. It would help our whole community go beyond the minimum requirements of mass education, and go beyond the education that is required for employment. There must be more to our lives than that.

I would like to see the following things in our system of education and socialization.

Modeling - We are not true role models for our children until we consciously order our lives to serve that function.

Respect - We must have an environment for our children where they can experience unconditional respect, where we listen to them, where we observe them closely, each and everyone.

Responsibility - We must provide environments for our children where they learn responsibility by being held responsible for real and important things.

Feedback - We must provide an environment for our children where they are well enough known by significant adults so that they can get mature feedback on what they do.

Recognition - We must provide an environment for our children where they can receive appropriate recognition for their efforts.

Love - We must provide an environment for all of our children where they experience love as they struggle to become the adults that we want them to be.

Can't you see an African community school where we teach the lessons of Toni Morrison's *The Bluest Eye,* including the sickness of self-negation, or Ayi Kwei Armah's *Two Thousand Seasons?* Such literature mirrors various types of adjustments that oppressed people make. Can't you see a school where the children get to read a true love story that models ideal Black male/female relationships, as in Zora Neale Hurston's *Their Eyes Were Watching God?* Our children ought to know how we lost our land and must be taught Walter Rodney's *How Europe Underdeveloped Africa,* and Chancellor Williams's *The Destruction of Black Civilization.*

The children and the wider community must see the movie *The Tallest Tree in Our Forest*, which is a biography of Paul Robeson, a role model of intellect, talent, courage, and commitment to the African family. They must hear the poetry of Mari Evans when she tells us to *Speak the Truth to the People*. We must also hear the recordings of Gil Scott Heron, Stevie Wonder, Bob Marley, Wynton Marsalis, who urge us to become culturally conscious and to know and appreciate our rich cultural heritage. We must read Black psychology such as W.E.B. Du Bois's *The Souls of Black Folk*, Franz Fanon's *Black Skin White Masks*, and Na'im Akbar's *Chains and Images of Psychological Slavery*. Then we must listen well to Harold Cruse in *The Crisis of the Negro Intellectual* and in *Plural But Equal*.

Do you see that I am talking family business? This is the business that the masses of our people—children as well as adults—do not have a chance to hear. Without these writers, artists, teachers, etc., and others like them, we can never develop any sense of wholeness in a society that sends a constant stream of degrading messages to us. Never in a million years will the things that I have suggested above be offered to us by someone outside the African family. They do not know these things. Further, these things do not hold the same meaning for them as they do for us. This is why we must take charge.

I want to see thousands of locally organized, volunteer-run, community schools and camps. I want to see enough of them so that not a single African American child misses the opportunity to participate. I want to see this as something that every African American adult feels a sense of obligation to support. I want to see hundreds of training and orientation centers to support community schools and camps. I want to see basic resource libraries of books and film to help local community schools and camps to get going fast. I want to see us move toward these things as if our lives depend on them, because in fact it does. My mother always says, "It's a poor dog that won't wag its own tail."

It does no good for us to become preoccupied with counting the walking wounded or counting corpses just so that we can say, "Ain't it awful!" Greater accuracy in presenting the statistics of "self-destructive behavior" will not give us insight into the causes of the behavior. It leads to victim blaming. We do not reject the numbers. However, we need the numbers on many of the causal factors or situations that have been overlooked. If we are to solve the problems that we and our children face, we must ask the right questions. If we only repeat the questions asked by strangers to our communities, we will have failed our people.

For example, here are some questions that are seldom asked, questions about the nature of the treatment that our children have received. Where are the statistics on treatment (input) and on treatment related to effects (output)? What adult contact and what type of daily contact is there for our children between the hours of 3:00 P.M. and 10:00 P.M., on weekends, and during the summers? What is the preparation and point of view of the adults who serve our children, if they are served at all? Are our children in trouble because they rejected caring and competent adult leadership and supervision? I predict that the answers to these questions will show that our children have been culturally malnourished, culturally neglected, and culturally abused. Many of them have actually been abandoned by us from their earliest years. Therefore, when children raise themselves or raise each other, we should not be shocked at the results.

The salvation for the children that we seek must start with a focus on parenting and on the parenting function that may be served by any adult. It takes special preparation for a community to serve in a parental role. Therefore our target must be the cultural socialization of parents and community in order to enhance our ability to do our job.

The only real self-destructive behavior is cultural homicide or cultural suicide. This will set up the essential conditions of vulnerability that will result in the symptoms that we have been seeing as problems.

The first crucified savior in human history was Asar (Osirus). He was tricked and killed by his evil brother, Set. His wife, Ast (Isis), found his body twice after Set had attempted to get rid of it, the second time cutting it up into 14 pieces. Ast found all of the pieces except for the penis, the symbol of the creative principle. Ast was successful in bringing the dead Asar back to life. Asar became lord of the underworld, mated with Ast, and became the father of an avenging son, Heru (Horus). Heru was regarded as the resurrected Asar. He and his father were one.

The body of African people has been crucified, cut into pieces, and scattered throughout the world. Yet it can be made whole and resurrected. In the words of the honorable Marcus Mosiah Garvey, *"Up You Mighty Race! You Can Accomplish What You Will!"*

Conceptual Confusion
and the Persistence of Group
Oppression Through Education

Wan Bon (One Tree)

One tree
So many leaves
One tree

One river
So many creeks
All are going to one sea

One head
So many thoughts
Thoughts among which one good one must be

One God
So many ways of worshiping
But one Father

One Suriname
So many hair types
So many skin colors
So many tongues
One people
R. Dobru

The above passage was written by a man who was not only the national poet of the South American country Suriname, he was also a leader of the revolution that resulted in Suriname's independence. Many visitors to Suriname agree that this country displays the finest examples of a comfortable cultural pluralism found anywhere on the globe. Distinct African, American Indian, Asian, Dutch, and Indian populations exist side by side in relative peace and harmony, with mutual respect. In addition, large numbers of all of these groups have blended into a multicultural and multiracial mix. Dobru expressed an ideal: the possibility for the simultaneous existence of national unity and diversity among cultural groups. This ideal has yet to be reached in most parts of the world. Indeed, in many parts of the world it has yet to be expressed.

Easily forgotten in the history of the United States are conditions such as the colonial domination of, and even genocide among, the native American Indian population; participation in the depopulation of Africa and the enslavement of large numbers of Africans; systematic resistance to the immigration of southern and eastern European populations; the exploitative use of migrant labor populations from China, the Philippines, and Mexico; and the systematic oppression of these groups. In addition, the government has sometimes overtaken territories outside the continental United States. The massive scale on which these events have occurred over many generations has produced pervasive and continuing distortions of social, political, philosophical, religious, and economic structures, as well as in normal and natural social relations among people.

For the greater portion of the nation's history, the frequently verbalized commitment to the ideals of liberty, equality, and fraternity has been realized by only a small subset of the total United States population: northern and western Europeans, and even then with some exceptions. What has existed in our nation during virtually all of its history is a social system that has guaranteed privilege to certain cultural groups, but it has oppressed some others. Every facet of the social system has been mobilized to produce the society that both the privileged and the oppressed experience; education is merely one facet of that complex social system.[1]

It is important to acknowledge at the onset that as long as there has been both privilege and oppression, there has also been agitation and activity against them. During slavery, there was the abolitionist movement. During the period of segregation, there was the desegregation movement. Since 1954, the year of the Supreme Court decision outlawing school segregation, *Brown v. Topeka Board of Education*, many different types of activities by many different individuals, agencies, and groups have been initiated to deal in one way or another with some aspect of equity. These include affirmative action programs in hiring, human relations training programs, multicultural education staff development programs, equal opportunity programs funded by the federal government, and legal assistance and class action suits on behalf of oppressed groups. Therefore, we may say that the problem has never existed in the absence of activity.

In my opinion, the more serious problem is the absence of comprehensive and rational planning to make these various activities more efficient and effective. Thousands of citizens from all walks of life have engaged in remedial activities, but no one has yet developed a clear conceptual base and theoretical framework from which to operate. At this point, we stand at a crossroad where we can choose either to continue the "ad hocracy" of practice or to undertake the difficult conceptual work that, if done well, can result in significant improvements in education for millions of pupils.

Privilege and Oppression Through Education

During the course of our history, a system of overt and covert education emerged to produce the social system desired by the groups in power.[2] The system of education included specific inequitable features. The Supreme Court decision of 1954, *Brown v. Topeka Board of Education,* outlawed the legal basis for certain manifestations of privilege and oppression in education. Before the "Brown" decision, the following inequities were present within the educational system:

1. An ideology of White supremacy and racism permeated virtually all school practices, including the formal curriculum.[3]
2. The control of education for oppressed populations was almost totally in the hands of members of privileged populations.
3. There was a systematic denial, distortion, and disrespect for the history, culture, and identity of oppressed groups; reciprocally, there was an inflated affirmation of respect and a distortion of the history, culture, and identity of privileged groups.
4. There was a deliberate inequitable distribution of resources for education, with the greatest amount of resources supporting the education of the privileged, and the least supporting the education of the oppressed.

5. A system that came to be called "segregation of the races" was developed; it was reflected in the operation of schools.

Thus, the system of privilege and oppression in education included six major interrelated functions:

* Ideology
* Political control
* Uses of history and culture
* Uses of group identity
* Uses of financial and human resources
* Physical segregation

The *Brown v. Topeka Board of Education* decision only focused on physical segregation. It assumed that by the mere elimination of a formal dual system of segregated education, equality of opportunity would follow. After the decision, it became clear that the complex system of privilege and oppression was far more intractable.[4] New procedures were implemented that provided differential and inequitable treatment:

1. An applied pseudoscience of mental measurement emerged in the schools, although there is little evidence that applied mental measurement activities in education can be tied to improved achievement outcomes for children.[5]
2. Systems of "ability" tracking emerged, many of which had the same consequences as the previous system of segregation by race.
3. The number of African American teachers and administrators, especially the latter, declined in the southern states.
4. New and degrading euphemisms for African American and other cultural minority children have emerged, because the names of programs were applied to the children as if the program names can be equated with group identity: "Chapter 1 children," "culturally deprived children," "culturally disadvantaged children," "latchkey children," "children from broken homes." Not only are these euphemisms degrading, they also submerge any positive ethnic or race identity of the children.
5. Cosmetic changes in the schools' curricula have been implemented in response to pressure from oppressed groups. With few exceptions, fundamental curriculum revisions have not been carried out by those who are qualified to do so.

Conceptual Confusion

The above list indicates that the problem of "segregation" is only a very small part of a general, pervasive system of privilege and oppression. It may not even have been the most important component; perhaps it was merely a symptom of deeper ills. However, during the last 30 years, the primary preoccupation of many judges, politicians, and educators has been with a variety of remedies for "segregation." In general, the substance of interrelated functions of equity remains unaddressed, or addressed only at a minimal level. One may assume that the courts, and others responsible for the design of education programs, did not conceptualize the other features of the system of privilege and oppression. It appears that the courts, politicians, and educators considered the other features to be less important than the issue of segregation. Perhaps they believed that mixing children of different groups together would somehow automatically ensure that fair and equivalent treatment would take place in the desegregated schools, and the other interrelated functions of the system of privilege and oppression would simply remedy themselves. If advocates for equity were aware of the full list of interrelated functions, such awareness has not been reflected in either their literature or their rhetoric.

"Desegregation" came to be understood as a remedy for "segregation," which in turn came to be seen as the entire problem. On the other hand, "desegregation" may be seen simply as the elimination of the legal basis for "segregation." But the advocates of "desegregation" and their legal supporters looked for something more, something that could serve as proof that "segregation" did not continue to exist. "Integration" then came to be seen as a kind of opposite to "segregation."

Once the privilege and oppression problem is framed in the terms "segregation," "desegregation," and "integration," a conceptual difficulty exists. None of these terms—individually or collectively—lead us to the entire list of interrelated functions. For example, one of the functions is the "ideology of White supremacy" that is taught by direct or indirect means in the schools. Taking "integration" as merely the opposite of "segregation" would make it possible to satisfy the demands of "integration" as currently understood without giving any systematic attention to the eradication of formal or informal manifestations of the "ideology of White supremacy." It is for this reason that some generic term or terms, must be developed to cover the total list of features and practices. I have chosen the terms "privilege," "oppression," and "inequity" since they are far more inclusive than "segregation," "desegregation," and "integration." It was an unfortunate tactical and conceptual error to define the inequity problem merely as "segregation," rather than one of privilege and oppression.

Something else must also be said about the concept of "integration." In fact, "integration," meaning the equitable or proportionate physical mixtures of cultural groups in schools, may actually result in a group cultural disintegration that is disproportionately borne by an oppressed group, with privileged cultural groups being permitted to maintain themselves more or less intact. Few educators or writers utilize the term "integration" to mean the creation of some entirely new cultural group to which all previous cultural groups would now belong. Frequently, "integration" only means providing access to membership in a dominant culture group for members of a previously excluded cultural group.

I believe that our difficulty with the term "integration" comes about because we have yet to develop a sincere, pluralistic, political, and social national ideology that allows us to conceive of the condition of simultaneous legitimacy for diverse cultural groups. Cultural assimilation, rather than cultural democracy, has always been the major implicit agenda within the nation. There is little rhetoric about cultural democracy, even within many oppressed groups. Cultural assimilation meets the needs of many citizens. Yet there are many others who will demand the right to both political and cultural freedom. Equity does not mean identity.[6]

Jordan Ngubane correctly pointed out that the primary goal during colonial oppression in Africa and in other parts of the world was much broader than the simple physical control of indigenous populations by outside colonizers. The final victory and ultimate aim for the outside colonizer was to change the colonized people by forcing an alienation between group members and their cultural and historical traditions. This alienation promotes destruction of individual and group identity, thus disabling them politically as well. The original challenges to privilege and oppression in the United States did not include the desire by African Americans for cultural surrender. Rather, the desire was to challenge all the functions of oppression.[7]

It must be noted that not all victims or beneficiaries of an inequitable system follow conscious, active, and calculated patterns of participation. In any situation where people "play by rules," Williams and Mitchell suggest that we may think of several levels of participation:

1. Game Makers design the rules of the system. A few members of the privileged groups know the design, and most others may not even be aware that a "game" is being played.
2. Game Advocates are policymakers, formal or informal, who can determine if the game will be played. They may decide that the game must be played, even if they do not understand its purpose or its design.
3. Game Dealers merely manage the game according to the rules and procedures they have been taught. They usually do not have the power to decide if the game will be played, or what the design of the game will be.
4. Pawns in the game simply play the game or have games played on them. They do not make the game; they do not decide if the game will be played; they do not manage the game. Frequently, they cannot even decide whether to play the game or not.[8]

If this analytical framework has any validity, it can be seen that there are different levels of participation by members of privileged and oppressed groups. For example, a European American family whose children attend the segregated schools might well claim that they were not the designers of the system. To do so, however, left them privileged but impotent, since they enjoyed the benefits, while remaining ignorant of the system's design. The oppressed people in the system may actually serve in any of the lower three levels, although they are usually on the bottom. For example, members of oppressed groups are frequently appointed by the privileged to say the things that their mentors wish them to say. Clearly, the remedial treatment of persons at each level in the game must reflect the nature of their participation in the system.

The above distinctions suggest why most popular labels for inequitable practices in education cover only a small part of the whole "game." For example, a calculating designer of a system of racial oppression should not be described by the benign title of "stereotyper" any more than the mindless dealer in an oppressive system should be accused of designing the system.

Consequences of Misconstruing the Problem and Euphemistic Labeling

The problem of privilege and oppression or inequity in education is sometimes cast as a problem of stereotyping, intergroup ignorance, or miscommunication. Stereotyping, ignorance, or miscommunication may, in fact, be problematic. However, these "problems" are merely manifestations or components of a total system that is much more complex and pervasive. Consequently, the educator who restricts his or her attention and activity to the elimination of stereotyping, intergroup ignorance, and miscommunication contributes to the appearance of problem solving when in fact, little of importance may actually be accomplished. Stereotyping, intergroup ignorance, or miscommunication become euphemisms for the deeper problems of privilege, oppression, or inequity, which are much more difficult to address.

Such euphemisms developed precisely because we are dealing with highly sensitive matters. They are sensitive because anyone who examines and analyzes the problems is an interested party in the emotionally charged situation, and no one can be neutral in a system where everyone is tied, in some way, to either the privileged or the oppressed. However, the use of euphemisms serves to reduce psychological and social tension. It does this in two ways: the euphemism may reduce the perceived scope of the domain being considered, or it may reduce the intensity of the negative perception of the topic. For example, euphemisms reduce the scope of the domain when the privilege and oppression problem is referred to as simply a segregation problem. One of the aspects of the original problem that might be left out would be some response to the conscious or unconscious "ideology of White supremacy," or some response to the destruction of the history and culture of a particular group.

We might also conceive of the use of euphemism in this way. "Oppression" could be relabeled "race relations," and in turn relabeled "intergroup relations," which might become "intergroup communications" or "interpersonal miscommunication." It is much easier to engage a school district in implementing a program to improve "interpersonal communications" than to focus on problems associated with privilege and oppression. Well-meaning educators and public policymakers succumb to the seduction of euphemisms since they reduce internal and external pressures, soothe sensitivities, and provide the illusion of progress toward important goals.

There have been many positive attempts over the past few years—human relations, multicultural education, and antiracism workshops and conferences, ethnic studies course development, guidelines to eliminate stereotypes, etc. However, if we examine the activities conducted under any or all of these headings, there is the general absence of a historical and theoretical base, and the absence of valid remedial strategies for activities undertaken. In other words, a plan of remedial action should be based upon some knowledge or theory as to what the problem is, how it came about, what maintains it, and how it can be changed. Some valid notion of causes related to effects must be explicated.

Let's take the example of multicultural education. When a program of multicultural education is launched, what is the precise nature of the problem that it attempts to address? Are the problems of privilege and oppression traceable to cultural misunderstanding alone, or are there other causes such as greed, fear, or ideology that make some members of one group attempt to oppress others? If the latter is the case, then one would be hard pressed to explain how training in a particular type of multicultural education addresses the root causes of the problem. As I examine present multicultural training activities, it is clear that, for the most part, professional practice is arbitrary, in a virtual state of anarchy, devoid of theory, and not grounded in historical context. Consequently, many well-meaning people may be expending enormous energy in what is essentially nonproductive work. For example, what is the cause of the "ideology of White supremacy?" How can it be changed? To what should it be changed? A comprehensive answer to these questions is essential before remedies can be designed and implemented.

For a variety of reasons, it is very difficult to address the "ideology of White supremacy." First, discovering the existence of such an ideology contributed to neurotic perceptions and guilt feelings. Second, since few of the resources of the education research community have been directed toward examining the impact of the "ideology of White supremacy" on school practice, there is limited empirical data on this subject. This condition exists in spite of the fact that the supremacy ideology has been a central feature of United States culture and its system of education for many decades. Finally, there is insufficient political pressure to address the present issue.[9]

We have little of the basic preparation that is necessary to mount a comprehensive assault on the problem of privilege and oppression in the schools. An examination of commonly used educational psychology, philosophy of education, and history of education textbooks will reveal that there is almost no examination of and theorizing about racist behavior. Racist behavior is neither described fully nor analyzed systematically. Indeed, the lack of analysis is almost as old as the system of racism itself. Many of the greatest leaders in education appear to have been blind to this central feature of privilege and oppression. For example, John Dewey, one of the most revered philosophers of American education, appears to have failed to recognize the need for leadership in this area.

Weinberg reported on John Dewey's trip to South Africa.[10] In the summer of 1934, John Dewey, who was accompanied by his daughter Jane, attended a conference on South African education. It was sponsored by a group called the New Education Fellowship, an international body established in 1915 to bring together teachers, parents, social workers and others who wanted to foster education more suited to changing needs. The conference was sponsored and supported by a number of government agencies, educational institutions, churches, and civic organizations throughout South Africa.

The first conference was held in Cape Town, starting on July 2nd, and lasting until the 13th of July, and the second one, in Johannesburg, beginning July 16th and ending on the 27th of July. Approximately 4,000 persons attended two sessions and more than 300 formal addresses were delivered by approximately 145 speakers. John Dewey was one of 25 people who had been specially invited as a speaker from the United States, and his expenses, and those of his daughter, were paid for by the Carnegie Cooperation of America.

The general theme of the conference was adapting education to meet the rapidly changing needs of society, with special attention to South Africa. The main issues that they discussed were the ultimate aim of education, the problem of method, and the problem of curriculum. Dewey spoke at each of these sessions, and he chose as his subjects the need for a "philosophy of education, what is learning, and growth in activity."

There were several tours provided at the conference so that attendees could observe firsthand the pattern of life prevailing in South Africa as well as programs that were aimed at improving the lot of the masses. John Dewey and his daughter, Jane, took advantage of many of these tours, and also went on unscheduled trips. According to John Dewey's daughter, they had a good deal of time for travel, and saw much of the country. They visited many missionaries, medical and religious, to see what was going on in the education of the natives of South Africa, and to improve their condition. Jane recalled that the agent for native reservations took them on very interesting trips, probably very much to the detriment of their regular work. They took whole-day tours, and according to Jane, saw more than they could have seen on their own. What is striking about this experience is that John Dewey did not record his impressions of South Africa when he returned, as he had done when he visited Japan, China, Turkey, Mexico, and Russia.

It is interesting that Dewey's discussion subjects reflected no special recognition of or attention to the virulent form of education under apartheid that operated in the Union of South Africa at that very time. Not only did Dewey fail, for whatever reasons, to record those impressions, but as Weinberg has indicated, neither he nor other great defenders of the common school spoke out against racism and oppression in American education.[11]

How can we explain this and other failures by frontline educational theorists and historians to deal with racism and group oppression? How can we explain why behavioral scientists who write books on teacher education, also avoid the issues of racism and group oppression? Perhaps psychological mechanisms are at play here. Is it denial? Rationalization? For a few educators and behavioral scientists, it may well be conscious and intentional. There is continued failure to come to grips with the real world of inequality. This failure remains symptomatic of the inability of educators to deal with substantive and sensitive root problems associated with privilege and oppression in education.[12]

At present, there are limited contemporary analyses of education related to privilege and oppression. As indicated earlier, when such analyses are performed, they tend to be under the rubric of euphemistic concepts. Such euphemisms do not suggest or reveal the calculated malevolent intent of the privileged and oppressive system; further, they fail to reflect the fact that many of our contemporary educational problems are the direct or indirect residuals of previous explicit designs to maintain privilege and oppression.

Although the Supreme Court decision of 1954 legally outlawed segregation in education, the practices associated with "de facto" desegregation have been almost impossible to eliminate. For example, White flight, tracking within schools, and continued containment of handicapped children in special classes are but a few of the techniques that have contributed to the maintenance of the status quo. Moreover, the law could not, and did not, deal with the minds that produced segregation in the first place, nor the extent to which overt and covert behavior was directed toward perpetuation of the status quo. To what extent have thoughtless and perhaps innocent inheritors of the system mindlessly continued patterns of behavior that maintain the status quo?

It is my belief that the system of privilege and oppression, as manifested in education, was systematically designed and applied over many decades. It seems unlikely that such a pervasive system can be dismantled in the absence of a comprehensive, equally well designed and implemented program. Cosmetic changes are simply inadequate.

Constructing a True Democratic Thrust in Education

Although we are dealing with a deeply ingrained system, it can be corrected. Conceptual clarity is a step forward, but alone it will result in little, especially if the dynamics of the defense mechanisms of those who support such a system are not understood. The person who has a vested interest in the maintenance of a system of privilege and oppression tends to have a perceptual system that denies undesirable information. For example, it was not the shortage of information that produced the widely accepted myth of the intellectual superiority of Europeans over other populations in the world; it was the propensity to prefer propaganda over scientific information that kept otherwise truth-seeking individuals blindly attracted to racist thought.[13]

If educators and policymakers are to make substantive changes in the undemocratic educational system, such changes must be based upon clear and specific conceptual analyses.

No meaningful response to the problems can be developed as long as they are poorly defined. Further, the scale and scope of the remedy must match the scale and scope of the problem. We will know that serious attention is being given to solving the problems of privilege and oppression in education when the great minds of our time recognize and analyze them. Present responses to the equity problem are initiated most often by litigation and by injured people who form pressure groups. When affirmative action and human relations are paramount responsibilities of school governance boards and their chief executive officers, that is, not merely priorities of their adjunct support staff, then we will be on the road to real progress. School leaders must have a clear and accurate description of how inequity functions in the educational system, as well as a valid theory of its origins. It is the "dynamics" of inequity that the educator must understand, rather than the mere fact of inequality itself.

When a serious problem is perceived, it must be treated seriously. Key leaders and policymakers must make a conscious commitment to mobilize appropriate resources, and to establish clear priorities for action. This means that

1. a map is constructed of the entire domain of the interrelated functions.
2. leadership is exercised to provide vision, inspiration, and support.
3. goals, timelines, and specific outcome criteria are established.

4. specific responsibilities are assigned to meet all contingencies.
5. means are established for holding school executives accountable.

The responses of school system executives and policy-makers to the problems of inequity are typically ad hoc. Although often well-meaning, they usually come as a consequence of pressure groups, court mandates, and legislation. Even assuming the best of motives, a coherent and comprehensive plan of action is not likely to emerge under such diverse and uncoordinated circumstances. For example, how does a school superintendent combine all of the following into a comprehensive and coordinated response: court-ordered busing to achieve integration, a court-ordered prohibition of the use of culturally and racially biased intelligence tests, a legislative mandate for mainstreaming all children into the least restricted environment (Public Law 94-142), a task force for integrated education, demands for human relations and race relations training, and a review of textbook selections and the elimination of stereotypes in curriculum materials.

The conception of the problems and the solutions are disassociated in the minds of those who have the authority and resources to act. This means that the initiative for action and the conceptualization of the problems are not symbiotically associated with problem solving behaviors of educational leaders. Existing school leaders must become highly informed and must construct the total map of what must be done if meaningful change is to take place. At this point, however, the matter of how a complete conceptual map is to be drawn is overshadowed by the fact that nothing remotely resembling such a map exists.

It is my purpose here to suggest the work that must be done to construct such a map. No one person can carry out this work alone. Yet with the appropriate support, a group of collaborators could do it. The comprehensive approach needed to eliminate educational inequities should include the following components:

1. A complete history of the types of inequities that have been found in education
2. A full description of the present context in education, with specific attention to societal forces (e.g., racism, poverty, sexism, etc.) that result in inequity in the schools

3. A comprehensive set of theories to explain the phenomenon of inequity in education

Collectively, these theories should address the following dimensions:

* Probable causes and forms of privilege and oppression
* Dynamics of privilege and oppression
* Manifestations of privilege and oppression
* A repertoire of valid remedial strategies based upon explanations
* Understandings derived from the previous components

A few examples should help to clarify the meaning and utility of the components listed above.

History - Most Americans, privileged or oppressed, are only familiar with their own direct experiences with equity matters. Such experiences cannot be used as a primary source of accurate information about the real world. The extent of inequity and patterns within the practice of inequity would be lost to anyone who relied only on his or her personal experiences, no matter how extensive. For example, one could easily be misled into thinking that racial oppression in the United States, while extensive in the past, and residual in present form, has always followed a pattern of incremental reduction. The analysis of African American history by C. Vann Woodward reveals that, in fact, the phenomenon of racial oppression has followed the pattern of a pendulum, going forward and then backward. Thus, the segregation of African Americans in the United States followed a period of relative freedom after slavery.[14]

Frequently, participants in the race relations workshops I have observed will deplore racism, make a commitment to fight it, but see it as mainly accidental. Some educators, ignorant of history, will be unable to comprehend the premise that not all inequity in education is accidental, and that some of it has resulted from calculated and intentional activity to deprive some groups of their rights and freedoms. Specific attention to the history of deliberate group oppression has been given by a number of historians. Educators who are not familiar with the substance of these written histories cannot construct a holistic map of the equity territory. Therefore, subsequent theory and practice must be regarded as naive, immature, and unsophisticated. History must inform theory.[15]

Context - Context may be thought of as the history of the present. Those who live in the present, like those who lived in the past, are not automatically aware of patterns of privilege and oppression beyond their own personal experiences. For example, almost all popular large-scale evaluation research in education is based upon the unfounded and erroneous assumption that there is a universal school experience to which all children are equally exposed. Even a cursory observation of schools and neighborhoods will show the vast differences in school treatment that is accorded to different cultural, racial, or ethnic groups. Yet little empirical data are collected to illustrate that fact. In the absence of such empirical data, some researchers deny that inequity in school treatment exists. Empirical observations by participant observers or stenographers in classrooms give abundant information about the real world of our children. No serious leader who confronts the equity problem can be effective if he or she is ignorant of details of the real world experiences of children and their families.[16]

Theories - Educational practices tend to be atheoretical. Equity practices are even more so. Although theories about equity exist, educators appear to make little or no use of them. Thus, remedial strategies are doomed to be arbitrary and ad hoc in the absence of some theory to explain the causes of privilege and oppression. To avoid such "ad hocracy," educators must first answer questions such as the following. Does racist behavior begin within individuals or within society? Is it natural or is it produced? Is it amenable to intellectual or political approaches? Many remedial activities may be irrelevant and involve a serious waste of resources simply because they are not based upon an understanding of causes, dynamics, and manifestations of inequity.[17]

A Repertoire of Valid Strategies - Abundant proposals and practices exist to deal with various aspects of inequality in education. Unfortunately, there are few meaningful criteria available that enable the wise and prudent educator to select practices that follow naturally, logically, and scientifically from the study of history, context, and the development of theory.

As I analyze the diverse strategies that have been proposed or utilized to eradicate the uneven impact of privilege and oppression in education, it appears that most are directed toward the symptoms of problems rather than toward their roots. For example, a very popular strategy for the remediation of equity problems is to focus on the use of stereotypes in teaching practices and teaching materials. The general strategy is to instruct teachers and students how to identify stereotypes and replace them with more appropriate images. I have yet to encounter educators who employ strategies to eliminate stereotypes and who also deal explicitly with the origin or causes of the stereotypes. In my opinion, stereotypes are merely symptoms of deeper dynamics. I have little faith that a massive program to change stereotypes or symptoms will also remove the root causes that produce them. If the root causes remain, other manifestations will appear even after stereotypes are eliminated.

Strategies must be developed that flow from an understanding of the history, context, and causal theories, and these strategies must be tested and evaluated. Too much of what is now being done that is accepted as effective strategy is nothing more than a selection from an array of untried and unproven strategies. This may be a function of "desperation." Educational leaders and other vested interests within school communities who are aware of massive inequities in their schools, are often so eager to promote democratic thrusts in education that they frequently adopt strategies without properly analyzing them. These hastily adopted strategies may offer little prospect of success for several reasons:

1. The proposed strategies may be unrelated to the interrelated functions that are major forces in the inequity problem.
2. The proposed strategies may be related logically, but may not have a demonstrable empirical connection with desired behavioral changes in students or school staff.
3. The proposed strategies may not be justifiable on philosophical grounds.

In the final analysis, we must look at the impact on student outcomes as the primary evidence of the validity of strategies for eradicating inequity. To borrow a familiar saying, "The operation is not a success if the patient dies." Decisions to adopt proposals and practices from the repertoire of valid strategies must be contingent upon empirical evidence of their demonstrated connection to promoting equitable student outcomes.

The problems of privilege and oppression in education can be solved. We have sufficient professional knowledge to successfully eradicate both problems from our schools. That is to say, there are no secrets about how to successfully teach students from any racial, cultural, or ethnic group. In addition, no credible evidence exists to dispute the fact that, given the same educational treatment, all groups will succeed in school subjects equally well. The problem is that all groups do not receive the same educational treatment. It is politics, not pedagogy, that prevents school officials from doing their best with all pupils. It is also the absence of conceptual clarity and theoretical grounding that keeps us from seeing that inequity problems are political by nature. Thus, the content of the school experience can be transformed to one that is appropriate for all pupils.

Conceptual clarity alone is insufficient to produce complete remediation. Further, complete solutions to identified inequity problems will require much more than school officials can do alone. Nevertheless, significant progress is possible if both conceptual clarity and complete solutions are pursued with energy and commitment by school officials and other interest groups in the national community. We can achieve the promises associated with this nation's democratic ideology only when it is shared by all of our citizens.

Segregation and other forms of group oppression are the problems that we must seek to address. National unity is possible either under conditions of cultural democracy, cultural assimilation, or a combination of the two, as the case of Suriname shows us. In short, the political commitment to a truly democratic society can be followed by a transformation of society and all social institutions. Education is one of the social institutions in need of transformation. It is never neutral and will always serve some master. If that master is democratic principles, then inequity will be eliminated.

Behavioral Style, Culture, and Teaching and Learning

In 1976, I wrote a technical report on work that I had done for the California State Department of Education. It was entitled, *Alternatives to I.Q. Testing: An Approach to the Assessment of Gifted "Minority" Children.* One aspect of that work involved taking a close look at the matter of behavioral style, which included but was broader than cognitive style. I was exploring the idea then that behavioral style might help to explain the gap in test performance between White and Black students, or between any two groups of students, for that matter. The assumption was that two groups of students that actually have the same intellectual potential would, because of diversity in cultural socialization, develop habits and preferences that would cause them to manifest their mental powers in somewhat different ways.

The research that I was doing at that time was focused on testing and assessment issues. It did not focus on the matter of the use of testing and assessment data for the design of instruction in settings that could be characterized as culturally diverse. However, I fully expected then, just as I do now, that diversity in behavioral style, which also is correlated to group behavior among cultural groups, would be a meaningful phenomenon to be taken into account in the delivery of instruction. Naturally, the utility of behavioral style for instructional planning is dependent upon systematic study of the nature and potential of that style.

Since 1976, I have pursued other research interests, at least one of which was a part of the 1976 study. That area of interest is African and African American history and culture. In addition, I have also studied effective instructional strategies. While cultural behavioral style, including cognitive style, remains an area of interest to me, it has not been my priority area of research. However, I have kept up fairly well with some of the best literature in the area.

In 1976, and since that time, abundant and overwhelming data have accumulated in a variety of academic disciplines to show that behavioral styles exist among individuals. In addition, abundant and overwhelming data exist to show that cultural groups vary with respect to style. The academic disciplines that contain the evidence include anthropology, psychology, and linguistics.

My research in California focused on African and African American culture in contrast to European and European American culture. As indicated in my technical report, I could have selected any one or more dimensions of human experience for closer study for the purpose of this contrast. I chose to review the literature that would allow for a comparison between African American and European Americans in the following areas: religion, language, and music.

My study was undertaken in full recognition of the fact that the precise attribution of a cultural identity to individuals is certain to be fraught with error. I wrote rather, of central tendencies within groups. As I indicated in the paper, a given individual may be very much like most of the members of his or her historical groups of reference. In fact, most individual African Americans are very much a part of a core African American culture. Yet some may operate on the margin of the historical group of reference. Also some may operate in a way that is quite outside their historical group of preference. All of this is dependent upon the nature of the cultural socialization process to which they are exposed.

I hasten to add that I refer to culture, rather than to race, or class, even though there may be some correlation among all three variables, because of political and economic realities. For example, African Americans have for years been segregated and confined in general to a common space and to common economic conditions, resulting in a high degree of within-group socialization.

I found in 1976, and I have seen nothing since that time to challenge that finding, that a unique African

American core culture could be described empirically, and that most African Americans share this core culture to a greater or lesser degree. It has been interesting that even a few European Americans share this core culture to a greater or lesser degree. It has been interesting that some European American and some African American commentators seem to be threatened by the very idea that an African American culture exists. Some even deny that African Americans have a culture, only a "culture of poverty." Clearly, such a position could only be taken by someone who has not studied African American history and culture systematically. Students of political and economic problems are seldom students of history and cultures.

Advertisers in the private business sector are well aware of cultural diversity. Without such awareness they would fail miserably in many ethnic markets. Since there are few if any penalties for the failure of teaching in education, such as profit loss in business, we have had the luxury of ignoring meaningful phenomena.

It is one thing to determine that behavioral style exists and that cultural behavioral style also exists. It is quite another thing to make valid pedagogical applications of the information about style. In fact, it could be the case that style could exist (behavioral style, cultural style, learning style) and that there might be no meaningful implications for instruction at all. On the other hand, an understanding of style may very well help us to solve some of the stubborn pedagogical problems that exist today.

In 1976, I wrote the following comments at the end of my paper under a section entitled "Cautions and Interpretation." It is critically important that those who use the information presented here be aware of the following points:

1. We do not regard style as in any way equivalent to IQ or "intelligence." We simply regard style as the vehicle through which intelligence is expressed.

2. We do not posit the notion of style as an excuse to explain why some children do not learn in some subjects. In fact, we believe that there is evidence to indicate that any content may be learned by any style user. The question is simply one of how a given style user will approach the task and whether the approach that a given style user uses is compatible with

that of the teacher or the institution that provides instruction.

3. Finally, it is our opinion that the evidence indicates that style *is*. However, there is no intent here to take sides in any debate over whether style should or should not exist. That would be a separate discussion and would be resolved in terms of the aims of society and education.

But what are we to do with the information about style in the instructional process? I believe that it is useful to think of the possible response as falling into two general categories. First, there are responses about which we may feel a reasonable degree of certainty. Then there are responses about which we may feel less certain, and where more information is needed.

Clear Pedagogical Consequences

It is my opinion that there are three clear problem areas that can be informed by what we know now about style. They are as follows:

1. The misunderstanding of cultural behavioral style leads to errors in the estimation of a student's or a cultural group's intellectual potential. The consequences of such errors are enormous. This leads to mislabeling, misplacement, and mistreatment of children.

2. The misunderstanding of cultural behavioral style leads to errors in estimates of learned abilities or achievement in academic subjects such as reading. For example, it has been shown that some teachers who are unfamiliar with the storytelling style of African American children are actually unable to follow the children's story, failing to detect the inherent order of the story, even to the extent of believing that the children's orderly stories have no order at all.

3. The misunderstanding of cultural behavioral style leads to errors in estimates of the language abilities of the students.

In general, the literature on teacher expectations is clear. The images that teachers and others hold about children and their potential have a major influence on the use of the teacher's full range of professional skills. For example, if a teacher believes that a student's intellectual potential is low, research shows that the teacher will "teach down" to the estimated level. They will simplify, concertize, fragment, and slow the pace of instruction. They will fail to offer abstract conceptually oriented instruction to the child. So we see that it is not the learning style of the child that prevents the child from learning. It is the use of the children's style by the teacher as a sign of incapacity that causes the teacher to reduce the quality of instruction offered.

Students can master any style of instruction, provided that they are given the opportunity to develop the new repertoire. In my experience, expanding the students repertoire to include learning academic content within a new style of instruction can be accomplished within a reasonably brief period of time. Styles are more like habits, values, and preferences or predispositions than they are like biological dispositions. Students have an incredible capacity for developing the ability to use multiple styles, in much the same way that multiple language competency can be accomplished.

Potential Pedagogical Consequences

The issue associated with cultural behavioral style is not at all a matter of the students' capacity to accommodate the style of the school. I have shown in my 1976 technical report that the traditional American school is quite rigid and encapsulated in a particular style . Mainly, the traditional school mimics the traditional cultural style of European Americans. Yet this is not the only way to teach. What is even more important, it may not even be the best way to teach for European American children. The real question is what is the pedagogical value to all children and teachers of providing stylistic diversity in the schools?

Unfortunately, we tend to treat the stylistic mismatch between some students and the schools as a student deficiency or problem requiring the students to change. We fail to see the potential for enriching the school experience for all children. Moreover, we fail to see that the traditional school style has severe limitations. Business and industry leaders are well aware of the fact that it takes a great deal more than our stable conforming educational process to produce the flexible and creative risk takers that they often require. Millions of dollars are spent in large corporations today trying to expand the stylistic repertoire of rigid sales people, managers, researchers, and supervisors.

Limitations of the Traditional American School

As it is in general	*As it could be*
(Analytical, "Obsessive-Compulsive")	(Relational, "Hysterical")
Rules	Freedom
Standardization	Variation
Conformity	Creativity
Memory for specific facts	Memory for essence
Regularity	Novelty
Rigid order	Flexibility
"Normality"	Uniqueness
Different equals deficit	Sameness equals oppression
Preconceive	Improvise
Precision	Approximate
Logical	Psychological
Atomistic	Global
Egocentric	Sociocentric
Convergent	Divergent
Controlled	Expressive
Meanings are universal	Meanings are contextual
Direct	Indirect
Cognitive	Affective
Linear	Patterned
Mechanical	Humanistic
Unison	Individual in group
Hierarchical	Democratic
Isolation	Integration
Deductive	Inductive
Scheduled	Targets of opportunity
Thing focused	People focused
Constant	Evolving
Sign oriented	Meaning oriented
Duty	Loyalty

The justification for doing something about style in teaching is therefore not merely a question of equity for poorly served groups. The diverse cultural groups that make up the school population are a rich resource. They have much to teach the schools that are dominated by traditional practices about which we have done too little reflection.

We can be certain that behavioral cultural style variations in the schools will create the potential for significant problems in communication between teachers and some of the children that they serve. These communications problems are likely to be most acute when it comes to standard approaches to testing and assessment and the interpretation that is made of results.

The communication problem may also be present in other parts of the teacher-student interaction. For example, the ability of a teacher to establish rapport and to establish the desired teacher-learner bond can be affected by the way that the incongruent styles are managed. At present, we have much more data on style and assessment than we do about style and communication in education. Anthropologists have gone much further than educators in developing an understanding of the meaning of style in human communications. For example, see Edward T. Hall's book, *Beyond Culture,* and Thomas Kochman's *Black /White Styles in Conflict,* among others. So once again, it is less a matter of style influencing learning than it is that style influences teaching, which influences learning.

Perhaps the most significant thing about the discussion of styles and learning is that it provides the opportunity to raise issues pertaining to general pedagogy that would not be raised otherwise. If African American and Hispanic children were not performing at too low a level, we might be tempted to leave the school situation as it is, believing it to be adequate for the European American students who seem to be doing well. Yet a look at the workplace and at the general way that many Americans tend to live their lives suggests that there is cause for deep concern.

As shown in the table above from my 1976 technical report, I contrasted the characteristics of schools as they appear to be in the majority of cases today with some alternative characteristics. Over the years, many educators have had occasion to examine the two lists of characteristics side by side. Almost without fail, there is a tendency for educators to verbalize a preference for school systems to operate on the basis of more flexible, creative, improvisational, spontaneous, and less rigid principles. In fact, the list of potential characteristics for schools is usually associated with the image that most educators hold about the operation of "gifted" programs. In interviews, educators tend to favor personal professional behaviors that are like the second "as it could be" list to the first "as it is" list.

Clearly, if for no other reason than that the image of the school that teachers and school leaders want is different from the schools that we have, we can use the current situation in New York as a springboard for far-reaching reforms. Such reforms can serve the needs of poorly served cultural groups. The fringe benefit is, as usual, that anything that benefits the poorly served students always works to the benefit of all.

Teachers and Cultural Styles in a Pluralistic Society

I
s matching teaching styles to students' cultural learning styles the answer to low achievement among "minority" students, or an excuse not to teach all students in effective ways, or both?

Educational dialogue in recent years has given substantial attention to the question of the importance and precise meaning of "style" in teaching and learning, particularly for "minority" groups. Style differences between teachers and students and between students and the curriculum have been cited as explanations for the low academic performance of some "minority" groups—just as, "one person's meat is another person's explanation, is another person's excuse."

Predictably, a debate has ensued over the part, if any, that style plays. There has, however, been little opportunity for a rigorous and systematic scrutiny of applied pedagogy that incorporates insights from the style theorists. As a result, much of the discussion about style have taken on more of the character of rhetoric than of scientific pedagogy.

In education, we frequently do not enjoy common professional terminology. We use the same words some of the time, but we do not have common meanings for those words. This problem is particularly acute when the topic is style. We clearly need to find a new way to talk about a somewhat complex set of realities. Before we proceed, certain relevant questions must be answered: Does style exist? What is style? Is style the property of groups, of individuals, or of both? Can any group be identified by a particular style? Is the style of a group pedagogically meaningful?

Educators sometimes appear to be caught on the horns of a dilemma. They are called upon to be sensitive to the styles that the students in their classes present and warned not to stereotype groups of people. All individuals deserve, we are told, to be able to reveal themselves as they really are. We are not to prejudge students. Are these directives in conflict with each other?

Culture, Race, and Class

Definitions of culture differ widely, even among professionals such as anthropologists. I will offer a simple working definition that contains the essence of others. This definition does not attempt to enumerate all the parameters of culture or offer a theory of its dynamics, yet it should be useful here.

Paulo Freire, the gifted Brazilian educator, has defined culture as "anything that human beings make." In essence, Freire sought to make primary the distinction between what is "nature" and what is culture, between what is made by humans and what is not. This definition should leave the user with a certain sense of the arbitrariness and the equivalence of the many things that many different peoples make. For example, the Chinese, English, and African peoples all make music, but each does it differently. Similarly, each people has a distinctive way of making languages, philosophy, music, symbols, stories, poetry. It is an error to think of one group's cultural creativity as superior to that of another. The two merely differ.

People choose to make things out of the elements available to them in their environment, in keeping with their motivation to do so and their historical frame of reference. Any cultural characterization of a person or group is, then, a statement about the results of human choice, not about natural properties, such as mental capacities.

Above all, an understanding of culture should bring a sense of the profound difficulty of coming up with cultural universals. Some educators and behavioral scientists have committed what social psychologist Wade Nobles has called the scientific "error of transubstantiation." That is the error of attempting to interpret the cultural substance of one group in terms of the cultural substance of another. In psychology, for example, measurement with culture-bound instruments may be thought to provide information about intellect, cognition, personality, or self-concept. It might in fact, however, simply assess cultural assimilation or similarity.

A human group shares ways of doing things. Simply put, groups share cultural patterns. Culture is what gives ethnicity its strength and meaning. Culture provides group members with a deep sense of belonging and often with a strong preference for behaving in certain ways.

Other means of designating groups may not generate this type of identity and feeling at all. For example, belonging to the group of Americans who are eighteen years of age, who owe library fines, who are five feet eleven inches tall, and who moved to Washington State last year may not be accompanied by any real group feelings at all.

The cultural dimension then, is very important to our discussion of style. Discussions of cultural matters in education, unfortunately, suffer from a widespread tendency to confuse race and class with culture. These may be associated, but they are not synonymous. A person of the Black race, for example, may or may not be closely identified with the mainstream of traditional culture in the Black community. In any given society, members of a race that tends to share a common culture may, because of racism or other forms of oppression, tend to occupy the bottom rung of the economic and political ladder. But the culture of the group is not defined by its class: there are many cultural groups within every class level, just as members of one cultural group may represent different classes.

Knowing race and class then, the professional is obligated to look further if a student is to be understood. In a classic 1977 book about culture and style, Edward T. Hall emphasized a very important characteristic of culture. It is, he says, "invisible." Most of us are profoundly unaware of our cultural patterns. We experience them as normal or natural ways of acting, feeling, and being. According to Hall, we are most able to know ourselves culturally when we immerse ourselves in exotic cultures—cultures so different from our own that we are forced to understand that there is more than one way to be "natural."[1]

Such insights help us begin to appreciate the subtler differences among racial and ethnic groups in the United

States, which tend to overlap each other culturally to such an extent that the cultural commonalities tend to drown out the equally potent cultural uniquenesses. Any meaningful discussion of style thus requires a highly sophisticated sense of cultural dynamics.

Style

Human beings have an infinite variety of options in organizing and using the environment. Over time, individuals and groups tend to develop habitual ways of responding to experience. In individuals, we call the sum of these patterns "personality." Perhaps the best way to think about culture—or that aspect of culture we call "style"—is to consider it the "personality" of a group.

Scientists from many academic disciplines have reported amazingly similar findings based upon their observations of different aspects of group styles. They still, however, use different terminology. Brain researchers talk about "left-brain" and "right-brain" behavioral patterns. Psychologists such as Rosalie Cohen talk about "analytic" and "relational" cognitive styles. Anthropologists such as Warren Tenhouten have spoken about "science" and its "mirror image." Psychiatrists such as David Shapiro have noted "obsessive compulsive" versus "hysterical" behavioral styles. Strikingly, the specific descriptors of the behaviors that fall under the various labels for style are quite similar—sometimes identical—to one another.

As a simple definition of style, I propose "consistency in the behavior of a person or of a group that tends to be habitual"—the manifestation of a predisposition to approach things in a characteristic way.

Although a few investigators seem to be interested in seeking a biological basis for style, I have found it more useful to focus on the cultural basis. Style is learned. Our understanding from learning theory therefore applies here. For example, learned patterns can be either changed or augmented.

Educators have had a difficult time accepting the existence of varieties of culture and style. Many Americans have had a kind of ideological commitment to the notion of the nation as a "melting pot," as both an ideal and a reality. Some have a very hard time simultaneously managing the ideas of democracy on the one hand and cultural pluralism on the other. Yet there is no conflict between these two concepts. In fact, one test of a democracy may well be the degree to which it provides an environment within which religious pluralism, political pluralism, and yes, cultural pluralism can exist. In any event, ample empirical data attest to the reality of cultural pluralism.

Cultural style, then, cannot be ignored. But precisely what are we to make of it? Several important things may be said about style. First we must remember that style should be considered on its various levels: cognitive, learning, and behavioral. The following general points may be made:

1. Styles are learned, not innate.
2. Like other learned behaviors, styles can be changed.
3. A person can learn to use more than one style, and to switch when appropriate. When this talent is applied to languages, linguists call it "code switching."
4. Style tends to be rooted at a deep structural level and so may be manifest in a highly generalized way. For example, you can predict that cognitive learning, and general behavioral style will follow the same rules.

We may say, then, that behavioral style is an aspect of culture—"group personality"—and says certain things about the nature of style. What does this mean for teaching and learning?

A Question of Style or of Expectations

It is one thing to show that "invisible culture" is real. It is quite another thing to show that culture is meaningful in pedagogical terms.

It is widely assumed that the mere presence of style requires a pedagogical response, especially at the point of applying specific teaching strategies. It is also widely believed that there already exist well-articulated, appropriate teaching strategies that are differentiated from each other and that can also be characterized in stylistic terms—that good matches can be made between teaching and cognitive or learning styles. It is widely believed, moreover, that such matches ought to be made and that when they are made, teaching and learning will be more successful.

These ideas, while not necessarily held by a majority of teachers, are nevertheless intuitively satisfying to many.

But precisely where in the teaching and learning interaction does style inform pedagogy?

I have been an educator for more than 30 years. During most of that time, I have been a teacher educator. I have had the opportunity to observe thousands of teachers. I have had the opportunity to read extensively in the area of teaching strategies. I have been interested in locating teachers and schools where students who are normally expected to be low achievers are actually helped to be superior achievers. Many of the students who have been helped are the same students who, some argue, require a unique pedagogical style to match their cognitive or learning styles.

Since I have been interested in behavioral style and have conducted research on the topic, I have taken every opportunity to focus my observations and to query teachers—both successful and unsuccessful ones—in order to determine, if possible, the role that style considerations play in the work of teachers.

What I have learned is that the behavioral style issue is important and useful in some limited circumstances (I will address them later), but it is very premature to draw conclusions for classroom strategy based on style, or to prescribe pedagogical practice in a general way.

I do believe that greater sensitivity to style issues will make meaningful contributions to pedagogy in the future. Yet I remain unconvinced that the explanation for the low performance of culturally different "minority" group students will be found by pursuing questions of behavioral style. Since students are adaptable, the stylistic difference explanation does not answer the question of why "minority groups" perform at a low level.

In short, I believe that the children, no matter what their style, are failing primarily because of systematic inequities in the delivery of whatever pedagogical approach the teachers claim to master—not because students cannot learn from teachers whose styles do not match their own.

In fact, there is a protocol of interactive behaviors of teachers who, for whatever reasons, have low expectations for students. Excellent evidence for this conclusion can be found in the research summarized by Jere Brophy and cited by Eva Chun in 1988. The research shows that teachers tend to

1. demand less from low-expectation students ("lows") than from high-expectation students ("highs").
2. wait less time for lows to answer questions.
3. give lows the answer or call on someone else rather than try to improve the lows' responses through repeating the question, providing clues, or asking new questions.
4. provide lows with inappropriate reinforcement by rewarding inappropriate behaviors or incorrect answers.
5. criticize lows more often than highs for failure.
6. praise lows less frequently than highs for success.
7. fail to give feedback to lows' public responses.
8. pay less attention to lows and interact with them less frequently.
9. call on lows less often than highs to respond to questions.
10. seat lows farther away from the teacher than highs.
11. use more rapid pacing and less extended explanations or repetition of definitions and examples with highs than with lows.
12. accept more low-quality or more incorrect responses from lows.
13. attempt to improve more poor responses from highs than from lows.
14. interact with lows more privately than publicly.
15. give highs, but not lows, the benefit of the doubt in borderline cases in administering or grading tests or assignments.
16. give briefer and less informative feedback to the questions of lows than to those of highs.
17. use less intrusive instruction with highs than with lows, so that they have more opportunity to practice independently.
18. use less effective and more time-consuming instructional methods with lows than with highs when time is limited.

This range of behavior toward low-performing students is only one aspect of an even larger reality. Another aspect has to do with the real world of pedagogy.[2]

I believe most educators operate on the belief that our pedagogy is systematic, that there is a generally accepted professional practice. As mentioned above, we tend to believe that this practice can be differentiated. We imply exactly that when we group children in tracks or assign them to special education categories. But this assumption simply does not fit the empirical facts. The most accurate description we can give of present circumstances is that teachers generally have the freedom to create their own unique and ad hoc approach to designing instructional strategy. Uniform strategies are generally not required. This fact alone would make it difficult to change in any consistent way the manner in which all teachers react to various styles, assuming that it were desirable to do so.

There may be very good reasons for using what we know about style in the design of teaching. This has less to do with matters of inequity, however, than with making pedagogy better for all. The traditional approaches to pedagogy have tended to be rigid and uncreative. They are far from exhausting the wonderful possibilities for teaching and learning.

The Uses of Style

Where then, does this leave us? What can now be said about the utility of the style phenomenon for educators? I believe that the meaning of style for us at our present level of understanding can be found in four main areas.

First, the misunderstanding of behavioral style leads educators to make mistakes in estimating a student's or a cultural group's intellectual potential. The consequences of such errors are enormous, producing mislabeling, misplacement, and the ultimate mistreatment—inappropriate teaching—of children. If stylistic differences are interpreted as evidence of capacity rather than as an expression of preference, a long chain of abuses is set in motion.

Some children, for example, develop a habit of focusing on the global characteristics of a problem rather than on its particulars. Others do the reverse. Ideally, a student would be flexible enough to do either. Since schools traditionally give more weight to analytical approaches than to holistic approaches, however, the student who does not manifest analytical habits is at a decided disadvantage.

Second, the misunderstanding of behavioral styles leads educators to misread achievement in academic sub-

jects such as creative expression. Orlando Taylor, a sociolinguist and dean of the School of Communications at
Howard University, has shown, for example, that there is
often a gross mismatch between the storytelling styles of
African American children and those of their teachers.

Many teachers from Eurocentric cultures have a linear
storytelling style. Many African American children, on the
other hand, exhibit a spiraling storytelling style, with
many departures from an initial point, but with a return
to make a whole. Many teachers of these children are
unable to follow the children's coherent stories. Some
teachers even believe that the children's stories have no
order at all. Some lose patience with the children and
indicate that they're doing badly.[3]

Third, the misunderstanding of behavioral style can
lead educators to misjudge students' language abilities.
When students and teachers differ in language, teachers
sometimes use their own language as a normative reference. They are regarding common English as "language,"
instead of "a language." As a result, any child who speaks
a different version of English is seen as having a "language
deficiency" rather than a "common English deficiency."
This judgment makes a big difference in how the problem
is defined. On the one hand, there is a deficiency in the
student; on the other, there is an objective for instruction,
with no suggestion that the student is somehow impaired.

Finally, the misunderstanding of behavioral style can
make it difficult to establish rapport and to communicate.
The literature on teachers' expectations of students is
generally very clear. The images that teachers and others
hold of children and their potential have a major influence on their decisions to use the full range of their
professional skills. If a teacher mistakes a child's different
style for lack of intellectual potential, the child will likely
become educationally deprived as the teacher "teaches
down" to the estimated level. As I have mentioned, this
involves simplifying, concertizing, fragmenting, and slow-
ing the pace of instruction.

What We Know of Style

There is something we can call style, a central tendency
that is a characteristic of both individuals and groups. This
style is cultural—learned. It is meaningful in the teaching
and learning interaction. A student's style is not, however,

to be used as an excuse for poor teaching or as an index of low capacity.

It is too early for us to say how or whether pedagogy (classroom teaching strategy) should be modified in response to learning styles. A proper sensitivity to style can provide a perspective for enrichment of instruction for all children and for the improvement both of teacher-student communications and of the systematic assessment of students.

Educators need not avoid addressing the question of style for fear they may be guilty of stereotyping students. Empirical observations are not the same as stereotyping. But the observations must be empirical, and must be interpreted properly for each student. We must become more sensitive to style out of a basic respect for our students, for their reality, and for their tremendous potential for learning.

Fabrication:
The Politics and Sociology of Knowledge in the Study of Ancient Kemet (Egypt) and the Greek and Roman World

In going through the ancient Greek texts, one cannot escape the idea that in the eyes of these old authors, Egypt was the cradle of all knowledge and all wisdom. The most celebrated among the Hellenic wise men or philosophers crossed the sea to seek, with the priests, initiation into new knowledge. And if they never went, their biographers hastened to add to the episodes of their life this voyage which had become as traditional as it was necessary...

Nevertheless, it is not to describe some vague spiritual heritage, not to emphasize what "Greece owes to Egypt," that we have recalled these voyages of the philosophers. Nor is it to establish, after the classic sources, the places where Egyptian science was developed: the voyagers informed themselves on what interested them, no more, and we will see later that besides geometry and astronomy, theology and history, the Egyptian priests cultivated a host of other disciplines of which our tourists say nothing. . . . There is an added point; the philosophers of Greece, as celebrated as they were, won still more popular admiration when one could find an Egyptian sojourn at the source of their knowledge.

—Serge Sauneron

One of the more curious academic debates of our times deals with the origin, the race and the influence of the ancient Kemetic people, Egyptians. The Kemetic people referred to themselves by the name Kemet, or they called their land *The Beloved Land*, Tamerry. It was the Greeks who changed the name of the country to Egypt. Not only was the name of the country changed from Kemet or Tamerry to Egypt, virtually every other significant thing that had a name in

Kemet was also changed. The names of the gods and goddesses were Grecianized. For example, Asa or Asar became Osiris. Ast became Isis. Jehuti became Thoth. The names of the cities were changed. For example, Menefer became Memphis. Waset became Thebes. The names of monuments were changed. Horemaket became The Sphinx. Even the proper names of people including the pharaohs and queens were changed. For example, Mena became Menes. Senwosret became Sesotris. Amenhotep became Amenophis.

Some may regard these changes as mere superficialities, however, in a very real way they symbolize the fundamental distorted treatment of Kemetic reality, and the general reality of African people by European scholarship over time. In the case of names, it is easy to see how tampering with the true record has occurred. However, when it comes to more intangible things, such as the interpretation of cultural data, or taking a position on the race and origin of the ancient Kemetics themselves, it is no longer clear just how or when the changes take place.

After much struggle, Martin Bernal finally got a publisher for his blockbuster book, *Black Athena*, in London. The lack of interest in publishing such a significant book in the United States is a story that needs to be told and examined carefully. It was not a blockbuster because he advanced something new. Dozens of scholars internationally, both African and European, had come to some of the same conclusions as Bernal much earlier: to wit, that the ancient Kemetic people were a native Black African people, and that the culture and civilization of Kemet was widely influential in the Greco-Roman classical world.[1]

It takes nothing away from the value of Bernal's excellent scholarship to say this. In fact, he has been quite up-front in saying the same thing. Bernal's work is important because for a variety of reasons, it now appears difficult to ignore him. His work cannot be written off as academically unworthy. His academic credentials are intact. He even has the pedigree that comes from being the grandson of one of the greatest Egyptologists ever, Sir Alan Gardiner. He has used a wide range of information, primarily historical and linguistic. And yet there are other scholars, notable among them, Dr. Cheikh Anta Diop, who used an even broader range of data, and who performed even more magnificent multidisciplinary analyses than did

Bernal. As those who study the field know, Cheikh Anta Diop, an African Egyptologist, used data from his extensive research in paleontology, linguistics, history, cultural anthropology, microbiology, mathematics and other academic disciplines. Parenthetically, Dr. Diop was well prepared in each area. For example, he had worked with the best nuclear physicists and chemists in France. Yet his seminal work has yet to have a fair hearing among his peers.

It is important to note that when Dr. Cheikh Anta Diop of Senegal and his colleague Dr. Theophile Obenga of Congo, finally got their opportunity, on neutral ground, to present their data in support of native Black Kemet, their rock solid arguments shook the traditional Egyptological establishment. It has never been the same since that time. The official report of the details of the meeting said the following:

> Although the preparatory working paper sent out by UNESCO gave particulars of what was desired, not all participants had prepared communications comparable with the painstakingly researched contributions of Professors Cheikh Anta Diop and Obenga. There was consequently a real lack of balance in the discussions.[2]

It is hard to imagine a more telling conclusion. What type of empirical data had supported the age old idea of a White Egypt? Did the traditional Egyptologists expect to prove a case for it by relying on their prestige? What other data and interpretations can be challenged when the door is opened for new topics and for scholarly opinion that is normally ignored or excluded? Notice that traditional Egyptologists who used to argue for a White Egypt now have retreated to an argument for a *mixed* Egypt, without any more new data than before. It is because serious attention by European and European American Egyptologists is seldom paid to the work of such formally trained African Egyptologists as Cheikh Anta Diop and Dr. Theophile Obenga, at least publicly, that *Black Athena* seems so shocking.

I am very impressed with the work that Martin Bernal has done, giving due credit to Africa for its best known ancient civilization, and for recognizing the influence of Africa in the ancient world. However, I am most impressed with a specific aspect of that work. To me, more important than all of his conclusions about the ancient Kemetic people is the work that he did in chapter 4, which reveals the impact of the social and political context within which the research on ancient Kemet was done, especially in the eighteenth century.

Bernal's chapter 4 is entitled "Hostilities to Egypt in the 18th Century." Dr. Bernal has definitely made his case that there has been more than one story about the origin and influence of the ancient Kemets. His "ancient model," the model of interpretation applied by the classical scholars of Greece and Rome was certainly quite different than that which emerged in eighteenth century Europe. In chapter 4, Martin Bernal called attention to the political climate in Europe, especially in Germany, and particularly the effect of that climate at Goettingen University, which may have given rise to and seemed to explain the fundamental change in the ancient story, a change that occurred for the most part without the benefit of significant new data. Bernal tells us that some scholars at Goettingen may also be the seminal force behind racist ideology. Bernal says that many of these influential scholars tried to distort Kemetic history and also *fabricated* a Greece without Kemet. This is most a most serious charge. It begs to be considered for what it meant for Egyptology then and what it may mean now.

> We are now approaching the nub of this volume and the origins of the forces that eventually overthrew the Ancient Model, leading to the replacement of Kemet (Egypt) by Greece as the fount of European civilization.[3]

Martin Bernal identifies four political and ideological forces that were responsible for the change, forces that did not include fresh empirical data on Kemet.

* Christian reaction
* The rise of the concept of *progress*
* The growth of racism
* Romantic Hellenism

According to Bernal, Christian reaction referred to the hostility and tension that existed because of the competition between the Christian religion and the Kemetic religion. This competition continues in residual form even into the 1990's. The Ast (Isis) religion of Kemet was at its height in Greece and Rome from 300 B.C. to 325 A.D., more than 600 years.

The concept of *progress*, as Martin Bernal says, was a paradigmatic interpretation that implies later or newer is better than older. The growth of racism during the eighteenth century as a justification for slavery, and later for colonialism, in the nineteenth century should require little explanation.

> In the long run we can see that Egypt was also harmed by the rise of racism and the need to disparage every African culture; during the 18th century, however, the ambiguity of Egypt's racial position allowed its supporters to claim that it was essentially and originally *White*. Greece, by contrast, benefited from racism, immediately and in very way; and it was rapidly seen as the *childhood* of the *dynamic* European race.

The romanticism that Bernal saw occurred within the context of a particular political setting.

> First Germany: during the early part of the 18th century, Germany went through one of its most acute crisis of national identity in striking contrast to France, Holland and England. For more than a century following the end of the 30 years war in 1648 there was continued military devastation, political fragmentation and economic backwardness. The same period saw the military and cultural rise of France to a point where it seemed about to become *New Rome*, capable of absorbing all Europe. The language and culture of the German courts, including that of Frederick the Great of Prussia was French; most of the books published in Germany in the first half of the century were in Latin and French. *Thus there was a reasonable fear voiced by the late 17th century philosopher and mathematician Leibniz and later patriots, that German would never develop into a language capable of being used for cultural and philosophical discourse;* it might even, like their Germanic Frankish language spoken by the early of French, disappear altogether in the face of French. German culture and the German people were seen as being in mortal danger.

The most significant response to this crisis on the part of the German romantics was the attempt to return Germans to their cultural roots, and to create an authentic German civilization from the German soil and the German people. *German thinkers including Kant, Fichte, Hegel and the Schlegels, provided a firm basis for the chauvinism and racism of the following two centuries.*[4]

We have seen a similar situation here in the United States, as far as nationalistic motivation and scholarship are concerned. Dr. John Gilkerson and Morton Susna wrote a very revealing history of the National Endowment for the Arts and of the National Endowment for the Humanities.

> . . .the founders of the endowment hoped it would help resolve long-standing debates and doubts about the nature and quality of American civilization. They wanted to define a distinctively American culture that would capture the democratic spirit and counter totalitarianism in the rest of the world.

> . . .the desire to promote a unique national culture had "heavily shaped the creation of the National Foundation for the Arts and the Humanities, and continues to influence the operation of both endowments today."

> . . .In the 19th century, he said, many Americans feared the United States was too young, too egalitarian, and too obsessed with business to create a "high culture." But they hoped those same features might produce a culture that would be uniquely American.

> . . .some Americans became concerned about competing with the Soviet Union, not just in military and foreign affairs, but in cultural matters as well.

> . . .in 1964, the American Council of Learned Societies, the Council of Graduate Schools, and the united chapters of Phi Beta Kappa jointly issued a report recommending that the government create a federal foundation to support both the arts and the humanities. The report "was itself a cultural nationalist manifesto. . . ."

> After World War II, as relations with the Soviet Union deteriorated, humanists hoped to define "a joint culture" that would unite Americans from different backgrounds and help them resist the lure of totalitarian ideology. . . .

> One problem is that American cultural nation-
> alists have often reduced pressing social and
> economic issues to matters of culture," he said.
> That has led them to use the humanities endow-
> ment to combat cultural trends they do not like.[5]

Time will tell if Martin Bernal's thesis holds. However, time will tell only if scholars give their attention to the same questions as did he.

It is very interesting that while Martin Bernal's thesis has made a stir, most of the reaction, positive and negative, seem to be focused on the questions of origin and influence of the Kemets on the classical world, *not on the political sociology of academic inquiry*. Significantly, I know of no one who has challenged Bernal on the racist and biased scholarship issue. There seems to be an extreme reluctance and lack of interest by academics to delve into these highly sensitive matters at all, an area which when exposed has the capacity to undermine the foundation of racist thought in the academic world.

Generally speaking, Africa is the home of Black people, and, generally speaking, Europe is the home of White people. There is nothing inherent in those two realities that generates tension between individuals or among peoples. However, place a great civilization on the African continent, place native Africans at the root and branches of that civilization, show that that civilization occupied a leadership role in the world for centuries, do that in the context of a European White supremacy belief system and world view that has for centuries painted Africans as inferior beings, and you then have the makings of a situation in academe where truth becomes a scarce commodity.

Objectivity and neutrality is definitely a scientific ideal; however it is seldom a social reality. When scholars come exclusively from one ethnic, racial, or national group, dominating a field, the likelihood of ethnic chauvinism in science is magnified. When we add the economic and political self-interest (the enormous profits of slavery and colonialism) of such groups to that mix, a prudent person would approach such resulting scholarship with caution, even with extreme caution.[6]

Few Americans have any idea just how intentional, systematic, intensive, prolonged and widespread was the *defamation* process directed toward African people and the descendants of African people all over the world during the slavery, colonial, and racism periods. They are generally unaware of the role that scholarship played. Bernal was right about the racist context for scholarship, then and later. A few examples follow:

Benjamin Franklin, while viewing the inferiority of Blacks as purely cultural and completely remediable, nonetheless expressed the hope that America would become a domain of Whites, undiluted by less pleasing colors.

> I could wish their numbers were increased. And while we are, as I may call it, scouring our planet clearing America of woods, and so making this side of our globe reflect a brighter light to the eyes of inhabitants of Mars or Venus, why should we... darken its people? Why increase the sons of Africa, by planting them in America, where we have so fair an opportunity, by excluding all Blacks and tawnys, or increasing the lovely White and red?[7]

Thomas Jefferson

> I advance it, therefore, as a suspicion only, that the Blacks, whether originally a distinct race or made distinct by time and circumstance, are inferior to the Whites in the endowments of both body and mind.[8]

David Hume advocated both the separate creation and innate inferiority of non-White races.

> I am apt to suspect the Negroes and in general all the other species of men (for there are four or five different kinds) to be naturally inferior to the Whites. There was never a civilized nation of any other complexion than White, nor even any individual eminent either in action or speculation. No ingenious manufacturers among them, no art, no sciences.[9]

George Curvier, widely hailed in France as the Aristotle of his age, and a founder of geology, paleontology, and modern comparative anatomy, referred to native Africans as "the most degraded of the human races, whose form approaches that of the beast and whose intelligence is nowhere great enough to arrive at regular government."[10]

Louis Agassiz, (Harvard) Leading Naturalist

> This compact continent of Africa exhibits a population which has been in constant intercourse with the White race, which has enjoyed the benefit

of the example of the Egyptian civilization, of
the Phoenician civilization, of the Roman civilization, of the Arab civilization...and nevertheless
there has never been a regulated society of Black
men developed on the continent. . . .[11]

Abraham Lincoln

There is a physical difference between the White
and Black races which I believe will forever forbid
the two races living together on terms of social
and political equality, and inasmuch as they
cannot so live, while they do remain together
there must be the position of superior and inferior, and I was much as any other man am in
favor of having the superior position assigned
to the White race.

. . .Negro equality, Fudge! How long, in the
government of a God great enough to make and
rule the universe shall there continue knaves to
vend and fools to equip, so low a piece of de-
magogism as this.[12]

Arnold Toynbee wrote,

When we classify mankind by color, the only one
of the primary races, given by this classification,
which has not made a creative contribution to
nay of our twenty-one civilization is the Black
race.[13]

Georg Wilhelm Friedrich Hegel

This is the land where men are children, a land
lying beyond the daylight of self conscious history, and enveloped in the black color of night.
At this point, let us forget Africa not to mention
it again. Africa is no historical part of the world.
. . .[14]

Richard Burton

The study of the Negro is the study of man's
rudimentary mind. He would appear rather a
degeneracy from the civilized man than a savage
rising to the first step, were it not for his total
incapacity for improvement. He has not the ring
of the true mental. There is no rich nature for
education to cultivate. He seems to belong to
one of those childish races never rising to man's
estate, who fall like worn out limbs from the
great chain of animated nature.[15]

Samuel Baker, an explorer looking for the source of the
Nile said,

Human nature viewed in its crudest state has seen among African savages is quite on the level with that of the brute, and not to be compared with the noble character of the dog. There is neither gratitude, pity, love or self denial, no idea of duty, no religion, nothing but covetousness, ingratitude, selfishness and cruelty.[16]

Putnam's Monthly (Author Unidentified)

The most minute and the most careful researchers have, as yet, failed to discover a history or any knowledge of ancient times among Negro races. They have invented no writing; not even the crude picture-writing of the lowest tribes; they have no gods and no heroes; no epic poems and no legend, not even simple traditions. There never existed among them an organized government; they never ruled a hierarchy or an established church.[17]

George F. Will

"Eurocentricity" is right, in American curriculums and consciousness, because it accords with the facts of our history, and we—and Europe—are fortunate for that. The political and moral legacy of Europe has made the most happy and admirable nations. Saying that may be indelicate, but it has the merit of being true, and the truth should be the core of any curriculum.[18]

P.T. Bauer

. . . .Most people do not appreciate the low level of economic achievement of the indigenous human resources of Africa. If they know it, they tend to feel responsible, or are made to feel responsible for it.

In historical times the achievement of Black Africa (i.e., most of the continent of Africa) has been negligible compared with that of Asia and Europe....

. . . .Before the closing decades of the nineteenth century Professor Mazrui's erstwhile Garden of Eden was without the rudiments of either civilized or of modern life....

. . .African backwardness amidst ample natural resources is only one conspicuous example of the fact that material progress depends on personal qualities, social institutions and mores,

and political arrangements which make for en-
deavor and achievement, and not simply physical
resources. . . .

. . .Professor Mazrui would like Africa to mod-
ernize, but without Westernization. . . this is not
possible. The concept of material progress, of
steadily increasing control of man over his environment, is Western, as are the modes of conduct which derive from it. Progress and its
conditions and manifestations may not be laudable or conducive to happiness. But the idea of
modernization without Westernization is self-
contradictory.[19]

No wonder an honest scholar with great courage would
challenge his peers.

Speaking at the annual meeting of the organization of
American historians, *Leon Litwack,* Professor of History at
the University of California, Berkeley, indicted past historians for perpetuating racism. He called on his present-
day colleagues to heal that wound. . . .

No group of scholars was more deeply implicated
in the mis-education of American youth and did
more to shape the thinking of generations of
Americans about race and Blacks than historians.
. . whether by neglect or distortion, the scholarly
monographs and texts they authored perpetu-
ated racial stereotypes and myths.[20]

These few quotations demonstrate the vicious and defamatory way in which some of the most prestigious European and American scholars have viewed African people,
have written about them, influencing heavily scholarly and
public opinion. It is because of such observations that a
Bernal book becomes necessary.

There is more to the story than this, however. Not only
were such opinions generated and published widely, active attempts were made by many public officials and
scholars alike to prevent the education of African populations in general and in particular about themselves. Philanthropists collaborated and played a major role in the
design in what Carter G. Woodson called a *miseducation*
process.[21]

Kenneth King has done brilliant work in his book *Pan
Africanism and Education,* documenting the miseducation
role played by those who had the responsibility for the
education of African people, not only on the continent of

Africa, but throughout the world. Similarly, the book by Donald Spivey, *Schooling for the New Slavery* follows up on Kenneth King's treatment by showing the role and function of Black industrial education in the United States as a way of keeping African people away from the data needed to interpret their own cultural and historical reality. It cannot be emphasized too strongly that this activist scholarly miseducation role was a world-wide phenomenon. Examples of the overt aspect of this role still remain in South Africa today. In addition, there has been no in-depth systematic purge of false information from bodies of mainstream scholarship.

In other words, looked at from the point of view of an African, we can see the defamatory role that some scholarship has played in the reporting of historical reality. Such defamatory presentations are often not merely the musings of the cloistered academics. They can and have created deadly climates that trigger negative activism.[22]

Recently, we have seen the emergence in academe of a new imperative in scholarship among a small, but influential group of conservative scholars. At least the imperative is new in the sense that it is being stated explicitly. This imperative in academics is anti-intellectual, anti-democratic and anti-scientific. I refer to the growing group of scholars, who say that their role in higher education is to *defend the West.* According to a report in the *Chronicle of Higher Education,* former Secretary of Education William Bennett went to Stanford University to protest Stanford University's revision of the Canon, (an interesting term for university studies) in freshman studies. He gave four reasons why the Stanford Faculty, and presumably others in higher education, should defend the West:

1. It is ours.
2. It is complex.
3. It is good.
4. It is under attack.

This assumes the validity of the perception that there is a *West,* that is under attack simply because it is the West, and that scholars should be mobilized to defend it (as religion or scholarship?) This position can be found in the writings of such people as the group of professors who took out an unsigned ad in the November 8, 1989 issue of the *Chronicle of Higher Education* as "the National Association of Scholars." This suggests a peculiar role for higher education in view of the traditional stated goal of a search for truth.

This position has lead to a unique kind of activism by some of those scholars that should be of interest to academic inquiry. The character of this newly emerging *defense system* is that it is the product of private dialogue and is propagandistic, strident and venomous. Many recent editorials (since November 1989) by right wing conservative news columnists appear to espouse the same rhetoric. They seem to have been written by the same person, or developed in the same think tank. Note the following: (a) the anecdotal citations they use as stimulus materials, (b) the uniform range and mix of topics or targets they select to address, (c) the bitter tone in which they are written, and (d) the focus of their dialogue, which fails to acknowledge or address the true and full positions of their targets. These scholars appear to desire that whole categories of topics be ruled off-limits to scholarly inquiry, topics such as the role of scholars in the design of an oppressive society.

Some scholars go so far as to say that "we should only study those things that bring us together." They want to leave untouched any negative elements in the history of the nation, even though they are true. This has the ring of censorship and propaganda. Of course, the goal of harmony among all of the world's people is laudable, and academics should make their contribution to that harmony. However, the suppression of truth seems hardly to have the potential for serving those ends. We do not need academic George Wallaces to stand in the university door to block the free flow of information and dialogue.

In order to maintain the operative concept of immaculate or autochthonous *Western Civilization,* it is necessary to avoid studiously whole bodies of relevant and valid scholarship. For example, we can reveal to students the rich literature on Kemet and Mesopotamia and can articulate the parameters of these high civilizations that were the antecedents of Western Civilization. Moreover, we can compare them to the Greco-Roman Civilization, while documenting the teacher-student relationship between the older civilizations of Kemet and Mesopotamia and those of Greece and Rome, as a prelude to the discovery in the West of the inherited parameters of Africa and Asia. Moreover, what is called Western Civilization has been under the constant influence of international forces, not the least of which was the 700 to 800 years of Moorish control and influence in Europe.

One is not quite sure when scholars speak of *the West* whether what is meant is

* the White race,
* a value system associated with the West,
* the science and technology in its later evolution in the West,
* the humanities tradition of the West, or
* something else.

Does the contemporary injunction to defend the West, categorically, apply to the defense of all of the above? The whole thing becomes more ludicrous in light of the fact that what is perceived as an attack on the West, as I am aware of criticisms, are really attacks on the role and productions of some scholars who have created the ideology of White supremacy, and those who have advocated and become activists toward those ends. The victims of racial oppression in the West have experienced it for hundreds of years of slavery, segregation, and racism. Certainly this is not the aspect of the West to be defended as *ours* and *good*. On the other hand, no one attacks the positive aspects of the western experience indiscriminately. However, the victims of oppression do attack the position of those who say that they represent the West, when they are coercive towards cultural groups that have every right to exist as ethnic groups, and who have the responsibility to remember their holocaust.

We must be aware of the fact that cultural oppression was the primary tool in the arsenal of colonials and slavers. The well-understood effect of this cultural oppression was to destroy the unity of a group so that it would be unable to defend itself or to mobilize to solve its problems. The history of the use of scholarship devoted toward these ends can be documented without effort. Consequently the universal *unilateral decree of what is normative culture, or what are the normative values of "civilization" deserves our careful attention, as Franz Fanon has said*. As far as African and African Americans are concerned, I know of no recommendation or insistence that what is called Western Civilization be eliminated from the schools. The insistence is that critical challenges to any content in the schools must not be suppressed.[23]

Bernal is to be thanked for including in *Black Athena* the data on the sociopolitical aspect of the scholarship on Greece and the African and Asian world.

1. There are those scholars of greatest integrity who attempt to report the truth as they see it, letting the chips fall where they may.
2. There are those scholars who possess an *unconscious* cultural bias that colors and shapes their creativity.
3. There are those scholars who deliberately distort the human record for explicit political purposes.
4. There are those scholars who proceed with their work in ignorance of all of the above.

I have my own position about the data that are presented in the study of the origin of and influence of the ancient Kemetics, and I believe that there is overwhelming support for the fact that these were native Africans. It was not necessary and was certainly unparsimonious to attempt to explain the great civilization of Kemet (Egypt) by positing (with no documentation) the notion of some alien interplanetary travelers, or some foreign population who moved into Africa, built the great African civilization of Kemet, left with no trace and failed to build a similar civilization anywhere else on the earth. To accept such a notion is to explain away the linguistic and cultural unity of ancient Kemet with the other existing African population, and the physical unity exhibited in skull studies, melanin dosage tests, osteological measures, etc.[24]

As exciting as such discussions are, from my point of view, the most important priority for scholarship in this sociopolitical environment is that structures be created to minimize the distorting influences of ignorance, falsehood, and chauvinism. The United Nations' efforts to provide a more truthful and balanced history of the continent of Africa is a good example of what can be done. *Multidisciplinary, multinational specialists from all over the world collaborated in the development of an excellent work.* This represents a balancing of perspectives, a type of academic check and balance system. Politically powerful nations and groups are in a position to impose their view of the world on the entire world. While they may make political sense,

it does not make scholarly sense. Scholars must acknowledge at the outset the role that the sociopolitical context
plays in research and teaching. The depth of this influence argues strongly for a vigorous and extensive attempt
to prevent bias in the future.

Do We Have the "Will" to Educate All Children?

I t is clear from the title that the knowledge and skills to educate all children already exist. Because we have lived in a historically oppressive society, educational issues tend to be framed as technical issues, which denies their political origin and meaning. This chapter attempts to illustrate that there are no pedagogical barriers to teaching and learning when willing people are prepared and made available to children.

If we embrace a will to excellence, we can deeply restructure education in ways that will enable teachers to release the full potential of all our children.

Between 1953 and 1955, a young instructional assistant at Cornell University was completing graduate work. Because, as he puts it, "I was blessed with a logical mind and an inclination to make things simple, plain, and real," Abdulalim Shabazz was frequently selected to serve as a teacher or tutor to his peers when his professors could not be present. This was nothing new for Shabazz. After all, he had graduated from the famous Dunbar High School in Washington, D.C., an all-African American high school from the segregation era that had produced some of the finest scholars in the history of the United States. There too, when his mathematics teacher had to be absent, Abdulalim Shabazz was often called upon to take over the class.

Later, Shabazz would earn his doctorate in mathematics and would serve as a faculty member at two historically Black institutions, Atlanta University in Atlanta, and Tuskegee University in Alabama.

"Give Me Your Worst Ones"

One period of his illustrious career as a research scientist and professor is of particular interest. It was between 1956 and 1963 when Professor Shabazz was Chair of the Mathematics Department at Atlanta University. During that time, 109 students graduated with masters degrees in mathematics. Thereafter, more than a third of that 109 went on to earn doctoral degrees in mathematics or mathematics education from some of the best universities in the United States. Of considerable significance is that many of them produced students who later earned doctoral degrees in mathematics and mathematics education. It is estimated that nearly 50 percent (about 200) African American mathematicians presently in the United States, resulted either directly or indirectly from Atlanta University's production of the 109 master degree recipients between the seven-year period from 1956 and 1963. This is an extraordinary record. Shabazz is either directly or indirectly linked to the production of more than half of the African American recipients of doctoral degrees in mathematics. That fact deserves notice. What is even more important, however, is that a significant segment of the 109, according to Shabazz, began their student careers with serious academic deficiencies, not only in mathematics, but also in language art skills as well!

Recently, Shabazz returned to Clark Atlanta University and assumed the Chair of the Department of Mathematics. Once more, and in a very short period of time, he has initiated changes that seem to be leading toward another productive era. At one point, when stimulating the faculty to greater productivity, and in response to some expressed doubts by some faculty members about the abilities of Clark Atlanta University students to do higher mathematics, Shabazz challenged his peers to *"Give me your worst ones and I will teach them!"*

Aware of Shabazz's track record, and perhaps in reflection on their own summary judgments, many faculty members took up the challenge themselves. The fruits of their work are already becoming apparent.

In an interview, Shabazz shared with me the contents of recent letters from several of his former students who had written to him to express appreciation for his key influence on their academic development. When discussing these testimonials, not only was it clear that *SAT and ACT scores had almost no meaning for him,* he also had a focused set of goals of excellence that shaped his approach to dealing with all students. His goals are the following:

1. To *teach understanding* rather than merely to teach mathematical operations;
2. To *teach mathematical language* for the purpose of communicating in mathematics and not merely as a way to solve textbook problems;
3. To *teach that math was not at all a fixed body of knowledge,* but that it was a experimental enterprise in the truest sense of that word, and that their approach to the solution of mathematical problems then, and in the future, should be to try a variety of strategies;
4. *To have students believe as he did that mathematics, "is nothing more than a reflection of life and that life itself is mathematical."* He wanted them to know that the symbols used in mathematics approximate the reality of human experience and cosmic operations;
5. *To give his students a sense of hope* that they could become superior performers.

Shabazz also emphasized teaching his students problem solving, and then just as important and perhaps even more so, teaching them the skill to "write up" what they had done "in a beautiful way." When students did this, and most did, he would point out to his students that they had, after their deep study, "seen things that had not been there before," that they had actually seen what mathematics is all about, not merely the manipulation of numbers *but perceiving* "patterns." Shabazz's overall goal was to involve students in *being mathematicians,* not merely to learn formulas.

Shabazz bristled when teachers "taught down" to students, even those students with a history of low academic performance, "treating them like babies." He decried some teachers who started the year by announcing to their class that, "at least one half of the students in this class will fail." Rather than approach his students in a frightening manner, his approach was to "appeal to the intellect" of each and every student, "to their humanity" and "to their reasoning" rather than emphasize the mastery of algorithms.

Shabazz lamented the fact that the society in general has *internalized a false paradigm about learning,* especially in mathematics, that comes from late nineteenth century Social Darwinism. The tenets of this belief system include the idea that high levels of conceptually oriented mathematics achievement are accessible to a few, and that even this few will not include many, if any, African Americans, Hispanic Americans and certain other cultural minority groups.

Shabazz mentioned in passing, almost apologetically, that he had never had a course in teacher education.

Practice, Practice, and More Practice

Another example of successful teaching of minority students is the work of Jaime Escalante at Garfield High School in Los Angeles.[1]

During the past 10 years, at this one high school, over 500 students, mainly Hispanic, mostly low income, have been taught well enough that they passed the *Advanced Placement SAT Calculus* test. How many other high schools in America can boast of such a record, "inner city" or not?

Escalante said that he did not recruit students by reviewing their test scores, nor were his students necessarily among the gifted or in any kind of high IQ track. He believed that tracking was unworkable and unproven as a guarantee that students would be channeled into the program of classes that were best for them. "My sole criterion for acceptance into this program is that students want to be a part of it and sincerely want to learn math."

Escalante said that in 1979, when the junior high school teachers would tell him to take a particular student because he was gifted in math, he would almost always ignore them. That type of recommendation was almost a certain guarantee that the child would be passed over. If the child was actually gifted, then Escalante thought that that child would need less help from the teacher. In addition, he felt that very few of the "gifted" were appreciably different from the average except in their ability to score high on tracking tests. So as a result, he often chose the students who were considered to be "rascals" and students who were "discipline problems," as well as those who simply liked math. He said that he found that the class cut-ups were often the most intelligent, but were extremely bored because of poor teaching, and they were disillusioned because they saw the work that they were doing as a dead-end. Sometimes they showed themselves to have the most "ganas" when their "learning light" was finally turned on.

There is no shortcut for minorities at Garfield High School. In order for students to even sit for the advanced placement exam, they must have completed algebra I, geometry, algebra II, trigonometry or math analysis, calculus for first year, and/or calculus for second-year college. Some students also took analytical geometry or precalculus during the program. Most of these students had never taken algebra prior to the program.

In spite of their astonishing success, like Shabazz, Escalante and his colleagues found themselves struggling with the system. This teacher, with an extraordinary track record, found himself fighting just to get appropriate textbooks. Escalante said that because of the cost of the textbooks was often much greater than the amount of money allowed, he found himself in conflict with the administration. He said that he got his first introduction to Title I when he requested textbooks that he felt he needed to raise students' scores to the minimum standard of competency. But he was told, "No, Jaime, these books do not qualify for Title One; they are clearly not remedial." Escalante said that this was the same person who told him in complete seriousness, "Jaime, if you get better test scores for these kids, then they are not going to qualify for Title One money." He said he had to fight many battles to convince others that the more expensive books were a vital necessity and were not an extravagance at all.

Escalante emphasized the value of hard work. Practice, practice, and more practice is demanded from each student. In addition, Escalante and his colleagues emphasized the necessity for exposing students to the high-tech math world and to successful role models.

One of the beauties of the Escalante experience is what it suggests about the design of teacher education. Ben Jimenez was a young math teacher at Garfield High School in the mid-seventies when Escalante arrived, and he was about to quit his job, because he felt his students were out of control. Escalante said that he helped Jimenez to learn techniques for control and discipline, and after that he was free to concentrate on building his skills as a teacher.

Jimenez came to be an award-winning mathematics teacher just as Escalante, contributing many students to the total number of advanced placement calculus passes each year.

Releasing the Genius in Children

Here, then, is another teacher who teaches students of families who are mostly below the poverty line. I continue to be shocked at the fact that so many professional educators are quick to insult the skill and hard work of such teachers as Escalante and Shabazz by labeling them "charismatic." They imply that charisma is magical and therefore beyond the reach of "ordinary" teachers. They also imply that only charismatic teachers can help low performers. These professionals have changed children's lives with their own *sweat, blood* and *tears.* Other professionals who prepare well and work as hard can do the same thing.

As I have reviewed the work and comments of dozens of great teachers, their conversations sound right for true professional teachers. They seem to share in a true educator's *ethos.* Common discussions of education—all too often—are characterized by uninspired technical barrenness, and are shaped by the bureaucracy and a *structured ideology* that permeates the society, which causes many of us to doubt the fundamental human potential of the masses of our children. Our faith in the students and in ourselves is often so low that our approach to the teaching task lacks the vitality so typical of natural human teaching-learning encounters. To me, the Shabazzes, and the Escalantes exhibit more of the characteristics of informal mother-child learning dyads in healthy societies than they do of factors most talked about in teacher training. Maybe our professional conversations are on the wrong topics! Maybe we are looking in the wrong direction for school improvement. The valid change process just may be more direct, straightforward, and less complicated than we think.

I keep asking myself, is there anything in the current educational reform agenda that would lead us to the *philosophy,* the *thought,* the *effect,* the *energy* and *results* of the most productive pedagogs in the field, like Shabazz and Escalante? Do we even have the capacity to conceive of these teachers of excellence as our models? I want us to engage the problem of how to structure an approach to education that aims to *release the genius* that is common in the masses of our children, just as these good teachers do! First, we must believe that the genius is there. Do we really believe that it is?

It is hard to take seriously the idea that the masses of our children are geniuses when we embrace the wrong pedagogical paradigm—in spite of new rhetoric to the contrary. We have been historically committed to the same paradigm that we had when public school education began in the United States, ascribing genius to a select few. We have embraced a related *prediction* paradigm that tells us that the major task of assessment professionals is to *forecast* future performance, not to assist with problem solving in teaching and learning. We have continued to embrace the *tracking* paradigm. Even when children have been untracked organizationally, they remain "gifted," "average," and "retarded" in our minds. Otherwise, our national achievement results would leave us with a greater sense of urgency than we now manifest.

Research on Infants and Complex Thinking

Sometimes, where educators are concerned, I wonder if the real meaning of the research findings on infant thinking has begun to sink in. Think of all the years that we have thought about thinking. For many of us, the model for human thought included the false concept of *tabula rasa* or the "blank slate." As students of teacher education, many of us were taught that infants were not really capable of thinking complex thoughts, which was regarded as being due to maturation and long-term nurturing. One famous researcher on infancy told a Chicago audience of early childhood educators that, "There just isn't much there until babies are six months old." What has become increasingly well documented, however, is that while maturation and nurturing may explain some parts of thinking, teaching, and learning, babies start from a cognitive baseline that is nothing short of awesome. In the November 1990 issue of The American Psychological Association *Monitor,* Lori Denton reported that contrary to the findings of many developmental psychologists, such as Jean Piaget, babies as young as three and a half months old actually understand some of the physical and spatial properties of hidden objects. According to researcher

Renee Baillargeon at the University of Illinois, *very young infants share the physical reasoning ability of adults.* They actually understand that objects exist even when hidden. They understand that objects cannot move through the space that is occupied by other objects, and that they cannot be at two separate points in space without traveling from one point to the other.

In reading about Professor Baillargeon's work, I recalled the wonderful book, *Children's Minds.* In that book, Margaret Donaldson, a cognitive psychologist, demonstrated that by constructing more sophisticated and appropriate tasks for infants and young children, it was possible to demonstrate that they reach standard levels of intellectual development months and years earlier than those suggested in the research of Piaget. In other words, our judgment about the level and complexity of mental functioning of infants, is based, in many cases, on data that were *artifacts of the form in which interrogation proceeded,* which is a true representation of what infants could do.[2]

Denton says that Baillargeon used visual tasks in her experiments rather than the manual search task that Piaget had used, because infants might perform poorly not because of their misunderstanding about hidden objects, but because they have limited ability to plan and execute the search task. Then she did some more experiments and found that the infants learn to solve qualitative problems before they learn to solve the quantitative problems, and that they use the qualitative strategies to assess the effect of quantitative variables, because they had not learned to reason quantitatively about them. "The inability to reason quantitatively has little to do apparently with the mental ability, and more to do with the possession of accumulated experiential content upon which quantitative can be performed. That is a matter of time and exposure, not intelligence."

One of the highly significant things about the infant research is that the infants are examined at a stage in their development *prior to the impact of inequitable cultural socialization.* Baillargeon then delivers the bombshell:

> No matter what their socioeconomic background, race or gender, babies of similar ages tend to perform similarly on the basic test. . . . Adults' memories differ from infants primarily because they process information much more

rapidly and have many more memories to make associations with.

She said that the findings are surprising, because the neuropsychologists have been doubting the capability of infants to represent in their memory, information about setting or place until their hippocampus is formed somewhere around eight or nine months of age. "The neuropsychologists are going to have to revise their ideas," she said.

Teachers as Mediators of Student Potential

I have been convinced for a long time that the meaning of the findings of this type of research, when considered in the context of the powerful teaching performances of such teachers as Shabazz and Escalante, is that there is a universal genius among human beings. Teachers are the "mediators" who provide, or fail to provide, the essential experiences that permit students to release their awesome potential.

We all have an enormous mental capacity to do the things that are required of us in either a high-tech or a low-tech society. There simply is no reality base whatsoever for the pessimistic human attitude that is so widespread. In other words, the ubiquitous question about the intellectual capacities of students that has preoccupied American educators for the past 80 to 90 years, and which continues to be central in our thought structure is for our purposes at this point, *virtually meaningless* for powerful pedagogy! The constant preoccupation with mental assessment and labeling, deters and distorts critical analysis of professional services, prevents the improvement of professional practice, and impedes the execution of valid strategies. Why can't we abandon harmful or meaningless professional practice, or replace them with valid ones?

Saying that the evidence for human genius is overwhelming, is not to say that all people are identical in their abilities to do intellectual tasks. There may very well be cognitive differences among learners. However, our concern for these differences should come only after our students have reached an academic achievement level far beyond that which we reach now. Our current ceiling for students is really much closer to where the floor ought to be.

The Beauty and Promise of True Restructuring

The restructuring that educators need to do, then, is much more a matter of *theory, philosophy, perception, conception, assumptions,* and *models* than it is a matter of rearranging the technical and logistical chairs on the educational titanic. It is not a matter of the *amount of time,* of *middle schools or junior high schools,* of *site-based management,* of *schools of choice,* of *behavioral objectives,* of *access to technology. Deep restructuring* is a matter of drawing up an appropriate vision of human potential, of designing human institutions, of creating a professional work environment, of linking school activities with community directions, of creating human bonds in the operation of appropriate socialization activities, and of aiming for the stars for the children and for ourselves academically and socially.

The fundamental problem in deep restructuring has more to do with *aim* and *appropriate practice* than it does with additional resources. If we apply criteria from appropriate deep restructuring to existing practice, we will surely find and eliminate gross misuse of precious physical and human resources. Who could deny for example, that we have wasted incredible resources trying to answer the capacity question for the past 70 years, and that in doing so, we have used the results to cripple the capacity of schools to serve the children. In addition, we have dragged professionals into practices that are not only inappropriate, but are professionally unrewarding, debilitating, demeaning, and depressing as well.

The beauty and promise of true restructuring is that it will provide us with the opportunity to create the educational systems that never have existed before, not because they were hard to create, but because we have not yet manifested the vision, or tried to create them. If the 1990s is to offer anything to education, it would be a new vision of what it is that we are supposed to do and a new commitment to create educational systems that prepare students *both* for their economic role in society *and* for their social, intellectual, and spiritual enhancement as well.

For example, I have long wondered why it took us so long to "discover" "cooperative learning," an approach that is well known among many peoples in the world, and why once having "discovered it," it has become so difficult to execute. At least one reason must have to do with the fact that *we do not have a cooperative philosophy in the general culture.* The pervasive commitment to vouchers and school choice suggests a competitive philosophy rather than a cooperative one. We no longer accept, it seems, the idea that we are our "brothers' and sisters' keepers."

Tapping the Potential of Teachers

While I am convinced that a large part of our difficulty has to do with the way we think about educating our children, that issue is connected to an even more basic problem: the way we teach and the way we regard our educators, especially our teachers. Just as there is a vast untapped potential, yes, genius among the children, there is also a vast untapped potential among teachers who serve the children. I believe that the intellectual and professional potential of our teachers has been drastically underestimated as a consequence of the same paradigm that causes us to underestimate the intellectual and professional potential of our students.

Some of us challenge those who have little faith in the intellectual capacities of the average student. A project in Chicago, sponsored by the National Endowment for the Humanities, does the same thing for teachers. Senior professors from the University of Chicago, Northeastern University, and Chicago State University—from the fields of classics, Egyptology, and Assyriology—in addition to the Chicago School of Inner-City Studies, have organized an intellectual banquet for regular classroom teachers at the middle school level. In a year-long seminar, these teachers are treated to the great literature of the ancient world. They compared the literatures of ancient Egypt, Mesopotamia, and Greece. As regular classroom teachers read and talked about these great bodies of literature, I was struck by the intellectual awakening among them, and how it became apparent in subsequent course preparation and their teaching.

Teachers need their own intellectual and emotional hunger fed. They need to experience the joy of *collaborative discussion, dialogue, critique* and *research.* An enriched academic foundation is definitely a prerequisite for an enriched pedagogical foundation. Together, the two provide a level of comfort for the teacher that supports professional dialogue as well as teacher-student dialogue. The primary roles that the teacher ought to play in service to children are enhanced by the development of the teacher's intellectual power and professional socialization. Such roles include the following:

* The teacher as a *member of an intellectual learning community* both general and specialized
* The teacher as a *stakeholder in the community* that he or she serves
* The teacher as a *community advocate* and not merely as a student advocate
* The teacher as a *participant in goal setting* for children and their communities

As you can see, this view contrasts sharply with that of the teacher as a mere technician in an environment characterized by lack of esteem and trust in professionals.

A Will to Excellence

In order to restructure, we must first look deeply at the goals that we set for our children and the beliefs that we have about them. Once we are on the right track there, then we must turn our attention to the delivery systems, as we have begun to do. Untracking is right. Mainstreaming is right. Decentralization is right. Cooperative learning is right. Technological access for all is right. Multiculturalism is right. But none of these approaches or strategies will mean anything if the fundamental belief system does not fit the new structures that are being created.

The risk for our children in school is not one associated with their intelligence. Our failures have nothing to do with I.Q., nothing to do with poverty, nothing to do with race, nothing to do with language, nothing to do with style, nothing to do with the need to discover new pedagogy, nothing to do with the development of unique and differentiated special pedagogies, and nothing to do with the children's families. All of these are red herrings. The study of them may ultimately lead to some greater insight on the instructional process, but at present, they serve to distract attention from the fundamental problem facing us today. We have one and only one problem: *Are we truly willing to see each and every child in this nation, develop to the peak of his or her capacities?*

If our destination is excellence on a massive scale, not only must we change from the slow lane to the fast lane, we must change highways. Perhaps we need to abandon the highways altogether and take flight, because the highest goals that we can imagine are well within reach for those who have the *will to achieve excellence.*

The Meaning of KMT
(Ancient Egyptian) History for
Contemporary African American
Experience

A REVOLUTION in the study of KMT (Egypt), a native Black African civilization, has been in progress. It began slowly during the closing decades of the nineteenth century. It has accelerated markedly during the past three decades or so. This revolution can and will have great meaning for African Americans and for people of African descent all over the world.

Two important concepts are the foundation of considerations about the meaning of KMT. These two concepts are fundamental challenges to traditional Egyptology and to racist scholarship associated with the European colonial period. They are the following:

1. Ancient KMT from its beginning and during its greatest periods of cultural development was an indigenous Black African civilization. Its birthplace was inner equatorial Africa.
2. Ancient KMT remained at its core culturally unified with the rest of ancient Africa. African cultures had more similarities than differences. As a result, KMT must be considered as an African classical civilization.

KMT is the name for the country that was used by the ancient African people in what we now call Egypt. It means "the Black land" or "the Black people of the land." KMT is sometimes written as Kemet. The letter "e" is sometimes inserted as a convention by Egyptologists, and is entirely arbitrary since the original vowels are unknown. The currently accepted date for the beginning of KMT is 3100 B.C.

This nation was founded by a king from the south who unified the northern or lower part of the land with the southern or upper part of the land. (The Nile River flows from the south to the north.) Twelve native African dynasties were in power for more than one thousand years. This included the Pyramid Age. At least two more of the most important dynasties, the Eighteenth and the Twenty-Fifth, were initiated by kings from the south. Kemetic civilization, the earliest recorded, lasted for nearly three thousand years.[1]

Some scholars have divided the history of KMT into 30 dynastic periods, the last being a period of Greco-Roman political domination just before and after the time of Christ. It was after this period, or more precisely, it was after the time of the first Councils at Nicea in the fourth century A.D. that the knowledge of Ancient Kemetic civilization was lost to Europeans. This was due primarily to their sustained systematic efforts to destroy the remnants of Kemetic cultural forms, which had been strong influences and which remained as powerful influences on European culture, even during the period of Greco-Roman political control of KMT. Over a period of two hundred years or so following the Councils at Nicea, the Romans gradually succeeded in closing the Kemetic temple/universities and destroying the Kemetic priesthood/professorate, in an attempt to declare their total intellectual and spiritual independence from Africa.[2]

The revival of widespread European interest in Ancient KMT began with Napoleon Bonaparte's conquest in 1798. Napoleon is said to have taken nearly two hundred academic specialists with him. These specialists were given the opportunity to study various aspects of Kemetic history and culture, ancient and modern. Perhaps the single most important outcome of this scholarly attention was the discovery at Rosetta on the mouth of the Nile, a stone that proved to be the key to the decipherment of the Mdw Ntr (hieroglyphics). The credit for this decipherment in 1822 is given to Jean Francois Champollion le Jeune. After Champollion, it took years to translate the vast ancient writings to be found on the walls of temples, tombs, monuments, coffins, and on papyri. That work is not yet completed. Therefore, it can be understood why it would be in the later decades of the nineteenth century before the stunning impact of those translations on the interpretation of the influence of KMT on Western and world civilization would be revealed. The more KMT was studied, the more astonishing were the findings that showed its culture to be antecedent to developments in world science, religion, education, art, architecture, etc.[3]

Beginning with W. E. B. Du Bois, there was a gradual growing African American awareness of the greatness of KMT and of the fact that KMT was a civilization created by Africans who were Black people. From that time numerous African American scholars have extended the study of KMT. Many European and European American scholars also began to lift the veil of ignorance and to destroy racist ideas about KMT and the role of Africans in it.[4]

Perhaps no single scholar has had the impact on the recent direction of traditional Egyptology as has Cheikh Anta Diop. Almost single-handedly he took on the traditional Egyptological establishment in a frontal assault on cherished presuppositions about KMT as a White or non-African civilization. This multidisciplined genius led the fight to reconstruct conceptions of KMT.

Diop's original research in history, linguistics, archeology, paleontology and other disciplines, and his synthesis of a vast field of interdisciplinary literature has had its telling effect. For example, Diop even developed a simple chemical test to determine the melanin content in the skin of a mummy as a way of determining its "race." The mummies he tested from the Marietta excavations proved to be "Black." While many Egyptologists struggle to hold on to old conceptions of a non-African KMT, they have been forced by the data to give up much ground.

Nowhere is this more in evidence than in the recent volumes on ancient African history which were developed under the auspices of the United Nations Educational Scientific and Cultural Organization (UNESCO) by an interdisciplinary group of leading scholars from all over the world. Anyone who compares the writings of some of the authors (traditional Egyptologists) of chapters in the UNESCO publication with almost anything that those authors had written previously will see the shift toward Cheikh Anta Diop's thesis of a Black African KMT.

Most notable was the failure of Diop's opposing scholars to make any points in a UNESCO-sponsored debate held in Cairo in 1974. The debate centered on the origin of the ancient Egyptians. The results of that debate are best summed up by the official commentator's remarks:

> Although the preparatory working paper sent out by UNESCO gave particulars of what was desired, not all participants had prepared communications comparable with the painstakingly researched contributions of professors Cheikh Anta Diop and Obenga. There was consequently a real lack of balance in the discussions.[5]

It is necessary to set forth here a more fully developed list of certain operating assumptions that determine the framework for the discussion that follows. It is not possible to discuss each of these assumptions in detail in this paper. However, a number of authors have done so previously. These are the assumptions:

1. Mankind (hominids) began in Africa, near Lake Nyanza (Victoria), nearly five million years ago and was dark-skinned.
2. KMT (Egypt) is Africa's oldest recorded classical civilization and the world's oldest civilization.
3. KMT is the "child of inner Africa."
4. Egypt, like the rest of Africa, began as a Black civilization.
5. KMT is the world's second oldest recorded nation (Ta Seti in Nubia is currently documented to be at least two hundred years older than Egypt.)
6. Indigenous Africans were driven from Egypt by various invasions occurring after the twelfth th dynastic period, circa 1783 B.C., settling in other parts of Africa, including West Africa. There were also many other migrations of nilotic and equatorial Africans throughout the millennia.
7. KMT was a major influence on world civilization and is the main parent of "Western" civilization.
8. Ancient KMT is culturally unified to the rest of the African continent.[6]

The Uses of History and Culture

History and culture play central roles in national development. They also play central roles in the lives of cultural groups within given national boundaries. The leadership of nations and groups—especially viable nations and groups—is almost always acutely aware of the importance of history and culture. This can be understood in part when we examine internationally the tremendous national, state, and local investments in faculties of history in schools, in museums, in monuments, in holidays, and in symbols. This is especially true in the United States.[7]

The attitude of national governments toward history and culture is not casual. Often the teaching of history is required by law. Desirable cultural activities are supported by the provision of financial resources, e.g., the National Endowment for the Humanities and the Corporation for Public Broadcasting. In using legal and financial resources to support the development and retention of history and culture, governments make selected history and culture legitimate. At the same time, the mainstream's neglect of a particular history and culture may tend to minimize its significance unless independent efforts are made by minority or powerless groups who initiate activities to support their own heritage.

Israel is a modern-day example of historical and cultural rescue, and of using a rescued and refurbished history and culture as the basis for building a national identity for Jews throughout its diaspora. For example, Hebrew was virtually a dead language. It was largely a reading language for priests or rabbis. The remnants of this ancient language were insufficient to serve as a fully operating modern language. Yet, through the efforts of a single individual, the language was literally recreated. Although there were English, French, Chinese, and many other national languages that serve as the lingua franca for hundreds of millions of people worldwide, the State of Israel opted for a language that was spoken by few people in the world. Clearly, a national interest took precedence over the apparent practicality of selecting an existing international language.[8]

An extremely negative example of the function of history and culture at the national level is found in the Union of South Africa. The Dutch , who ruled, were dominated by the British, politically and culturally. Their history and culture were suppressed. The culture, especially the language of the Dutch, was stigmatized, with tremendous negative impact on the psyche of the Dutch people."[9]

> In other words, the Bond's primary motivation was to prevent the disappearance of the Afrikaner Volk as a separate political language social and cultural entity. The identity of the Afrikaner had to be insured at a time when economically and

culturally impoverished, he was faced with the
threat of being swamped and absorbed by the
stronger English group, which at that time regarded this as an inevitable process.

Although the constitution of the Union of South
Africa entrenched the language rights of both
White groups, and although in law, members of
each group enjoyed full equality, in practice, the
Afrikaner was in many ways a second-class citizen.

More bitter for the Afrikaner than the fact of
physical inequity was the English attitude of
superiority, arrogance, and contempt for the
Afrikaner and his language. At that stage, Dutch
was still the only other official language, and
would only be replaced by Afrikaners. . . it was
the time when many an Afrikaner's school child
came home with tears in his eyes because he had
been punished by the unilingual English teacher
for daring to speak Afrikaan on school grounds.
Such punishment not infrequently included
walking around with a board slung on your neck
which read: I am a donkey. I spoke Dutch.[10]

After the Dutch wrestled control of South Africa from
the British, they did not stop at the establishment of
political totalitarianism; they invested vast resources and
energies in establishing a cultural totalitarianism as well.
Government control of every aspect of South African cultural life has been ironclad and complete. The political
value of the sports program, the arts, education, religion,
and the Afrikaaner language is clearly understood by the
Broederbond (the Brotherhood), a secret group of South
Africans who control the nation. That control was and is
calculated and is a key part of the foundation of the
present social order.[11]

Leaders of all nations are conscious of the powerful
function of culture in groups. They take greater or lesser
actions to capitalize on it as a political resource At home,
it strengthens national unity. Abroad, it has been used as
a weapon to subdue militarily conquered peoples. No
conqueror has won a final victory over any people until his
or her memory of history and culture was destroyed. All
wars of conquest ultimately are cultural wars. Conquerors
must erase the memory of conquered people. They prevent the practice of indigenous culture. They change
names of conquered peoples and places. They destroy or

stigmatize the symbols of conquered people. As Fanon has observed, these actions are not accidental. They are the outcome of careful study of human group dynamics. Successful conquerors know that history and culture is the jugular vein and Achilles tendon of a people.[12]

Claims on Antiquity: Greece As Europe's Classical Civilization

The ubiquity of Greece and Rome in the European and European American historical and cultural image needs no documentation. This is true even though there is little historical justification for many non-Greek or non-Roman Europeans to identify so closely with "classical antiquity." Indeed, they did not always do so. For most of the period of Greek and Roman rule, there was no "Europe" as such. North Western Europe was considered to be the hinterlands. Later it became politically advantageous and psychologically satisfying to assert a strong cultural connection between all of Europe and the classical Greco-Roman world. In this case, the use of history and culture was carried out based on assumptions that bore little relationship to the truth. Yet the claims on antiquity served vital social and political functions nevertheless.[13]

Claims on Antiquity: KMT As Africa's Classical Civilization

According to Diop, "Egypt will play the same role in the rethinking and renewing of African culture that Ancient Greece and Rome play in the culture of the West."[14]

Unfortunately, even today it is necessary to deal with the fact that supposedly enlightened people hardly are aware of the physical presence of KMT on the African continent. More serious however is the fact that the ancient Kemetic population is often not seen as an indigenous Black African population. The evidence for a Black African KMT has been accumulating for some time. In recent years the floodgates have been opened and the data are overwhelming in support of KMT as a Black civilization and as a child of Cush or Ethiopia.[15]

Many people see KMT as alien to the rest of Africa. Diop provided the scholarly foundation to refute that notion. But more than that, Diop gave evidence and a framework for binding the history and culture of East Africa to the whole of the culture of the continent, and by extension to its diaspora. Diop described and documented the cultural unity of Black Africa. The recognition of that unity is an important step in understanding the meaning of KMT for African Americans. African Americans, Africans throughout the diaspora, as well as African continentals are the legitimate heirs of the world's oldest classical tradition Moreover, this tradition lives today in part, and is available for rescue and reconstruction in light of today's realities.[16]

We must also recognize that KMT is the world's oldest recorded classical civilization. As such, it influenced world culture. We may use Europe as an example, as the following section will show.[17]

Claims on Antiquity: The Kemetic Claim on Greco/Roman Antiquity

Recently, Martin Bernal, a professor at Cornell University and grandson of Egyptologist Sir Alan Gardiner, has written a penetrating analysis of the history of our ideas about Greek history. He has identified two theoretical models to explain the history of Greece and its relationship to Europe. The "ancient model" held sway until about two hundred years ago. Until that time, history and legend placed the origin of Greek civilization in Africa, specifically in KMT (Egypt). According to Bernal this story was held to be true by many classical authors, for example Herodutus Book VI, and was denied by none. Moreover, there is no ancient tradition of an invasion of Greece from the north. In Book VI of his *Histories,* Herodutus wrote:

> How it happened that Egyptians came to the Peloponnese and what they did to make themselves kings in that part of Greece has been chronicled by other writers: I will add nothing therefore, but proceed to mention some points which no one else has yet touched upon.[18]

According to Bernal, a second model, the "Aryan model," was invented at the Gottengen University by German and British professors. Without any new data, and in the teeth of the ancient writers, they proclaimed an "Aryan" origin of Grecian civilization. This was and still is without an empirical foundation.

And so we have before us not merely the fact of a Black presence in ancient Greece, but the possible fact that Kemetic Africa played the major creative role in the establishment of the cultural patterns that are uniquely thought of as Greek civilization! A few Black faces on the remnants of pottery do not begin to tell the whole story. Black Africans were deeply involved in the lives of the Greeks. Note the writings of Homer in the *Iliad* and the *Odyssey*. What may be more important than the presence and importance of Black Africans in Greco-Roman antiquity is the story of how the knowledge of their certain presence and importance was "lost."[19]

There are certain givens that can be derived from a fair study of the historical record.

1. It cannot be denied that African Kemetic (Egyptian) civilization is older than the Greco-Roman by at least 2,000 years.

2. It cannot be denied that many of the features that are identified as key elements in Greco-Roman civilization were well recorded in ancient African Kemetic civilization long before either Greece or Rome existed. For example, consider the 18 dynasty temples at Waset (Luxor) that are called Karnak (originally called Ipet Isut), and Luxor (Southern Ipet) temples. Compare these and even earlier Kemetic structures with the Parthenon and other later Greco-Roman colonnaded temples. Clearly KMT was first. Compare the ancient religion of Asar (Osirus), Ast (Isis) and Heru (Horus) to early Greek and Roman religion and even later to Greco-Roman Christianity. In fact, until the rise of organized Christianity, Kemetic religion was a major if not the major religion of the Greco-Roman world.[20]

3. It cannot be denied that Greece and Rome were in close geographical proximity to Africa, the birthplace of high civilization.[21]

In light of all the above, why would it be necessary or even rational to be surprised at a Black African presence in ancient Greece and Rome? Why have most scholars looked for Africans in Greece and Rome only as slaves? There is documentation to show some Africans as

1. founders of Greece,
2. emperors of Rome,
3. popes in the early Christian church, and
4. models of civilizations.[22]

Africa was the source of two major forces that greatly affected the development of Europe. The first was the impact of KMT during the first millennium B.C. The second was the impact of the Moorish (inheritors of the Kematic culture) invasion and settlement in Southern Europe from 711 A D. to 1492 A.D. The evidence for the impact of these two contacts is pervasive and overwhelming. When a more truthful and rational world history is widely known, the distortions and blind spots of colonial historians will be sources of amusement.

The "loss" of Blacks in antiquity is due to defective theoretical historical paradigms, chauvinistic historians, the legacy of the distorted scholarship of White supremacist professors, the failure to rely upon primary data sources, the consequent repetition of popular historical error, and the failure to allocate resources for the investigation of questions appropriate to the rediscovery of Black people in antiquity.[23]

The influence of Black Africa's cultural antiquity is not limited to Europe or even to the African continent itself. Africans in antiquity are to be found in a diaspora that stretches in a band that reaches around the globe, especially around its equatorial regions.[24]

Historians have been too tentative and too cautious in describing Africa's place in world history. When this picture is drawn properly Blacks in the antiquity of the infant civilizations of Greece and Rome will come as no great surprise. On the contrary, it would be a miracle if this were not the case.

The Uses of Ancient Kemetic Heritage

The civilization of ancient KMT may seem remote to many African Americans, in time, in physical location, and in relationship to meaningful priorities for today in the United States. Yet there is an urgent need for African Americans to rescue and reconstruct this and other parts of all African heritage. As shown above, KMT was an integral part of a culturally unified continent. It is, because of KMT's abundant records, the best window on the dynamics of African culture generally. African Americans and other Africans in the diaspora still retain some general African cultural forms. Therefore, it is wrong to consider African Americans as if their heritage is merely European or as if all their African heritage has been obliterated.

The existence of advanced African cultural developments in antiquity, continental cultural unity, and diasporan cultural continuities may be of interest to many.
However, it is the utility of these things that must be
considered here. History and culture are ongoing creative
processes that arise out of any group's struggle to survive.
For African Americans that struggle continues. As the
struggle continues, there are several clear uses for the
cumulative and continuing history and culture of our
people:

1. *The source of philosophy.* In the face of an integrated ancient philosophical/religious system, the parent of
   world systems, it would be foolish for its heirs to act
   in ignorance of it. There is no reason for heirs of African systems to be more impressed by the answers to
   questions given in other philosophical/religious systems than they are with their own. Ideas about worldviews (metaphysics), knowledge views (epistemology),
   and value views (axiology), have been fully developed
   by African ancestors. They still contain avenues to
   truths that are worthy guides to mental and spiritual
   life. In fact, they have guided European thought
   through such institutions as churches and fraternal
   orders such as the Masonic order.[25]

2. *A foundation for group unity and identity.* The destruction of group unity and identity is a precondition for
   the enslavement of a people. The absence of group
   unity and identity reduces the power of the group
   and individuals within it. Group cohesion is a prerequisite to effective action. Group cohesion is rooted in
   shared culture.[26]

3. *A source of resistance to alien domination.* Cabral was as-
   tute in his recognition of the role of indigenous culture in the practice of freedom. He saw that only by
   the organized, systematic, and effective repression of
   a people's culture could a foreign or alien power
   dominate a native or culturally distinct population. It
   is for this reason that colonizers and oppressors all
   over the world have always declared war on ethnic culture. Conquerors are fully aware of the power of history and culture.[27]

   > History teaches us that in certain circumstances, it is
   > very easy for the foreigner to impose his domination
   > on a people, but it also teaches us that whatever may
   > be the material aspects of this domination, it can be
   > maintained only by the permanent organized repres-
   > sion of the cultural life of the people concerned.
   > Implantation of foreign domination can be assured
   > definitively only by physical liquidation of a significant

part of the dominated population. . . . In fact, to take up arms to dominate a people is above all, to take up arms to destroy, or at least neutralize, to paralyze, its cultural life. For with a strong and indigenous cultural life, foreign domination cannot be sure of its perpetuation.[28]

4. *A basis for independence.* Once freedom is won it must be sustained. It is pitiful to see so many of those who have won their freedom, having paid a blood price for it, surrender their initiative and enter into voluntary cultural servitude. A free person or group must have an independent conception of identity, purpose, and direction. The history and culture of African people provide the foundation for the construction of independent visions, no matter where the sons and daughters of Africa are.

5. *A basis for creativity.* Many African Americans are rightfully suspicious of romantic calls for a return to the past. Clearly, what is needed is reality and not romanticism in the contemporary world. Moreover, no return to the past is even possible for anyone. Yet one's own past can and must be used in the present as building material for the future. Real romanticism appears when misguided African American people try to build their futures out of the alien heritage of others, as if it were their own.

The use of one's past is not a rejection of technological creativities. It may help to put technology into perspective and to shape it. To know one's past is not to live in the past or to be stymied in the present. The past contains the seeds for the future.

A computer without a memory is dysfunctional, even though it has available a sophisticated program. The program simply would have nothing to process. A people without a memory or with a false memory is a disabled people. They have nothing to process or more likely they have "garbage" to process. For too long African Americans have been deprived of a true history. This means functioning without a vital asset that any people requires. The rescue and reconstruction of Kemetic history is but one small part of what should be a grand design for the rescue and reconstruction of the full picture. The culturally disarmed cannot stand as peers in a culturally armed world!

50 Plus: Essential References on the History of African People

In 1990, the first Annual Conference on the Infusion of African and African American Content in the School Curriculum was held in Atlanta, Georgia. It was cosponsored by Georgia State University, the Southern Education Foundation, and the Atlanta Public Schools. Dr. Lucretia Payton and Dr. Asa Hilliard cochaired that conference. Dr. Herman Reese of the Southern Education Foundation was the conference coordinator.

This excellent conference with higher-than-expected attendance was held just at the time when a national backlash against pluralism in education was being organized by conservative scholars, such as the National Association of Scholars. We realized that it would be difficult to provide in depth information on our activities to the broad public, and we also realized that virtually everything that we had attempted to do and say had been distorted by a media that had muzzled our opinions while broadcasting those from the extreme conservative end of the spectrum.

We began to develop strategies to provide information to a broader base of serious people and to reduce the rhetoric about pluralism in education. We illustrated just how much of a gap there was between what is true and what is known about African and African American people. One way of doing this was to publish a list of books that provided comprehensive information about African people. We believed that any novice who read any 10 of the references cited would be shocked by the fact that so much is known, but missing, from the schools. We recommend the following annotated bibliography for the family reference library, for the student, for the lay reader, and even for the scholar who has only just begun studying the history and culture of Africans and African Americans. This bibliography could have included thousands of books; however, to be useful it was significantly pared down, to hopefully attract the attention of open-minded and serious educators.

The image of people of African descent worldwide today is the product of the periods of slavery, colonization, segregation/apartheid, and racism. The outcome is distortion and falsehood that can and must be corrected through valid scholarship.

These references are selected to serve as a sample of the voluminous bibliographical resources that, taken together, depict the comprehensive, longitudinal, evolution, and migration of African people all over the globe. With these references, we try to answer the following questions. Who are the African people? Where did African people come from? What has happened to African people en route? Where are African people now?

The second section is a carefully selected set of references that articulate the problem of what W. E. B. Du Bois has called "double consciousness," and what Carter G. Woodson has called "miseducation." The authors also propose solutions that will free the mind.

No list of a mere 50 or more essential references on the history of African people can do justice to a historical and cultural story that is chronicled in tens of thousands of volumes. The purpose of this short selected list is to provide the rare references that compel awakening, that stimulate independent research, and that pose a framework that can serve as the lens through which we can see a more complete and valid picture of people of African descent.

Andrews, George Reid. *The Afro-Argentines of Buenos Aires, 1800-1900.* Madison: University of Wisconsin Press, 1980.

Andrews reports on his extensive research to discover the cause of the virtual disappearance of Africans from Buenos Aires, who, at one time, made up nearly 40 percent of the population. What happened in Buenos Aires occurred on a slightly smaller scale throughout Spanish or Latin America. Many facts are uncovered. African people everywhere need to learn these lessons.

Asante, Molefi K. and Mark T. Mattson. *Historical and Cultural Atlas of African Americans.* New York: Macmillan Publishing Co., 1992.

Magnificent! Comprehensive, authoritative, beautifully illustrated, and up to date, this is a must reference for the Africanist. It will be an important reference work for teachers and of great interest to students.

Austin, Allan D. *African Muslims in Antebellum America: A Sourcebook.* New York: Garland, 1984.

Austin selected a few biographies from slave interviews and documents that illuminated the high level of educational development of many Muslims who were enslaved in America. The primary and secondary education systems in some places were virtually universal and were supported at public expense. These Muslim educational systems existed in West Africa alongside other literate African non-Muslim systems such as the Dogon, who inhabit present-day Mali.

Bell, Derrick A. *Race, Racism and American Law.* Boston: Little Brown, 1973.

Racism is a belief and behavioral system that subordinates one group to another. Bell documents the legal mechanisms for accomplishing this subordination. The extensive nature of legalized racism in the United States is amply demonstrated.

Bennett, Lerone. *Before the Mayflower: A History of Black America.* Chicago: Johnson Publishing Co., 1962.

Bennett provides a complete picture of the history of Africans in America. He traces the development of the Black experience over time rather than emphasize single events. This book is a classic.

Bernal, Martin. *Black Athena, The Afroasiatic Roots of Classical Civilization.* Vol. 1, *The Fabrication of Ancient Greece.* London: Free Association, 1987.
Following many African, American, and European scholars, Bernal documents the key role that ancient KMT (Egypt) played, along with some elements of Mesopotamian civilization, in the development of classical Greek civilization. The most prestigious scholars of Greece spent many years under the tutelage of Africans in KMT (Egypt). Central to this volume are documented efforts to hide Africa's influence, presumably to support and rationalize the nationalistic aspirations of an emerging Germany.

Blyden, Edward W. *Christianity, Islam and the Negro Race.* 1887* Baltimore: Black Classic Press, 1993.
Blyden covers the history of development in West Africa and the special role played by religion. He compares the fate of Africans who adopted the religion of Islam with those who adopted Christianity. Christian Africans were dehumanized by slave and colonial powers; Islamic Africans were rarely oppressed, and were more likely to be self-determined.

Branch, Taylor. *Parting the Waters: America in the King Years.* New York: Simon and Schuster, 1988.
Branch provides one of the best interpretations of Martin Luther King, Jr.'s role during the civil rights and nationalistic upheavals in America.

de Graft-Johnson, J. C. *African Glory: The Story of Vanished Negro Civilizations.* 1954* Baltimore: Black Classic Press, 1986.
African Glory is an indispensable chronicle of various interrelated African civilizations from earliest times. It puts continental history into perspective. Through de Graft-Johnson's well-written book, we experience the rise, fall, and change of African nations and cultures.

Diop, Cheikh Anta. *The African Origin of Civilization: Myth or Reality.* Westport, Connecticut: Lawrence Hill and Company, 1974.
The African Origin of Civilization is an excellent single source covering the seminal role that Africa played in the development of the world's early civilization. Cheikh Anta Diop marshals a massive amount of multidisciplinary evi-

dence to show that the civilization of ancient KMT (Egypt) was indeed a native Black African civilization.

_____. *The Cultural Unity of Black Africa: The Domains of Patriarchy and Matriarchy in Classical Antiquity.* Chicago: Third World Press, 1978.

Should we think African "peoples" or "people?" Should we think of the differences among Africans or the similarities? In this book, Professor Diop introduces the powerful construct, "cultural unity." He attempts to show that superficial diversity hides deep structural and cultural unity. This is a very important work, for continental and diasporan Africans as well.

_____. *Civilization or Barbarism: An Authentic Anthropology.* Westport, Connecticut: Lawrence-Hill Books, 1991.

Civilization or Barbarism is a comprehensive history of ancient KMT (Egypt), with arguments and documentation in support of its Africanness and its worldwide influence, especially its influence on the Greek and Roman world. This book is destined to become a cornerstone book on the history and culture of people of African descent.

Du Bois, W. E. B. *The World and Africa: An Inquiry into the Part Which Africa Has Played in World History.* New York: Viking, 1947.

Du Bois, who was influenced by the great anthropologist Franz Boas, summarized the story of Africa's participation in world history. Beginning with the origin of man in east Africa, and following with the civilization of ancient KMT (Egypt), Du Bois shows that African people have never been out of the mainstream of world history.

_____. *Black Reconstruction in America: An Essay toward a History of the Part Which Black Folk Played in the Attempt to Reconstruct Democracy in America, 1860-1880.* New York: Harcourt Brace & Co., [1935].

Du Bois reveals the complex and significant role African Americans played during Reconstruction, a role that has been usually forgotten, overlooked, or completely ignored in current writings of American history. For example, he shows the central role that African Americans played in the development of public schools in the South.

Forbes, Jack. *Black Africans and Native Americans: Color, Race and Cast in the Evolution of Red-African People.* London: Blackwell, 1989.

Forbes brilliantly and meticulously describes the close relationship between African Americans and Native Americans over hundreds of years. He also examines the relationship between Native Americans and Europeans from precolonial times to modern times. The documentation and bibliography alone are invaluable. No treatment in any other source except his earlier books, *Aztecas del Norte,* and *Native Americans of California and Nevada,* gives a better picture of this early history.

Garvey, Amy Jacques. *Garvey and Garveyism.* New York: Collier Macmillan, 1970.

The story of the development of Marcus Garvey's thought, action, and influence in the Western Hemisphere, in Africa, and the world is well told in this timely book. No history of the twentieth century, whether it is the history of African people, or others, is complete in the absence of an analysis of the role of Garvey and Garveyism. He led a worldwide movement of African people in the twentieth century.

Giddings, Joshua. *The Exiles of Florida: Or the Crimes Committed by Our Government against the Maroons, Who Fled from South Carolina and Other Slave States, Seeking Protection under Spanish Laws.* 1858* Baltimore: Black Classic Press, 1994.

It is hard to understand how a book as old and as important as this one could be so little known. Giddings describes the close partnership between Africans as "Maroons," and Indians as "Seminoles," in establishing a lengthy and effective movement against slavery in Florida. The collaboration among free Indians and Africans agitated the slave society, which was maintained by the United States. The United States' attempt to extinguish the flames of freedom in Florida and the heroic resistance by the Maroons and Seminoles should be dramatized. The book reads like a novel.

Harding, Vincent. *There Is a River: The Black Struggle for Freedom in America.* New York: Harcourt Brace Jovanovich, 1981.

Harding tells a comprehensive story of the freedom struggle in America by documenting the resistance of Africans to a variety of attempts to oppress them.

Harris, Joseph E., ed. *Pillars in Ethiopian History: The William Leo Hansberry African History Notebook.* Vol. 1. Washington, D.C.: Howard University Press, 1974.
Historian Joseph Harris collected these notes by his friend, William Leo Hansberry. Hansberry was a brilliant historian who perused original sources of classical writers to document the history of Africa. This volume covers a relatively unknown story of the history of Ethiopians. Their ancient history and influence should be the subject of further study.

_____. *Africa and Africans as Seen by Classical Writers: The William Leo Hansberry African History Notebook.* Vol. 2. Washington, D.C.: Howard University Press, 1977.
While Volume 1 covers the history of Ethiopia, this volume documents the classical world's belief about the history of the entire continent of Africa. The history of Africa presented here is different than the one told by racist historians. The courses of study instituted by Professor Hansberry at Howard University in the early twenties are considered forerunners of contemporary African Studies Programs.

Higginbotham, A. Leon. *In the Matter of Color: Race and the American Legal Process.* New York: Oxford University, 1978.
This book is an excellent complement to *Race, Racism, and American Law* by Derrick Bell, which was cited earlier. Since racism is deeply entrenched within the law of the land, White supremacy is, in fact, a structural aspect of the society. White supremacy is just one example of what some have called "institutional racism."

Hilliard, Asa G., Lucretia Payton-Stewart, and Larry Obadele Williams. *The Infusion of African and African American Content in the School Curriculum: First National Conference Proceedings October 1989.* New Jersey: Aaron Press, 1990.
The rationale for the infusion of African and African American content in the school curriculum is discussed in this document of the first national conference held in Atlanta in 1989. Six of the keynote addresses from that conference are included here. However, by far, the most

valuable aspect of this reference is John Henrik Clarke's four-part syllabus on *The Role of African People in World History*. This syllabus provides comprehensive and detailed bibliographical references documenting the history of African people, worldwide. It is one of the few sources that provides a true sense of the place of African people in world history.

Holtzclaw, Robert Fulton. *The Saints Go Marching in: A One-Volume Hagiography of Africans, or Descendants of Africans Who Have Been Canonized by the Church Including Three of the Early Popes.* Shaker Heights, Ohio: The Keeble Press, Inc., 1980.

Few people are aware that African people played a major role in the evolution of world religion. Holtzclaw's book will rectify that error. He describes the roles Africans played in the Catholic church, including those at the top of the hierarchy.

Houston, Drusilla Dunjee. *Wonderful Ethiopians of the Ancient Cushite Empire.* 1926* Baltimore: Black Classic Press, 1985.

This is a remarkable book written in 1926 by an incredible scholar. Houston presents one of the earliest comprehensive views of the place of African people in world history. Before the benefit of documents produced in the last 50 years, and even without access to scholarly networks, Houston developed an exceptional outline of global African history.

Jackson, John. *Man, God, and Civilization.* New York: University Books, 1972.

Jackson provides a classic reference on African people in world history. He starts with ancient Africa and shows ancient Africa to be the home of civilization itself. The African influence on world civilization can be seen here, as well as the development of culture on the African continent.

James, George G.M. *Stolen Legacy.* San Francisco: Julian Richardson, 1954.

James traces the (Kemetic, or Egyptian) origin of Greek philosophical thought. In many ways, his work is a predecessor to Bernal's *Black Athena*, cited earlier, with additional documentation from the field of linguistics.

King, Kenneth. *Pan-Africanism and Education: A Study of Race, Philanthropy and Education in the Southern States of America and East Africa.* Oxford: Clarendon Press, 1971.

King presents in detail the history of the educational mechanisms used to control African people in the United States and on the continent of Africa by a small group of influential Europeans. They were educational philanthropists who shaped the direction of education for people of African descent.

Lane-Poole, Stanley. *The Story of the Moors in Spain.* 1886* Baltimore: Black Classic Press, 1990.

The period from 711 to 1492 A.D. was not the dark age for Africa. In fact, in northwest Africa, African Moors and Arabs carried their civilizing mission into Spain and Portugal. For most Americans, this is an obscure period, if they know anything of it at all. Nevertheless, it was a major period in terms of the influence Africa had on Europe in Spain and also further north.

Lewis, David Levering. *The Race to Fashoda: European Colonialism and African Resistance in the Scramble for Africa.* New York: Weidenfeld and Nicholson, 1987.

David Levering Lewis analyzes the dynamics and mechanisms of colonial expansion in Africa. For those who wish to see how Africa was taken apart after 1884, this is the book. Without such a treatment, many teachers and students will not understand how African civilizations could have declined.

Litwack, Leon. *Been in the Storm So Long: The Aftermath of Slavery.* New York: Vintage, 1979.

Litwack examines a key period in American history. There are some surprises here as we learn the details of the continuing struggle for freedom after "emancipation."

MacRitchie, David. *Ancient and Modern Britons.* 2 vols. 1884* Los Angeles: William Preston, 1986.

Frequent mention is made of the "mixing" of Africans and Europeans in the United States. However, current notions neglect the fact that the European population was already mixing heavily with Africans for hundreds of years before its arrival in the United States. In 1884, this European historian, MacRitchie, documented the long-term presence of Africans in Scotland, Ireland, and England, by relying heavily on etymological and historical data. These Africans were settlers, and occasionally even royalty in these European lands.

Massey, Gerald. *Book of the Beginnings: Containing an Attempt to Recover and Reconstitute the Lost Origins of the Myths and Mysteries, Types, and Symbols, Religion and Language, with Egypt as the Mouthpiece and Africa as the Birthplace.* 2 vols. 1881* Baltimore: Black Classic Press, 1994.
Gerald Massey was an early researcher who documented the African origin of civilization. Using the texts from the monuments in KMT (Egypt) and a profound understanding of the African use of symbols and symbolic thought, Gerald Massey illuminates the ancient past and the centrality of Africa in it. This is an extraordinary book!

Obenga, Theophile. *Ancient Egypt and Black Africa: A Student's Handbook for the Study of Ancient Egypt in Philosophy, Linguistics and Gender Relations.* London: Karnak House, 1992.
It is important to know the nature of intellectual development in Africa prior to the presence of Greeks in order to understand why Greek philosophers and scientists found Africa so attractive. Obenga presents a fresh perspective on the level of sophisticated development of philosophy by native Africans before major influences outside the African continent. The last chapter on male-female relations links ancient KMT firmly within the African cultural tradition. This is the only major publication by Dr. Obenga that is currently published in the English language.

Parker, George Wells. "African Origin of Grecian Civilization." *Journal of Negro History* 2,3 (1917): 334-44.
This article predates George G. M. James' *Stolen Legacy* and Martin Bernal's *Black Athena,* and substantially uses the same approach. The author expanded this article a few years later when he published the pamphlet, *Children of the Sun,* which is now available from Black Classic Press.

Portland Public Schools. *African American Baseline Essays.* Portland, Oregon: Multinomah School District 1J, 1987.
The Portland Oregon Public Schools' *African-American Baseline Essays* was produced by approximately thirty scholars and edited by six. Each essay traces the history of

African people in the disciplines of mathematics, science, language arts, art, music and social studies from the beginning of time to the present. Collectively, they represent the story of African people. Used throughout the United States, these essays are a part of a limited number of sources that discuss the history and culture of African people in holistic terms.

Price, Richard, ed. *Maroon Societies: Rebel Slave Communities in the Americas.* New York: Anchor Books, 1973.
    Many Africans successfully resisted slavery. Some ran away from their captors and established independent communities known as maroon communities. Price tells an excellent story of some of those communities.

Rodney, Walter. *How Europe Underdeveloped Africa.* Washington, D.C.: Howard University Press, 1974.
    How Africa could be so great and fall so low is unknown to many. Rodney's book, along with David Levering Lewis' *The Race to Fashoda,* cited earlier, helps to unravel that mystery.

Rogers, J. A. *Nature Knows No Color Line: Research into Negro Ancestry in the White Race.* St. Petersburg, Florida: Helga M. Rogers, 1952.
    Rogers' work, like MacRitchie's *Ancient and Modern Britons,* cited earlier, documents the African ancestry in European populations over hundreds of years. He relies on many documents from Europe, including the registers of royal families and their crests. Like most of J. A. Rogers' works, this one is extensively illustrated with photographs of primary sources.

Saad, Elias N. *The Social History of Timbuctoo: The Role of Muslim Scholars and Notables, 1400-1900.* New York: Cambridge University Press, 1983.
    Saad gives historical details that are generally unknown about the families of scholars who worked at the internationally acclaimed West African Sankore University. This university predated and lasted throughout most of the slave trade and the beginning of the colonial period. It existed at the pinnacle of a broad secondary and elementary school system run by native Africans who had converted to the Muslim faith. Other West African university cities included Gao, Djenne, and Sokoto; all are precolonial. Austin's *African Muslims in Antebellum America,* cited

earlier, gives additional proof of the extent and quality of formal public education for Africans.

Serfontein, J.H.P. *Brotherhood of Power: An Exposé of the Secret Afrikaner Broederbond.* Bloomington: Indiana University Press, 1978.
Serfontein uncovers the repressive activities of the Broederbond, the secret Afrikaner brotherhood. This organization still dominates South Africa today.

Spivey, Donald. *Schooling for the New Slavery: Black Industrial Education, 1868-1915. Westport, Connecticut: Greenwood Press, 1978.*
Spivey discusses the role of philanthropy and higher education in subjugating African Americans. It exposes the failed attempt to use Black institutions of higher education as instruments of subjugation. This book is a companion to *Pan-Africanism and Education* by Kenneth King, cited earlier.

Temple, Robert K. G. *The Sirius Mystery.* New York: St. Martin's Press, 1976.
Temple describes the culture of the Dogon nation, who are a brilliant group of people in West Africa. M. Griaulle and G. Dieterlen in their book, *The Pale Fox*, extend the work of Robert Temple. Both books should be read in order to gain an appreciation for the high level of intellectual and general cultural achievements of groups of Africans who rejected conversion to Islam. The Dogon cultural system is still in operation today in Mali!

UNESCO. *General History of Africa.* 8 vols. Berkeley: University of California Press, 1981.
This eight-volume set on the general history of Africa was produced by a multinational group of scholars under the sponsorship of the United Nations. It is a good reference for undoing the distortions in African and world history.

Van Sertima, Ivan. *They Came Before Columbus.* New York: Random House, 1976.
This is Van Sertima's classic: the story of the African presence in America before the arrival of Columbus, and even before the time of Christ! Packed with documentation, it integrates data from such fields as linguistics, history, cartography, oceanography, archaeology, botany,

and shipbuilding. This book has been published many times in the United States and in many languages all over the world.

_____, ed. *Journal of African Civilizations: Egypt Revisited.* New Brunswick: Transaction, 1989.

This special issue of the *Journal of African Civilizations* contains state-of-the-art information about the history of ancient KMT (Egypt). It provides empirical evidence of the Blackness of the ancient Kemetic people (Egyptians) and their world leadership.

_____, ed. *Journal of African Civilizations: African Presence in Early Europe.* New Brunswick: Transaction, 1985.

Van Sertima presents startling data that documents the presence and role of African people throughout Europe from the earliest human migrations to the present.

_____, ed. *Golden Age of the Moor.* New Brunswick, New Jersey: Transaction, 1991.

Van Sertima furnishes evidence of the influence of the Moors on Western civilization. He exposes the processes of "Whitening" and "deafricanizing" the Moors. To fully understand north and west Africa and aspects of the Middle Passage, it is absolutely essential to know the role the Moors played in this experience. Careful research and extensive documentation, the hallmark of Van Sertima's works, will make this book another classic.

Van Sertima, Ivan and Larry Williams, eds. *Journal of African Civilizations: Great African Thinkers: Cheikh Anta Diop.* New Brunswick, New Jersey: Transaction, 1989.

Van Sertima and his colleagues discuss the life and scholarship of the late multigenius, Cheikh Anta Diop. This special issue of the journal contains the evidence that enabled Diop and his colleague, Theophile Obenga from Gabon, to dominate the Cairo Symposium in 1974. This was a United Nations (UNESCO)-sponsored debate on the racial origin of the ancient Egyptians. Diop and Obenga dominated the debate even though they were a minority of 2 out of 20 of the world's best Egyptologists. There had never been such a meeting before on this topic, nor has there been one since.

Van Sertima, Ivan and Runoko Rashidi, eds. *Journal of African Civilizations: African Presence in Early Asia.* New Brunswick: Transaction, 1988.

In this work, Van Sertima furnishes evidence of the presence and contributions of African people throughout early Asia.

Williams, Chancellor. *The Destruction of Black Civilization: Great Issues of a Race from 4,000 B.C to 2,000 A.D.* Chicago: Third World Press, 1974.

This masterpiece by Chancellor Williams tells a comprehensive story of the development, destruction, and suppression of the culture and civilization of the people of Africa. In addition, Williams proposes the self-help actions needed to restore African people as participants in world civilization.

Additional Reading

Each of the titles below details the consequences of slavery, colonization, apartheid, and racism on the thinking of African people. These are only a few of the many authors who have understood the psychology of physical slavery, colonization, and racism. Each author has shown that mental independence is the foundation for restoring, reclaiming, redeveloping, and enhancing the lives of African people.

Ani, Marimba. *Yurugu: An Africancentered Critique of Western Civilization.* Trenton: Africa World Press, 1994.

ben-Jochannan, Yosef. *Cultural Genocide in the Black and African Studies Curriculum.* New York: Alkebu-Lan, 1972.

Cheatwood, Kiarri T-H, ed. *The Race: Matters Concerning Pan-African History, Culture, and Genocide.* Richmond: Native Son Publishers, 1991.

Chinweizu. *Decolonizing the African Mind.* London: Pero Press, 1987.

Clarke, John Henrik. *Africans at the Crossroad: Notes for an African World Revolution.* Trenton: African World Press, 1991.

Cruse, Harold. *The Crisis of the Negro Intellectual.* New York: William Morrow and Company, Inc., 1967.

Du Bois, W. E. B. *The Souls of Black Folk.* New York: Signet Classic, 1969.

Fanon, Franz. *Black Skin, White Masks.* New York: Grove Press, 1967.

Hoskins, Linus A. *Decoding European Geopolitics: Afrocentric Perspectives.* African American Affairs: Monographic Series vol. 4, no. 2. Kent, Ohio: The Institute for African American Affairs, Kent State University, 1990.

Madhubuti, Haki. *Claiming Earth: Race, Rage, Rape, Redemption.* Chicago: Third World Press, 1994.

Wa Thiong'o, Ngugi. *Decolonizing the Mind: The Politics of Language in African Literature.* London: James Currey, 1987.

Wilson, Amos N. *Black on Black Violence: The Psychodynamics of Black Self-Annihilation in Service of White Domination.* New York: African World Infosystems, 1990.

Woodson, Carter G. *The Miseducation of the Negro.* Washington, D.C.: The Associated Publishers, Inc. [1933].

Yette, Samuel. *The Choice: The Issue of Black Survival in America.* Silver Spring, Maryland: Cottage Books, 1971.

*Indicates first year published.

Chapter Endnotes

Introduction

1. Diop, 1991; Van Sertima, 1989; UNESCO, 1978.
2. Herskovits, 1969; Thompson, 1981; Turner, 1969.
3. Serfontein, 1978; King, 1971; ben-Jochannan, 1989;
   Woodson, 1977.
4. Du Bois, 1969; Woodson, 1977; Chinweizu, 1987;
   Wa Thiong'o, 1987; Spivey, 1978; Arnold, 1978.
5. ben-Jochannan, 1989; Du Bois, 1969; Chinweizu, 1987;
   Cruse, 1967; Fanon, 1967; Wa Thiong'o, 1987; Woodson,
   1977; Yette, 1971.
6. Diop, 1978; Williams, 1974; Institute for Contemporary
   Studies, 1981.
7. Ngubane, 1979; Arnold, 1978.

Anecdotal and Other Material

1. Idowu, 1975; Mbiti, 1969.
2. Idowu, 1975.
3. Ibid.
4. Ibid.
5. Griaule, 1965.
6. Mitchell, 1975.
7. Ibid.
8. Idowu, 1975.
9. Mitchell, 1975.
10. Herskovits, 1969.
11. Mitchell, 1975.
12. Ibid.
13. Ornstein, 1975; Ramirez and Castaneda, 1974;
    Witkin, 1965; Tenhouten, 1973.
14. Jones (now known as Amiri Baraka), 1963.
15. Sidran, 1971.
16. Jones, 1963.
17. Jones, 1967.
18. Jones, 1963.

19. Ibid.
20. Sidran, 1971.
21. Jones, 1963.
22. Ibid.
23. Simpkins, 1989.
24. Jones, 1963.
25. Taylor, 1975.
26. Locke, 1969.
27. Jones, 1963
28. Oliver, 1970.
29. Jones, 1967.
30. Jahn, 1961.
31. Fanon, 1967.
32. Carroll, 1956.
33. Ibid.
34. Ibid.
35. Taylor, 1987; Harrison, 1972; Andrews, 1974; Birdwhistell, 1970; Scheflen, 1974; Goffman, 1969; Fisner, 1975; Farb, 1974; Hall, 1977.
36. Vygotsky, 1962.
37. Cohen, 1971.
38. Williams, 1975.
39. Ibid.
40. Sidran, 1971.
41. Williams, 1975.
42. Turner, 1969.

The Maroon Within Us

1. Clegg, 1979; Diop, 1974; James, 1976; Massey, 1994; Williams, 1974.
2. Clegg, 1979; White, 1970; Van Sertima, 1976; Fell, 1976; Taharka, 1979; Rogers, 1961.
3. Du Bois, 1972.
4. Hilliard, 1979.
5. Price, 1973; Whitten, 1974; Counter and Evans, 1981; Bastide, 1971.
6. Garvey, 1974.
7. Ellison, 1972; Cobb and Grier, 1968.
8. Fanon, 1967.
9. Nobles, 1976; Akbar, 1981; Hill, 1977; Diop, 1978.
10. Bengu, 1975.

11. Lasche, 1978.
12. Ibid.
13. Bengu, 1975.
14. Morrison, 1970; Baraka, 1979; Fanon, 1967; Hare, 1970;
Frazier, 1970.
15. Asante, 1980.

Dr. ET as Afrocentric Transformer

1. Erickson, 1968; Fanon, 1967; Lasche, 1978; Bengu, 1975.
2. Freire, 1973.
3. Diop, 1978; Griaule, 1965; Hilliard, 1976; Jahn, 1961;
Ngubane, 1979; Baraka, 1979; Fanon, 1967;
Hodges, Struckman, and Trost, 1975; Howard,1980;
Memmi, 1965; Counter and Evans, 1981; Hilliard, 1976;
Redmond, 1976; Turner, 1969; Vass, 1979.
4. Hall, 1977.
5. Lasche, 1978.
6. Achebe, 1959, 1960, 1967; Armah, 1979.
7. Chinweizu, 1975; Fanon, 1965; Williams, 1974.
8. Kotzwinkle, 1982.
9. Ngubane, 1979; Woodson, 1978; Wright, 1977.
10. Griaule, 1965; Jahn, 1961; Ngubane, 1979; Armah, 1979.
11. Budge, 1967, 1973; Frankfort, 1948, 1977.
12. Asante, 1980.
13. Freire, 1973.
14. King, 1980.
15. Armah, 1979; Asante, 1980; Counter and Evans, 1981;
Diop, 1978; Garvey, 1974; Ngubane, 1979; Semaj, 1980.

Pedagogy in Ancient Kemet

1. Diop, 1978.
2. Churchward, 1978.
3. Frankfort, 1969.
4. Jackson, 1974.
5. ben-Jochannan, 1988.
6. Jackson, 1974.
7. Drower, 1970.
8. Williams, 1980.
9. Mertz, 1978.

10. Diop, 1978.
11. DeGramont, 1977.
12. Deren, 1951.
13. DeGramont, 1977.
14. Frankfort, 1969.
15. Diop, 1978; Thompson, 1981; Jahn, 1961.
16. James, 1976; de Lubicz, 1977; Thompson, 1981; Churchward, 1978.
17. James, 1976.
18. Kamil, 1976.
19. Riefstahl, 1964.
20. Erny, 1968.
21. Sonyinka, 1984.
22. Stierlin, 1978.
23. Ibid.
24. James, 1976.
25. Reed, 1978.
26. Simpson, 1972.
27. Ibid.
28. Wilson, 1956.
29. Lichtheim, 1975; James, 1976.
30. Massey, 1994.

Kemetic Concepts in Education

1. James, 1976; Babbitt, 1969.
2. Griaule, 1965; DuBois, 1969; Ngubane, 1979; Jahn, 1961; Erny, 1968.
3. Griaule, 1965; James, 1976; de Lubicz, 1978.
4. Ngubane, 1979; Williams, 1974; Rodney, 1970; Padmore, 1969; Armah, 1979.
5. Steindorff, 1957.
6. Abdullah, 1984.
7. Hurry, 1928.
8. Myer, 1900.
9. Ibid.
10. Ibid.
11. White, 1970.
12. Budge, 1973.
13. Babbitt, 1969.
14. Bengu, 1975.

Conceptual Confusion

1. Woodward, 1966; Bell, 1973; Higginbotham, 1978; Jacobs, Landau, and Pell, 1971; Jordan, 1977.
2. Hilliard, 1978; Weinberg, 1977.
3. Bullock, 1967; King, 1971; Weinberg, 1977.
4. Powell, 1973.
5. Chase, 1977; Hilliard, 1982; Houts, 1977; Kamin, 1974; Slack and Porter, 1980.
6. Ngubane, 1979.
7. Ibid.
8. Williams and Mitchell, 1980.
9. Blauner, 1972; Pearce, 1971; Schwartz and Disch, 1970; Jacobs, Landau, and Pell, 1971.
10. Weinberg, 1977.
11. Ibid.
12. Chase, 1977; Kamin, 1974; King, 1971; Spivey, 1978.
13. Chase, 1977; Kamin, 1974.
14. Woodward, 1966.
15. Barzun, 1965; Chase, 1977; Gossett, 1973; Hirsch, 1981; Kamin, 1974; King, 1971; Schwartz and Disch, 1970; Serfontein, 1978; Spivey, 1978; Stanton, 1960.
16. Hilliard, 1982; Jensen, 1961; Rist, 1973; Rosenthal and Jacobsen, 1968.
17. Freire, 1973; Hilliard, 1978; Memmi, 1965; Pearce, 1971; Schwartz and Disch, 1970.

Teachers and Cultural Styles in a Pluralistic Society

1. Hall, 1977.
2. Chun, 1988.
3. Taylor, 1987.

Fabrication

1. Du Bois, 1972; James, 1976; Diop, 1974; Harris, 1974; Massey, 1994; Dow, 1937; Volney, 1991; Parker, 1917; Witt, 1971; Heyob, 1975; Brady, 1935; Williams and Hilliard, 1990; Williams, 1974; Houston, 1985.
2. UNESCO, 1981.

3. Bernal, 1987.
4. Ibid.
5. Winkler, 1990.
6. Berger and Luckmann, 1966; Kuhn, 1970.
7. Gould, 1981.
8. Ibid.
9. Ibid.
10. Ibid.
11. Ibid.
12. Ibid.
13. Ibid.
14. Davidson, 1984.
15. Ibid.
16. Ibid.
17. Nobles, 1987.
18. Will, 1989.
19. Bauer, 1981.
20. Black Issues in Higher Education, 1987.
21. Woodson, 1977; King, 1971; Spivey, 1978; Aptheker, 1973.
22. Weinreich, 1946; Chase, 1977; Kamin, 1974; Thomas and Sillen, 1972; Benedict, 1959.
23. Hirsch, 1987; Bloom, 1987.
24. Hilliard, 1989a; Hilliard, 1989b.

Do We Have the "Will" to Education All Children?

1. Escalante and Dirman, 1990.
2. Donaldson, 1978.

The Meaning of KMT

1. Diop (in Mokhtar), 1981.
2. James, 1976.
3. Budge, 1929.
4. ben-Jochannan, 1989; Carruthers, 1984; Du Bois, 1915, 1946; Houston, 1985; Jackson, 1974; Van Sertima, 1989; Williams, 1974; Churchward, 1978; Massey, 1994; Volney,1991;
5. Diop, 1973, 1974, 1978; Ki-zerbo, 1981; Diop (in Mokhtar), 1981.

6. Churchward, 1978; Diop (in Mokhtar), 1981; Houston, 1985; Jackson, 1974; Massey, 1994; Van Sertima, 1982; Diop, 1985; Williams (in Van Sertima), 1985.
7. Cabral, 1973; Serfontein, 1978; St. John, 1975.
8. St. John, 1975.
9. Serfontein, 1978.
10. Ibid.
11. Wilkins and Strydom, 1979.
12. Cabral, 1973; Fanon, 1965.
13. Bernal, 1984; Durkeim, 1977.
14. Jefferies (in Van Sertima), 1982.
15. Diop, 1974; Van Sertima, 1985; Diop (in Mokhtar), 1981; Houston, 1985.
16. Diop, 1978.
17 Rashidi, 1988.
18. Bernal, 1984.
19. Snowden, 1971.
20. Budge, 1973; Churchward, 1978; Freud, 1967; Meyer, 1900; Van Sertima, 1985.
21. Hilliard (in Van Sertima), 1985; James, 1976.
22. Bernal, 1984; Rogers, 1972; Holtzclaw, 1980; Diop, 1974; Jackson, 1974.
23. Bernal, 1984.
24. Rashidi, 1988.
25. Meyer, 1900.
26. Fanon, 1965.
27. Cabral, 1973.
28. Ibid.

Select Bibliography

Abdullah, Mahmoud. (1984) *Egyptologist and Tour Guide*. Luxor, Egypt: Seti I Travel.

Achebe, Chinua. (1959) *Things Fall Apart*. New York: Fawcett Press.

_____. (1960) *No Longer at Ease*. New York: Fawcett Press.

_____. (1967) *A Man of the People*. New York: Anchor Books.

Akbar, Na'im. (1981) "Mental Disorder Among African-Americans." *Black Books Bulletin* 72: 18-25.

Aldred, Cyril. (1965) *Egypt to the End of the Old Kingdom*. New York: McGraw-Hill.

Andrews, Malachi. (1974) *Psychoblacksology*. Berkeley: Achebe Enterprises.

Aptheker, Herbert, ed. (1973) *The Education of Black People: Ten Critiques, 1906-1960 by W.E.B. Du Bois*. New York: Monthly Review Press.

Armah, Ayi K. (1979) *Two Thousand Seasons*. Chicago: Third World Press.

Arnold, Millard, ed. (1978) *Steve Biko: Black Consciousness in South Africa*. New York: Random House.

Asante, Molefi Kete. (1980) *Afrocentricity: The Theory of Social Change*. Buffalo: Amulefi Publishing.

Babbitt, Frank C., trans. (1969) *Plutarch's Moralia*. Vol. 5. Cambridge: Harvard University Press.

Baraka, Amiri. (1979) *The Sydney Poet Heroical*. New York: I Reed Books. *See also*: Jones, LeRoi for additional works by this author.

Barzun, Jaques. (1965) *Race: A Study in Superstition*. New York: Harper and Row.

Bastide, Roger. (1971) *African Civilizations in the New World*. New York: Harper Torchbooks.

Bauer, P.T. (1981) *Equality, the Third World and Economic Delusion*. Cambridge: Harvard.

Bell, Derrick. (1973) *Race, Racism, and American Law*. Boston: Little Brown and Company.

Bellah, R. N. et al. (1985) *Habits of the Heart: Individualism and Commitment in American Life.* New York: Harper and Row.

Benedict, Ruth. (1959) *Race: Science and Politics.* New York: Viking Press.

Bengu, S. E. M. (1975) *Chasing Gods Not Our Own.* Pietermaritzberg, Natal Republic of South Africa: Shorter and Shooer.

ben-Jochannan, Yosef. [1971] (1988) *Africa: Mother of Western Civilization.* Baltimore: Black Classic Press.

_____. [1972] (1989) *Black Man of the Nile and His Family.* Baltimore: Black Classic Press.

_____. (1972) *Cultural Genocide in the Black and African Studies Curriculum.* New York: Alkebu-Lan.

Berger, Peter L., and Thomas Luckmann. (1966) *The Social Construction of Reality: A Treatise in the Sociology of Knowledge.* New York: Doubleday.

Bernal, Martin. (1984) "Black Athena, The Denial of the Afro-Asiatic Roots of Greece." Ithaca: Cornell University.

_____. (1987) *Black Athena, The Afroasiatic Roots of Classical Civilization.* Vol. 1, *The Fabrication of Ancient Greece.* London: Free Association.

Biddis, M. D. (1970) *The Father of Racist Ideology: The Social and Political Thought of Count Gobineau.* New York: Harper and Row.

Birdwhistell, Ray L. (1970) *Kinesico and Context: Essays on Body Motion Communication.* Philadelphia: University of Pennsylvania Press.

Black Issues in Higher Education. (1987) "Historians Blamed for Perpetuating Bias—Outgoing President Challenges Colleagues." *Black Issues in Higher Education* 4, no 4: 2.

Blake, J. Herman. (1984) "Doctor Can't Do Me No Good." In *Black Folk Medicine: The Therapeutic Significance of Faith and Trust.* Edited by Wilbur Watson. Atlanta: Clarke Atlanta University.

Blauner, R. Robert. (1972) *Racial Oppression in America.* New York: Harper and Row.

Bloom, Alan. (1987) *The Closing of the American Mind.* New York: Simon and Schuster.

Brady, A. (1935) "The Reception of the Egyptian Cults by the Greeks (330-30 B.C.)" *The University of Missouri Studies: A Quarterly of Research* 10, no. 1: 6-88.

Breasted, James Henry. (1937) *A History of Egypt from the Earliest Times to the Persian Conquest.* New York: Charles Scribner's Sons.

Budge, E. A. Wallis. [1926](1977) *The Dwellers on the Nile*. New York: Dover.

_____. (1967) *The Egyptian Book of the Dead: The Papyrus of Ans*. New York: Dover.

_____. [1911](1973) *Osirus and the Egyptian Resurrection*. New York: Dover.

_____. (1929) *The Rosetta Stone in the British Museum*. London: British Museum.

Bullock, Henry H. (1967) *A History of Negro Education in the South from 1619 to the Present*. New York: Praeger.

Cabral, Amilcar. (1973) *Return to the Source: Selected Speeches of Amilcar Cabral*. New York: Monthly Review Press.

Carlson, Lewis H. and George A. Colburn. (1972) *In Their Place: White America Defines Her Minorities, 1850-1950*. New York: John Wiley and Sons.

Carroll, John B., ed. [1927-41](1956) *Language, Thought, and Reality: Selected Writings of Benjamin Lee Whorf*. Cambridge: The MIT Press.

Caruthers, Jacob H. (1984) *Essays in Ancient Egyptian Studies*. Los Angeles: University of Sankore Press.

Cerny, Jaroslav. (1947) *Papers and Books in Ancient Egypt*. London: H.K. Lewis & Company, Ltd.

Chase, Alan. (1977) *The Legacy of Malthus: The Social Cost of the New Scientific Racism*. New York: Alfred Knopf.

Chinweizu. (1975) *The West and the Rest of Us: White Predators, Black Slavers and the African Elite*. New York: Vintage Books.

_____. (1987) *Decolonizing the African Mind*. London: Sundoor Press.

Chun, Eva Wells. (1987-88). "Sorting Black Students for Success and Failure: The Inequity of Ability Grouping and Tracking." *Urban League Review* 11, nos. 1-2: 93-106.

Churchward, Albert. [1913](1978) *Signs and Symbols of Primordial Man*. Westport, Connecticut: Greenwood Press.

Clegg, LeGrand, II. (1979) "The First Americans." *Journal of African Civilizations* 1, no. 1: 98-107.

Cobb, Price and William Grier. (1968) *Black Rage*. New York: Bantam.

Cohen, Rosalie. (1971) "The Influence of Conceptual Rule Sets on Measures of Learning Ability." *Race and Intelligence*.

Cole, Michael. et al. (1971) *The Cultural Context of Learning and Thinking: An Exploration in Experimental Anthropology*. New York: Basic Books.

Condon, J. C. and F. Yousef, (1979) *An Introduction to Intercultural Communications*. Indianapolis: Bob Merrill.

Counter, Alan and D. L. Evans. (1981) *I Sought My Brother: An Afro-American Reunion.* Cambridge: MIT Press.

Courlander, Harold. (1967) *The African.* New York: Crown.

Cruse, Harold. (1967) *The Crisis of the Negro Intellectual.* New York: William Morrow and Company, Inc.

Davidson, Basil. (1974) *Africa.* (videotape) Massachusetts: RM Arts Videotape.

DeGramont, Sanche. (1977) *The Strong Brown God: The Story of the Niger River.* Boston: Houghton Mifflin.

de Lubicz, R. A. Schwaller. (1977) *The Temple in Man.* Brookline, Massachusetts: Autumn Press.

_____. (1978) *Symbol and the Symbolic.* Brookline, Massachusetts: Autumn Press.

Denton, Lori. (1990) "Babies Grasp Idea of Concealed Objects." *Monitor* 8 (October): 4.

Deren, Maya. (1951) *Divine Horsemen: The Voodoo Gods of Haiti.* New York: Delta.

Diop, Cheikh Anta. (1973) "Pigmentation of the Ancient Egyptians: Test by Melanin Analysis." *Bulletin de L'institute Fondamental D'Afrique Noire,* Series B, Sciences Humaines, Tome XXXV, No. 3, Juilliet.

_____. (1974) *The African Origin of Civilization: Myth or Reality.* New York: Lawrence Hill.

_____. [1974](1978) *Black Africa: The Economic and Cultural Basis for a Federated State.* Westport, Connecticut: Lawrence Hill.

_____. (1978) *The Cultural Unity of Black Africa.* Chicago: Third World Press.

_____. (1991) *Civilization or Barbarism: An Authentic Anthropology.* Chicago: Lawrence Hill.

Donaldson, Margaret. (1978) *Children's Minds.* New York: W.W. Norton.

Dow, S. (1937) "The Egyptian Cults of Athens." *Harvard Theological Review* 30: 188-232.

Drower, Margaret. (1970) *Nubia: A Drowning Land.* New York: Atheneum.

DuBois, Felix. [1869](1969) *Timbucktoo the Mysterious.* New York: Negro Universities Press.

Du Bois, W.E.B.[1909] (1970) *The Negro American Family.* Cambridge: The MIT Press.

_____. [1915](1972a) *The Negro.* London: Oxford.

_____. [1946](1972b) *The World and Africa: An Inquiry into the Part Which Africa Played in World History.* New York: International Publishers.

_____. (1969) *The Souls of Black Folk.* New York: Signet.

Durkeim, Emile. (1977) 'Education and Society."In *Power and Ideology in Education*. Edited by Jerome Karabel and A.H. Halsey. New York: Oxford.

Ellison, Ralph. (1972) *Invisible Man*. New York: Vintage.

Erickson, Erik. (1968) *Identity, Youth and Crisis*. New York: W.W. Norton.

Erny, Pierre. (1968) *Childhood and Cosmos*. New York: Black Orpheus Press.

Escalante, Jaime and John Dirman. (1990) *Jaime Escalante Math Program*. Washington, D.C.: National Education Association (reprinted from the *Journal of Negro Education* 59, no. 3: 407-423.

Evans, Mari. (1977) "The Nature and Methodology of Colonization and Its Relationship to Creativity." *Black Books Bulletin* 6, no. 3: 10-17.

Fanon, Franz. (1965) *A Dying Colonialism*. New York: Evergreen.

_____. (1967) *Black Skin, White Masks*. New York: Grove Press.

Farb, Peter. (1974) *Word Play: What Happens When People Talk*. New York: Alfred Knopf.

Fell, Barry. (1976) *America B.C.: Ancient Settlers in the New World*. New York: Wallaby Pocket Book.

Feuerstein, Reuven. (1979) *The Dynamic Assessment of Retarded Performers*. Baltimore: University Park Press.

Fisher, R. L. (1968) "Thinking Style and Socio-economic Status." *Perceptual and Motor Skills* 26: 825-826.

Fisner, Seymour. (1975) *Body Consciousness*. New York: Jason Aronson.

Fitzhugh, George. (1971) *Cannibals All: Or Slaves Without Masters*. Cambridge: The Belknap Press of Harvard University Press.

Forbes, Jack D. (1977) "Racism, Scholarship and Cultural Pluralism." In *Higher Education*. Davis, California: University of California Native American Studies Tecumseh Center.

Frankfort, Henri. (1948) *Ancient Egyptian Religion*. New York: Harper Torch Books.

_____. (1969) *Kingship and the Gods: A Study of Ancient Near Eastern Religion as the Integration of Society and Nature*. Chicago: University of Chicago Press.

_____. (1977). *The Intellectual Adventure of Man*. Chicago: University of Chicago Press.

Frazier, E. Franklin. (1970) *Black Bourgeoisie*. New York: Macmillan.

Fredrickson, George M. (1971) *The Black Image in the White Mind: The Debate on Afro-American Character and Destiny, 1817-1914*. New York: Harper Torchbooks.

Freire, Paulo. (1973) *Education for Critical Consciousness*. New York: Seabury Press.

Freud, Sigmund. [1939](1967) *Moses and Monotheism*. New York: Vintage.

Garvey, Amy J. (1974) *Garvey and Garveyism*. New York: Collier Macmillan.

Garvey, Amy J. and E.U. Essien. (1977) *More Philosophy and Opinions of Marcus Garvey*. Vol. 3. London: Frank Cass.

Gay, John. (1973) *Red Dust on the Green Leaves*. Thompson, Connecticut: Intercultural Associates.

Gerry, A. L. and John Gluver. (1976) *Eye Color, Sex and Children's Behavior*. Chicago: Nelson-Hall Publishers.

Goffman, Irving. (1969) *Strategic Interaction*. Philadelphia: University of Pennsylvania Press.

Goody, Jack. (1978) *The Domestication of the Savage Mind*. Cambridge: Cambridge University.

Gossett, Thomas S.(1973) *Race: The History of an Idea in America*. New York: Schocken.

Gould, Stephen Jay. (1981) *The Mismeasure of Man*. New York: W. W. Norton.

Grant, Madison. (1924) *The Passing of the Great Race or the Racial Basis of European History*. New York: Charles Scribner and Sons.

Gratus, Jack. (1973) *The Great White Lie: Slavery, Emancipation and Changing Racial Attitudes*. New York: Monthly Review Press.

Graves, S.P. (1913) *Education before the Middle Ages*. New York: Macmillan.

Griaule, Marcel and Germaine Dietelin. (1965) *Conversations with Ogotemneli*. Oxford: Oxford University Press.

Hale, Daniel. (1982) *Black Children: Their Roots, Culture and Learning Styles*. Provo, UT: Brigham Young University Press.

Hall, Edward T. (1977) *Beyond Culture*. New York: Anchor.

Hall, Manly P. (1971) *Free Masonry of the Ancient Egyptians*. Los Angeles: Philosophical Research Society, Inc.

Hare, Nathan. (1970) *The Black Anglo-Saxons*. London: Collier Macmillan.

Harris, Joseph. (1974) *Africa and Africans as Seen by Classical Writers*. Washington, D.C.: Howard University Press.

Harrison, Paul C. (1972) *The Drama of Nommao*. New York: Grove Press.

Haskins, R. W. (1844) *The Arts, Sciences, and Civilization, Anterior to Greece and Rome*. Buffalo: A.W. Wilgus.

Heath, Shirley B. (1983) *Ways with Words*. Cambridge (Cambridge-shire) and New York: Cambridge University Press.

Heller, Kirby, Wayne Holtzman, and Samuel Messick. (1982) *Placing Children in Special Education: A Strategy for Equity.* Washington, D.C.: National Academy Press.

Herskovits, Melville J. (1969) *The Myth of the Negro Past.* Boston: Beacon.

Heyob, Sharon Kelley. (1975) *The Cult of Isis among Women in the Greco-Roman World.* Leiden: E. J. Brill.

Higginbotham, A. Leon. (1978) *In the Matter of Color: Race and the American Legal Process.* New York: Oxford.

Hill, Robert B. (1977) *Informal Adoption Among Black Families.* New York: National Urban League.

Hilliard, Asa G., III. (1976) "Alternatives to IQ Testing: An Approach to the Identification of Gifted 'Minority' Children." *Final Report, Sacramento: Special Education Support Unity, California State Department of Education.* (ERIC Document Reproduction Service No. ED 145-959).

_____. (1978) *Anatomy and Dynamics of Oppression: An Educator's Response.* New York: Columbia University. (ERIC Document Reproduction Services No. ED 163-126).

_____. (1978) "Equal Educational Opportunity and Quality Education." *Anthropology and Education Quarterly* 9, no. 2: 110-126.

_____. (1979) "Involuntary Servitude." Keynote presentation to Western Regional NAACP Conference, Monterey, California.

_____. (1982) "Culture, Treatment, and Belief." *Georgia Educational Researcher* 1, no. 1: 26-39.

_____. (1983) "Psychological Factors Associated with Language in the Education of the African-American Child." *Journal of Negro Education* 52 no.1: 24-34.

_____. (1989a) "The Eye of Ra and the Abode of Maat: The Pinnacle of Black Leadership in the Ancient World." *Journal of African Civilizations* 10: 211-238.

_____. (1989b) "Kemetic Historical Revision: Implications for Cross Cultural Research and Evaluation," *Evaluation Practice:* 7-23.

_____, ed. (1987) "Testing African-American Students." *Special Issue of Negro Educational Review* 38, nos. 2 and 3: 33-216.

_____. et al. (1981) *Behavioral Criteria in Research and the Study of Racism: Performing the Jackal Function.* Technical Reports 1-111, Office of Naval Research, Contract No. N00014-77-c-0183.

Hirsch, E.D. (1987) *Cultural Literacy: What Every American Needs to Know.* Boston: Houghton Mifflin.

Hirsch, Jerry. (1981) "To Unfrock the Charlatans." *Sage Race Relations Abstracts* 6, no. 2:1-67.

Hodges, John, Donald K. Struckmann, and Lynn Dorland Trost. (1971) *Cultural Bases of Racism and Group Oppression: An Examination of Traditional "Western" Concepts, Values and Institutional Structures Which Support Racism, Sexism and Elitism.* Berkeley: Two Riders Press.

Hofstadter, Richard. (1955) *Social Darwinism in American Thought.* Boston: Beacon Press.

Holtzclaw, Robert Fulton. (1980) *The Saints Go Marching In: A One-Volume Hapiography of Africans, or Descendants of Africans Who Have Been Canonized by the Church Including Three of the Early Popes.* Shaker Heights, Ohio: Keeble Press, Inc.

Hoover, M. R. L. Politzer and D. Taylor. (1987). "Bias in Reading Tests for Black Language Speakers: A Sociolinguistic Perspective." *Negro Educational Review* 38, nos. 2 and 3: 81-99.

Houston, Drusilla Dunjee. [1926](1985) *Wonderful Ethiopians of the Ancient Cushite Empire.* Baltimore: Black Classic Press.

Houts, Paul, ed. (1977) *The Myth of Measurability.* New York: Hart.

Howard, Joseph. (1980) "Toward a Social Psychology of Colonialism." In *Black Psychology.* Edited by R. Jones. New York: Harper and Row.

Hunter, William A. (1974) *Multicultural Education Through Competency Based Teacher Education.* Washington: American Association of Colleges of Teacher Education.

Hurry, J.B. (1928) *Imhotep: Vizier and Physician of King Zoser and Afterwards the Egyptian God of Medicine.* London: Oxford University Press.

Idowu, E. Bolaji. (1975) *African Traditional Religion: A Definition.* Maryknoll, New York: Orbis Books.

Institute for Contemporary Studies. (1981) *The Fairmont Papers.* London: Black Alternatives Conferences.

Jackson, John. (1974) *Introduction to African Civilizations.* Secaucus, N.J.: Citadel Press.

Jacobs, P., S. Landau, and E. Pell. (1971) *To Serve the Devil.* 2 vols. New York: Vintage Books.

Jahn, Janheinz. (1961) *Muntu: The New African Culture.* New York: Grove Press.

James, George G. M. [1954](1976) *Stolen Legacy.* San Francisco: Julian Richardson Associates.

Jefferies, Leonard Jr. (1982) "Review of Civilization or Barbarism: The Legacy of Cheikh Anta Diop." *Journal of African Civilization* 4, no. 2: 146-160.

Jensen, Arthur. (1961) *Bias in Mental Testing*. New York: Grove.

Jesperson, Otto. (1964) *Mankind, Nation and Individual from a Linguistic Point of View*. Bloomington: Indiana University Press.

Jones, LeRoi. (1963) *Blues People: The Negro Experience in White America and the Music That Developed From It*. New York: William Morrow and Company.

_____. (1967) *Black Music*. New York: William Morrow and Company.

Jordon, Winthrop. (1977) *White Over Black: American Attitudes Toward the Negro, 1550-1812*. New York: W. W. Norton.

Kamil, Jill. (1976) *Luxor: A Guide to Ancient Thebes*. New York: Longman.

Kamin, L. (1974) *The Science and Politics of I.Q.* New York: John Wiley.

Karabel, Jerome and H.H. Halsey, eds. (1977) *Power and Ideology in Education*. New York: Oxford.

Kessen, W., ed. (1976) *Childhood in China*. New Haven: Yale University Press.

King, Kenneth. (1971) *Pan Africanism in Education: A Study of Race, Philanthropy and Education in the Southern States of America and East Africa*. Oxford: Clarendon.

King, Lewis. (1980) "Models of Meaning in Mental Health Model Eight: The Transformation of the Oppressed." *Fanon Center Journal* 1, no. 1: 29-50.

King, Richard. (1981) "Black Dot: The Black Seed: The Archetype of Humanity." *Uraeus* 2, no. 1:18-34.

Ki-zerbo, J. (1981) *General History of Africa I: Methodology and Pre-history*. Berkeley, California: University California Press.

Kitano, Harry H. L. (1969) *Japanese Americans: Evolution of a Subculture*. Englewood Cliffs, New Jersey: Prentice Hall.

Kochman, Thomas. (1981) *Black/White Styles in Conflict*. Chicago: University of Chicago Press.

Kogan, N. (1971) "Educational Implication of Cognitive Style." In *Psychology and Educational Practice*. Edited by G.S. Lesser. Glenview, Il: Scott Foreman.

Kotzwinkle, W. (1982) *ET the Extra-Terrestrial in His Adventure on Earth*. New York: Berkeley Books.

Kuhn, Thomas S. (1962) *The Structure of Scientific Revolutions*. Chicago: University of Chicago Press.

Lacy, Dan. (1972) *The White Use of Blacks in America: 350 Years of Law and Violence, Attitudes and Etiquette, Politics and Change*. New York: McGraw Hill.

Lamb, R. D. and Rudolph C. Troike. (1972) *Language and Cultural Diversity in American Education.* Englewood Cliffs, New Jersey: Prentice Hall.

Lamy, Lucie. (1981) *Egyptian Mysteries: New Light on Ancient Spiritual Knowledge.* New York: Crossroads.

Landis, D., et al. (1976) "Word Meaning in Black and White." In *Variations in Black and White Conditions of the Social Environment.* Edited by H.C. Triandis. Urbana, Il: University of Illinois Press.

Lasche, Christopher. (1978) *The Culture of Narcissism: American Life in an Age of Diminishing Expectations.* New York: W. W. Norton.

Laurie, S.S. (1902) *Historical Survey of Pre-Christian Education.* London: Longmans, Green and Company.

Levi-Strauss, Claude. (1966) *The Savage Mind.* Chicago: The University of Chicago Press.

Lichtheim, Miriam. (1975) *Ancient Egyptian Literature.* Berkeley: University of California Press.

Locke, Alain. (1969) *The Negro and His Music: Negro Art Past and Present.* New York: Arno Press.

Marable, Manning. (1980) *From the Grassroots: Social and Political Essays Towards Afro-American Liberation.* Boston: South End Press.

Massey, Gerald. [1881] (1994) *Book of the Beginnings.* 2 vols. Baltimore: Black Classic Press.

Mbiti, John S. (1969) *African Religions and Philosophy.* New York: Praeger.

Memmi, Albert. (1965) *The Colonizer and the Colonized.* Boston: Beacon Press.

Mertz, Barbara. (1978) *Redland, Blackland: Daily Life in Ancient Egypt.* New York: Dodd, Mead & Co.

Meyer, Isaac, trans. (1900) *Oldest Books in the World: An Account of the Religion, Wisdom, Philosophy, Ethics, Psychology, Manners, Proverbs, Sayings, Refinement, etc... of the Ancient Egyptians.* New York: E.W. Dayton.

Mitchell, Henry. (1975) *Black Belief: Folk Beliefs of Blacks in America and West Africa.* New York: Harper and Row.

Mokhtar, Garmel. (1981) *General History of Africa II: Ancient Civilizations of Africa.* Berkeley, California: University of California Press.

Montague, Ashley. (1968) *The Concept of the Primitive.* New York: Collier Macmillan.

Montete, Pierre. (1964) *Eternal Egypt.* New York: New American Library.

Morrison, Toni. (1970) *The Bluest Eye.* New York: Pocket Books.

Ngubane, Jordan. K. (1979) *Conflict of Minds: Changing Power Distributions in South Africa.* New York: Books in Focus.

Nkrumah, Kwame. (1970) *Consciencism: Philosophy and Ideology for Decolonization.* New York: Modern Reader.

Nobles, Wade. (1976) *A Formulative and Empirical Study of Black Families.* Final Report to Department of Health Education, and Welfare, Office of Child Development, Contract No. 90-C-255.

_____. (1987) "Psychometrics and African-American Reality: A Question of Cultural Antimony." *Negro Educational Review* 38, nos. 2 and 3: 45-55.

Oakes, Jeannie. (1985) *Keeping Track: How Schools Structure Inequality.* New Haven: Yale University Press.

Oliver, Paul. (1970) *Savannah Syncopators: African Retentions in the Blues.* New York: Stein and Day.

Ornstein, Robert. (1975) *The Psychology of Consciousness.* Baltimore: Penguin.

Osgood, C. E., W. H. May, and M. S. Miron. (1975) *Cross Cultural Universals of Affective Meaning.* Chicago: University of Illinois Press.

Padmore, George. [1936] (1969) *How Britain Rules Africa.* New York: Negro Universities Press.

Parker, George Wells. (1917) "The African Origin of Grecian Civilization." *Journal of Negro History* 2, no 1: 334-344.

Pearce, Joseph. C. (1980) *Magical Child: Rediscovering Nature's Plan for Our Children.* New York: Bantam Books.

_____. (1985) *Magical Child Matures.* New York: E. P. Dutton.

Pearce, Roy. H. (1971) *Savagism and Civilization.* Baltimore: Johns Hopkins Press.

Poliakov, Leon. (1974) *The Aryan Myth: A History of Racist and Nationalist Ideas in Europe.* New York: Meridian.

Powell, Gloria. J. (1973) *Black Monday's Children: A Study of the Effects of School Desegregation on Self-Concepts of Southern Children.* New York: Appleton Century Crofts.

Price, Richard. (1973) *Maroon Societies:Rebel Slave Communities in the Americas.* New York: Anchor.

Ramirez, Manuel and A. Castenada. (1974) *Cultural Democracy, Bi-Cognitive Development and Education.* New York: Academic Press.

Ramirez, Manuel and O. Price-Williams. (1974) "Cognitive Styles of Children in Three Ethnic Groups in the United States." *Journal of Cross-Cultural Psychology* 5: 212-219.

Rashidi, Runoko, ed. (1988) *African Presence in Early Asia: Journal of African Civilizations.* New Brunswick: Transaction Press.

Redmond, Eugene. (1976) *Drum Voices: The Mission of Afro-American Poetry.* New York: Anchor Books.

Reed, Bika. (1978) *Rebel in the Soul.* New York: Inner Traditions International, Ltd.

Riefstahl, Elizabeth. (1964) *Thebes in the Time of Amunhotep III.* Norman: University of Oklahoma Press.

Rist, Raymond. (1973) *The Urban School: A Factor for Failure.* Cambridge: MIT Press.

Robeson, Paul. (1971) *Here I Stand.* Boston: Beacon.

Rodney, Walter. (1974) *How Europe Underdeveloped Africa.* Washington D.C.: Howard University Press.

Rogers, Joel A. [1946](1972)*World's Great Men of Color.* New York: The Macmillan Co.

_____. (1961) *Africa's Gift to America.* New York: Helga M. Rogers.

Rosenthal, Robert and Lenore Jacobsen. (1968) *Pygmalion in the Classroom.* New York: Holt, Rhinehart, and Winston.

Sauneron, Serge. (1969) *The Priest of Ancient Egypt.* New York: Grove Press.

Scheflen, Albert E. (1974) *How Behavior Means.* New York: Jason Aronson.

Schure, Edward. [1889] (1973) *The Mysteries of Ancient Egypt: Hermes/Moses.* Blauvelt, New York: Multimedia Publishing Corporation.

Schwartz, Barry, and R. Disch. (1970) *White Racism: Its History, Pathology and Practice.* New York: Dell.

Semaj, Leachim. (1980) "Rastafari: From Religion to Social Theory." *Caribbean Quarterly* 226, no. 4: 22-31.

Serfontein, J. H. P. (1978) *Brotherhood of Power: An Expose of the Secret Afrikaner Broederbond.* Bloomington, Indiana: Indiana University Press.

Shade, Barbara J. (1981) *Afro-American Patterns of Cognition.* Madison: University of Wisconsin Center for Education Research.

_____. (1981) "Racial Variation in Perceptual Differentiation." *Perceptual and Motorskills* 52: 243-248.

Sidran, Ben. (1971) *Black Talk.* New York: Holt, Rinehart & Winston.

Simpkins, Cuthbert O. [1975] (1989) *Coltrane: A Biography.* Baltimore: Black Classic Press.

Simpson, William K. (1972) *The Literature of Ancient Egypt.* New Haven: Yale University Press.

Slack, Warner V. and Douglass Porter. (1980) "The Scholastic Aptitude Test: A Critical Approach." *Harvard Educational Review* 50, no. 2: 54-175.

Smith, G. Elliott. (1916) "The Influence of Ancient Egyptian Civilization in the East and in America." Lecture at the John Ryland Library, March 10, 1915.

Smith, William A. (1955) *Ancient Education*. New York: Philosophical Library.

Smitherman, Geneva. (1977) *Talkin' and Testifyin': The Language of Black America*. Boston: Houghton Mifflin.

Snowden, Frank. (1971) *Blacks in Antiquity: Ethiopians in the Greco-Roman Experience*. Cambridge, MA: Belknap.

Sonyika, Dadisi. (1984) "Initiation." Paper presented at the first Annual Egyptian Studies Conference in Los Angeles, on African Education Systems.

Spindler, George D. (1987) *Education and Cultural Process*. Prospect Heights, Illinois: Waveland Press, Inc.

Spivey, Donald. (1978) *Schooling for the New Slavery: Black Industrial Education, 1868-1915*. Westport, Connecticut: Greenwood Press.

St. John, Robert. [1952](1975) *Tongue of the Prophets: The Life Story of Eliezer Ben Yehuda*. North Hollywood, California: Wilshire Book Company.

Stanton, William. (1960) *The Leopard's Spots: Scientific Attitudes Towards Race in America, 1815-1959*. Chicago: University of Chicago Press.

Steindorff, George and Keith C. Seele. (1957) *When Egypt Ruled the East*. Chicago: University of Chicago Press.

Stierlin, Henri. (1978) *The World of the Pharaohs*. New York: Sunflower.

Stoddard, Lothrop. [1921] (1971) *The Rising Tide of Color Against White World Supremacy*. Westport, Connecticut: Negro University Press.

Taharka. (1979) *Black Manhood: The Building of Civilization by the Black Man of the Nile*. Washington, D.C.: University Press of America.

Taylor, Orlando and Dorian L. Lee. (1987) "Standardization Tests and African-American Children: Communication and Language Issues." *Negro Educational Review* 38 nos. 2 and 3: 67-80.

TenHouten, Warren D. and Charles Kaplan. (1973) *Science and Its Mirror Image*. New York: Harper and Row.

Termu, A. and B. Swai. (1981) *Historian and Africanist History: A Critique*. London: Zed Press.

Thomas, Alexander and Samuel Sillen. (1972) *Racism and Psychiatry*. New York: Brunner Mazel.

Thompson, Robert F. and J. Cornet. (1981) *Four Moments of the Sun: Kongo Art in Two Worlds*. Washington, D.C.: National Gallery of Art.

Turner, Lorenzo D. (1942) "Some Contacts of Brazilian Ex-Slaves with Nigeria, West Africa." *Journal of Negro History* 27, no. 1: 55-67.

_____.(1969) *Africanism in the Gullah Dialect*. New York: Arno Press.

UNESCO. (1978) *The Peopling of Ancient Egypt and the Deciphering of the Mereotic Script*. Proceedings of the symposium held in Cairo from 28 January to 3 February 1974. Paris: United Nations Educational, Scientific and Cultural Organization.

UNESCO International Scientific Committee for the Drafting of a General History of Africa. (1981-) *General History of Africa*. 8 Vols. Berkeley: University of California Press.

Van Sertima, Ivan. (1976) *They Came Before Columbus*. New York: Random House.

_____, ed. (1982) *Egypt Revisited: Journal of African Civilization*. New Brunswick: Transaction Press.

_____, ed. (1985) *Nile Valley Civilizations: Journal of African Civilization*. New Brunswick: Transaction Press.

Vass, Claudia W. (1979) *The Bantu Speaking Heritage of the United States*. Los Angeles: Center for Afro-American Studies.

Volney, C.F. [1793] (1991) *The Ruins of Empires*. Baltimore: Black Classic Press.

Vygotsky, Les Semenovich. (1962) *Thought and Language*. Cambridge: The M.I.T. Press.

Wa Thiong'o, Ngugi. (1987) *Decolonizing the Mind: The Politics of Language in African Literature*. London: James Currey.

Weinberg, Meyer. (1977) *A Chance to Learn: The History of Race and Education in the United States*. New York: Cambridge University Press.

Weinreich, Max. (1946) *Hitler's Professors: The Part of Scholarship in Germany's Crimes Against the Jewish People*. New York: YIVO.

Will, George F. (1989) "Let's Face It Europe's Our Inspiration." *Daily News* December 19.

White, J. E. (1970) *Ancient Egypt: Its Culture and History*. New York: Dover.

Whitten, Norman E., Jr. (1974) *Black Frontiersmen: A South American Case*. New York: John Wiley.

Wilkins, Ivor and H. Strydom. (1979) *The Broederbond*. New York: Paddington Press.

Williams, Bruce. (1980) "The Lost Pharaohs of Nubia." *Archaeology,* September/October.

Williams, Chancellor. (1974) *The Destruction of Black Civilization: Great Issues of a Race from 4500 BC to 2000 AD.* Chicago: Third World Press.

Williams, F. (1970) *Language and Poverty: Perspectives on a Theme.* Chicago: Markham Press.

Williams, Obadele and Asa G. Hilliard, III. (1990) 'The Kemetic Influence in the Greco-Roman World." In *Reconstructing Kemetic Culture: Papers, Perspectives, Projects.* Edited by Maulana Karenga. Los Angeles: Sankore.

Williams, Robert L., ed. (1975) *Ebonics: The True Language of Black People.* St. Louis: The Institute of Black Studies.

Williams, Robert L. and Horace Mitchell. (1980) "The Testing Game." In *Black Psychology.* Edited by R. L. Jones. New York: Harper and Row.

Wilson, John A. (1956) *The Culture of Ancient Egypt.* Chicago: University of Chicago Press.

Winkler, Karen J. (1990) "Shaped by Nationalism and Ideology of Cold War, Humanities Foundation is Subject of New Studies." *The Chronicle of Higher Education* 18 (April): A1, A8.

Witkin, Herman A. (1965) "A Cognitive Style Approach to Cross-Cultural Research," *International Journal of Abnormal Psychology* 70, no. 5: 546-593.

Witt, R.E. (1971) *Isis in the Greco-Roman World.* New York: Cornell University Press.

Woodson, Carter G. [1933](1977) *Miseducation of the Negro.* Washington, D.C.: Associated Publishers.

————. (1978) *The African Background Outline: Or Handbook for the Study of the Negro.* New York: Negro Universities Press.

Woodward, C. Vann. (1966) *The Strange Career of Jim Crow.* New York: Oxford.

Worthy, Morgan. (1974) *Eye Color, Sex and Race: Keys to Human and Animal Behavior.* Anderson, S. C.: Drake House/Hallux.

Wright, Richard. (1977) *African Philosophy.* Washington, D.C.: University Press of America.

Yette, Samuel. (1971) *The Choice: The Issue of Black Survival in America.* Silver Springs, Maryland: Cottage Books.

Acknowledgements

Versions of the essays that appear in *The Maroon Within Us* have been previously published and presented in the following publications and conferences:
Anecdotal and Other Material to Illustrate the Expression of Behavioral Style in *Alternatives to IQ Testing: An Approach to the Assessment of Gifted Children*, California State Department of Education, 1976; **The Maroon Within Us: The Lessons of Africa for the Parenting and Education of African American Children** at Tennessee State University, April 1982, and later in *Journal of Black Studies* 1, no. 2 (Fall 1983); **In"Loco Parents" or Retrieving Responsibility** in *National Black Child Development Institute Newsletter*, 1982; **Dr ET as Africancentered Transformer** in *Fanon Center Journal: Perspectives on the Mental Health of Black Persons* 2, no. 1 (October 1984); **Pedagogy in Ancient Kemet** at the First Annual Ancient Egyptian Studies Conference in Los Angeles, California, 1984, and later in *Kemet and the African World View* (1986) Los Angeles: University of Sankore Press; **Saving Our Children** at National Alliance of Black School Educators Annual Meeting in Cleveland, Ohio, November 1984; **Kemetic Concepts in Education** at Morehouse College, Atlanta, Georgia, 1985, and later in the *Journal of African Civilizations* 6, no. 2 (1985); **Socializing Our Children for the Resurrection of African People** at the Annual Meeting of the National Black Child Development Institute in Detroit, Michigan, October 1987; **Conceptual Confusion and the Persistence of Group Oppression Through Education** in *Excellence and Equity* 21, no. 1 (1988) and also in *The Race: Matters Concerning Pan-African History, Culture, and Genocide*, edited by Kiarri T-H Cheatwood. (Richmond: Native Son Publishers, 1991); **Behavioral Style, Culture, and Teaching and Learning** at the New York State Department of Education in Albany, March 1988; **Teachers and Cultural Styles in a Pluralistic Society** in *NEA Today* 7, no. 6 (1989) and later in *Education Digest* 55, no. 2 (1989); **50 Plus: Essential References on the History of African People** in *Fifty Selected References on the History of African People* as a follow-up to the first Annual Conference on the African and African American Content in the School Curriculum in Atlanta, Georgia, 1990; **Fabrication: The Politics and Sociology of Knowledge in the Study of Ancient Kemet (Egypt) and the Greek and Roman World** at the conference on Martin Bernal's *Black Athena*, Temple University, October 1990; **Do We Have the "Will" to Educate All Children?** in *Educational Leadership* (September 1991); **The Meaning of KMT (Ancient Egyptian) History for Contemporary African American Experience** in *Phylon* 49 nos. 1,2 (1992).